D0382328

TANK
VERSUS
TANK

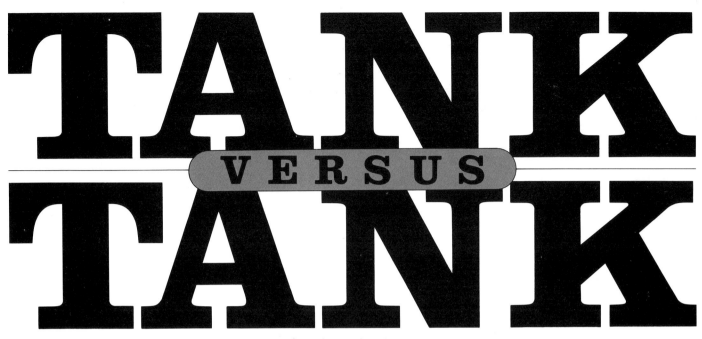

TANK *VERSUS* TANK

THE ILLUSTRATED STORY OF ARMORED BATTLEFIELD CONFLICT IN THE TWENTIETH CENTURY

KENNETH MACKSEY

Salem House Publishers

Topsfield, Massachusetts

Tank versus Tank was conceived and produced by
Grub Street, London

First published in the United States by Salem House
Publishers, 1988
462 Boston Street, Topsfield, MA 01983
Copyright © by Grub Street, London, 1988
Text copyright © by Kenneth Macksey, 1988
Artwork by Sarson and Bryan
Maps by Graeme Andrew
Designed by Jerry Goldie

Library of Congress Cataloging in Publication Data
    Macksey, Kenneth.
      Tank versus tank.
      1. Tank warfare   I. Title.
      UG446.5.M2249   1988   358′.18   87-35632
      ISBN 0-88162-282-6

Typeset by Chapterhouse
Printed in Italy by New Interlitho

BIBLIOGRAPHY

In the compilation of this book reference has been made to
official records as well as to articles in such well-informed
journals as that of the Royal United Services Institute, 'The
Tank' (Journal of the Royal Tank Regiment), and 'Armor'
(Journal of US Armor); and also to books in the select
bibliography below.

Anon—*Fifty years on tracks*—Holt Caterpillar Track Co
Fuller J F C—*Tanks in the Great War*—Murray, 1920
      —*Memoirs of an unconventional soldier*
      —Nicholson and Watson, 1936
Goutard, A—*The Battle of France*—Muller, 1958
Guderian, H—*Achtung! Panzer!*—UDV, 1937
      —*Panzer Leader*—Joseph, 1952
Herzog, C—*The Arab-Israeli Wars*—Arms and Armour
      Press, 1982
Horne, A—*To lose a battle*—Macmillan, 1969
Joachin, D—*History of the 4th Panzer Division 1938–1943*
Jukes, G—*Stalingrad*—Ballantine, 1968
      —*Kursk*—Ballantine, 1968
Lehmann, H—*Die Leibstandarte (Vol 3)*—Munin, 1982
      —(2 Vols)
Liddell Hart, BH—*The Tanks (Vol 2)*—Cassell, 1959
Macksey, K—*Guderian, Panzer General*—Macdonald, 1975
      —*Tank Warfare*—Hart-Davis, 1972
      —*A History of the Royal Armoured Corps
      1914–1975*—Newtown, 1983
      —*The Tank Pioneers*—Janes, 1981
Manstein, E—*Lost Victories*—Methuen, 1958
Manteufel, H. E. von—*Die 7 Panzerdivision im Zweiten
      Weltkrieg*—1965
Martel, G le Q—*In the wake of the tank*—Sifton Praed, 1934
Mellenthin, F von—*Panzer Battles*—Cassell, 1955
Milsom, J—*Russian Tanks 1900–1970*—Arms and Armour
      Press, 1970
Nehring, W—*Die Geschichte der Deutschen, Panzerwaffe
      1916–1945*—Propylaen 1969
Ogorkiewicz, R—*Armour*—Stevens, 1960
Pitt, B (Ed)—*Purnell's History of the Second World War*
      —Purnell, 1966
Rommel E (Ed Liddell Hart)—*Papers*—Collins, 1953
Schärfler, H—*Book of 35th Panzer Regiment*—Collins, 1983
Seaton, A—*The Russo-German War 1941–1945*—Barker, 1971
Starry, D.A.—*Armored Combat in Vietnam*—Blandford,
      1981
Stern, A—*A Log Book of a Pioneer*—Hodder and Stoughton,
      1919
Swinton, E—*Eyewitness*—Hodder and Stoughton, 1932
Teveth, S—*Tanks of Tammuz*—Weidenfeld and Nicolson,
      1969
Volakheim, Lt—*Deutschen Kampfwagen in Angriff 1918*
      —Mittler 1918
Williams-Ellis, C and A—*The Tank Corps*—Country Life,
      1919
Zezschwitz, G.P. von—*Heigl's Taschenbuch der Tanks
      (3 Vols)*—Lehmann, 1938 and 1971

The author would like to thank the following
for permission to use their photographs:
Grub Street, IWM, Popperfoto and TRH.

CONTENTS

CHAPTER ONE

WAR MACHINES, OLD AND NEW

IN DENSE FOG, THICKENED BY MORE THAN TWO HOURS' bombardment with high explosives and gas from German artillery, the crews of 14 weird and ungainly steel-encased machines, each weighing 32 tons, cranked their engines and made ready to advance against the British lines. Following these monsters, called A7Vs, came crouching infantry whose task of seizing the enemy trenches was to be eased by these, the first tanks built by Germany. They were the pawns in a conflict which was becoming dominated by major pieces of war material and by mechanization. Ahead lay their objectives, the villages of Villers Bretonneux and Cachy, each held in strength by British and Australian infantry and field artillery. Lying in ambush for a German attack which, for the past two or three days, had been anxiously expected, waited three British heavy Mark IV tanks, of similar size to those of the Germans, plus seven 14-ton Whippet tanks, capable of 8 mph, as compared with the 4 mph of the heavy machines. Groping their way with considerable difficulty in the opaque conditions and occasionally frustrated by mechanical troubles, the German tanks nevertheless succeeded for the most part in reaching their objectives. To the defenders' embarrassment, as well as their own, they arrived in Villers Bretonneux, and on the outskirts of Cachy, so far in advance of their own troops that they were compelled to turn back in order to quell by-passed opposition which now reasserted itself and stopped the German infantry dead.

Engrossed in the task of keeping their extremely unreliable machines running, in staying on course over unknown and shrouded terrain and giving help to the infantry who depended so much upon them, it came as a surprise to some among the German crews to find themselves confronted at short range, south of Villers Bretonneux, by their own kind – enemy tanks advancing aggressively, guns firing and bent on putting a stop to the A7Vs' depredations. In improving conditions of visibility and with the range opening up to nearly 400 m, the first tank-versus-tank fight had started.

THE WAR WAGONS

Since the invention of the potters' wheel in the Middle East as long ago, perhaps, as 3000 BC, man had adapted the idea to provide a means of transport. Built of wooden planks held together by copper clamps and sometimes rimmed with metal, the wheel made possible the construction of carts drawn by animals. Apart from their practical and commercial applications, carts could be employed to enhance the mobility of fighting men and, in favorable conditions, perform as combat vehicles in the heart of battle. The change from heavy, slow carts to light, purpose-built, fast chariots drawn by well-bred horses was a perfectly natural progression, stimulated by the invention of iron to replace copper and bronze in everyday use. Lighter and stronger spoked wheels, with more durable rims, bearings and axles, appeared at about the same time as the cutting properties of edged weapons were improved and as metal increasingly replaced skins as armored protection for men and beasts.

Yet from the start every warrior had to recognise certain basic factors which hampered the construction of armored fighting vehicles, the ancestors of the tank. Animals were severely limited in tractive power, carrying capacity and endurance. They required huge quantities of food and extensive rest in return for a relatively low output of work; and they were extremely vulnerable to attack, all the more so in face of the increasingly deadly longbows, crossbows and firearms which made their appearance in the Middle Ages. Indeed, it was the invention of gunpowder and the development of firearms in the 14th century which, faintly at first, tolled the knell of the horse as man's best source of mobility in war. The increased weight of thicker armor needed to withstand arrows propelled from the longbow or shot fired by a gun was such that the horse became overburdened, scarcely capable of a gallop and no longer a mobility asset. After the 15th century armor began to fall into disuse as soldiers came to the conclusion that their best chances of survival lay in agility to evade enemy missiles, and the adoption of heavy fire power against enemy weapon carriers as a guarantee of their own movement and survival on the battlefield. There ensued the paradoxical situation, over a period of about 300 years, in which fighting men, for their own good and effectiveness, virtually abandoned the erstwhile safety of personal armor.

Yet the desirability of armor protection remained paramount. Throughout the years of rising weapon power, the technology of fortification was drastically modified to withstand the heaviest artillery. The soaring stone edifices of the Middle Ages were superseded by deeply entrenched and barricaded defensive works located, for the most part, at strategic points which dominated communication systems and compelled the enemy either to commit himself to a prolonged siege operation or look elsewhere for an easier conquest. Attempts were also made to combine armored protection with mobility by building war wagons which could be towed by teams of horses from one place to another, forming themselves into circular, stationary laagers in the event of being threatened by attack on open ground. The most celebrated exponents of this technique, using modified farm wagons, were the Central European religious dissident Hussites, led in the Hussite wars (1419–34) by the half-blind but inspired John Žižka. With built-up, thickly timbered sides, portable boards which could be fitted at the halt to close gaps between wagons, and adap-

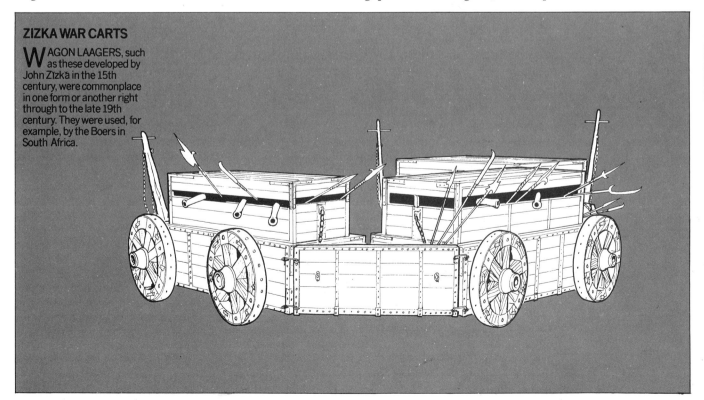

ZIZKA WAR CARTS

WAGON LAAGERS, such as these developed by John Žižka in the 15th century, were commonplace in one form or another right through to the late 19th century. They were used, for example, by the Boers in South Africa.

THE STEAM REVOLUTION

THE GRADUAL DEVELOPMENT OF STEAM traction engines, after James Watt had worked out more efficient methods of harnessing steam power in the 1760s, led inevitably to improved transport systems – such as powered railway and road vehicles.

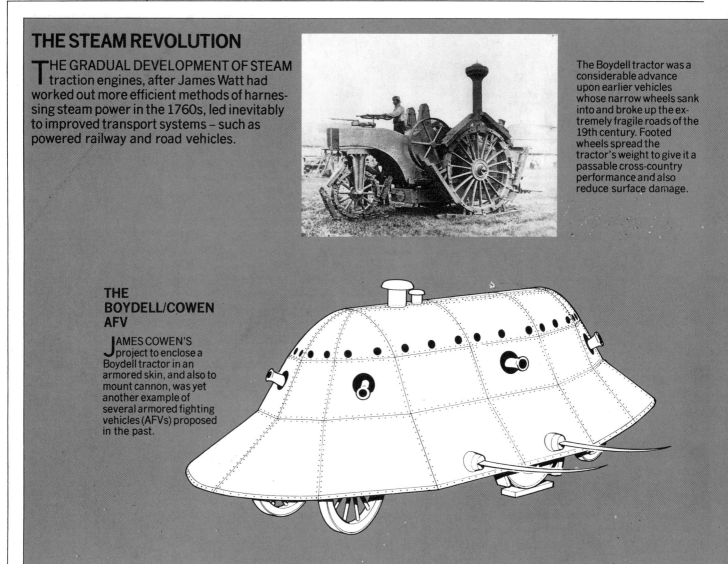

The Boydell tractor was a considerable advance upon earlier vehicles whose narrow wheels sank into and broke up the extremely fragile roads of the 19th century. Footed wheels spread the tractor's weight to give it a passable cross-country performance and also reduce surface damage.

THE BOYDELL/COWEN AFV

JAMES COWEN'S project to enclose a Boydell tractor in an armored skin, and also to mount cannon, was yet another example of several armored fighting vehicles (AFVs) proposed in the past.

tation as emplacements for crossbowmen and primitive artillery, their organization can be likened to that of latter-day tank formations. Moreover, at the battle of Kutna Hora war wagons actually did manage to win a great victory in mobility by fighting in close formation while on the move, bringing about the exhaustion and collapse of an enemy bent on attack but unable to penetrate their formation.

An effective means of propulsion lay at the heart of the problem of creating a universal weapon system which could impose upon the battlefield the basic requirements of decision – mobility, firepower and survivability. Guido da Vigevano's concept of a windmill-driven vehicle (1472) is merely the first known project of its sort, a machine upon which no more reliance could be placed than the presence of a wind strong enough to drive it. Leonardo da Vinci's hand-cranked model vehicle (1500), for all the ingenuity of its intricate geared pinions, could never, with manpower alone, contrive to develop sufficient power to shift its armored weight and still leave the crew fit for combat. Not until a practical steam engine was produced by James Watt in the late 1700s, and Nicholas Cugnot had demonstrated the first steam-driven road vehicle in 1769, were the seeds sown of the solution to the power plant problem. Inefficient and greedy in fuel consumption though the first steam engines were, by 1846 they had been developed sufficiently to make reasonably economic traction engines such as the machine designed by James Boydell, which became both a commercial and a military proposition. This tractor's

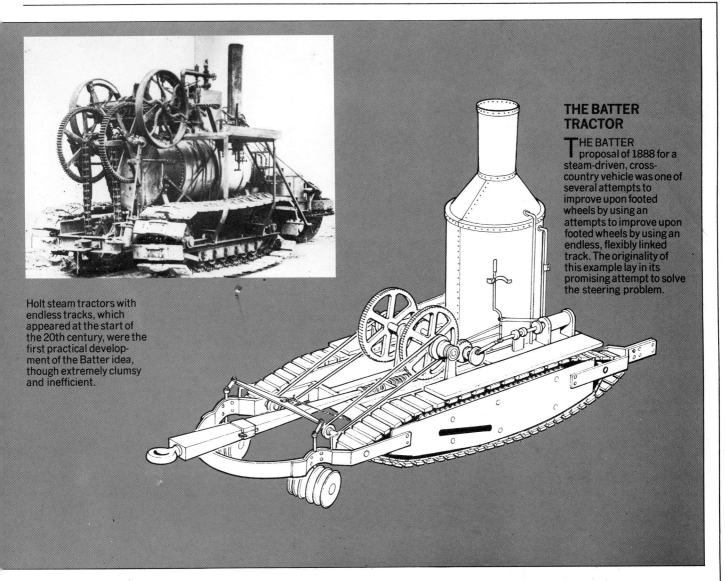

Holt steam tractors with endless tracks, which appeared at the start of the 20th century, were the first practical development of the Batter idea, though extremely clumsy and inefficient.

THE BATTER TRACTOR

THE BATTER proposal of 1888 for a steam-driven, cross-country vehicle was one of several attempts to improve upon footed wheels by using an attempts to improve upon footed wheels by using an endless, flexibly linked track. The originality of this example lay in its promising attempt to solve the steering problem.

advantages over many other land vehicles was the arrangement of its large, footed wheels which enabled it to spread its weight over a wider area and, thus, with the benefit of a relatively low ground pressure, cross uneven or soft surfaces. As a load carrier in the Crimean War (1854–56) it had its uses; but as an inspiration to other inventors over the next six decades, it was vital. Numerous proposals and models of 'continuous tracks' appeared. Most important of all was James Cowen's 1855 project for encasing the Boydell tractor in an iron, dome-like, outer casing (rather like da Vinci's model), fitting it with scythes and arming it with cannon to enable the men inside to advance in relative safety against the vastly increased firepower of the latest rifles and artillery. It mattered little that Britain's Prime Minister, Lord Palmerston, rejected it as 'uncivilised'. The concept of the tank had been born and would become ever less resistible as the killing power of weapons multiplied exceedingly.

MILITARY TECHNOLOGY ACCELERATES

The second half of the 19th century featured an astonishing acceleration in the pace of technical innovation and invention, allied to the further vast expansion of manufacturing capacity which had its instigation, to a considerable extent, in the stimulation to cheaper power production provided by James Watt's improved steam engine. The design and development of weapons contributed very significantly to this revolution. For example, at the root of the invention in 1856 by British gunsmith Henry Bessemer of his Converter method for making cheaper steel in large quantities, lay his desire to produce a new spun shell to compete for orders in an expanding armaments market created by the Crimean War. Finding that existing iron barrels would not withstand the required pressure, he was compelled to use steel which, prior to his method and the open-hearth system later invented by William Siemens, was too short in supply and too long in price. Likewise, the introduction of more rapid-firing, breech-loading firearms and cannon in the aftermath of the invention in the 1820s of the von Dreyse needle gun and improved cartridges gave encouragement and ideas to inventors who, for many years, had been searching for ways of producing a practical semi-automatic machine-gun. The hand-cranked models introduced in the 1850s, and first used in action during the American Civil War in the 1860s, were merely a second phase in the continuous amplification of killing potential. Alfred Nobel's more powerful, smokeless ballistic explosive, developed in the 1880s, made possible in 1885 Hiram Maxim's belt-fed, fully automatic machine-gun with its sustained rate of fire of 400 to 500 rounds per minute, a fusillade of enormous potential which professional soldiers were tardy to realise made almost hopeless man's survival, above ground, without some sort of armored protection.

Yet, by one of those paradoxes which so frequently complement or neutralize a significant advance in science or technology, the seeds of an antidote to the machine-gun and the latest rapid-fire artillery were simultaneously being sown. In 1882 Robert Hadfield's manganese steel was shown to provide far superior protection against shot than the wrought iron or mild carbon steel plates currently in use as armor. It was matched in 1885 by M Marbeau's nickel steel. Both gave good, if more expensive, protection against bullets and shell splinters. At the same time they set in motion a requirement for hardened projectiles to penetrate these latest steel alloy armors. More fundamental, however, was the demonstration in Germany in 1883 by Gottlieb Daimler of a small bicycle powered by a gasoline fuel, spark ignition four-stroke engine, based on the heavy power plant developed by the firm of Otto and Langen. In 1885 Daimler produced a four-wheeled vehicle. Seen from the outset as a substitute for the horse, the light petrol engine was also, at once, deprecated by horse lovers and denigrated on the grounds that it was noisy,

smelly, too slow and unreliable: all of which was true but overlooked the fact that every new machine needs time for development which, if the rewards are sufficiently attractive, will be carried through.

In the case of gasoline-engined vehicles, it took just 15 years for the point to be reached at which motor cars were running at 20 mph and at which strong demand was developing for radical improvements to the existing bad roads – all of which portended a transport revolution as well as a military one. For in 1899 F R Simms demonstrated in Britain a four-wheeled motor-cycle armed with a Maxim machine-gun, which was mounted behind an armored shield. A year later, in collaboration with the firms of Vickers and Maxims, he was showing off a fully armored, 'War Car', fitted with a 1½-pounder cannon, two machine-guns, 6 mm armor and capable of travelling at 6 mph on roads.

ARMORED CARS AND TRACTORS

In the decade to come various armored or simple armed cars were experimented with by several European firms. One variation was the mobile anti-balloon gun produced by the German firm of Ehrhardt in 1906 as a mounting for a 50 mm cannon for use against tethered balloons employed by armies to enable observers to see 'over the hill' into enemy territory. At the time any thought of vehicle versus vehicle combat was far from the minds of those stating the requirement, but the need for enhanced mobility was underlined with the appearance in the 1890s of airships driven by gasoline engines at speeds up to 17 mph. At that moment a balloon gun travelling at 20 mph seemed as good a defense as any against the first practical flying machines.

The extremely poor roads which were hampering the motor car and which, earlier, had prompted Boydell and others to design special wheels to cope with them, had also inspired a host of ideas centered upon 'continuous chain' tracks or 'endless railways'. Beginning with an idea by Buenos Aires-based Guillaume Fenders in 1883, there emerged a recognizably modern concept: a continuous, linked track driven by a sprocket, carried round an idler wheel and supporting the vehicle on rollers. Fenders' arrangement of endless cables and chains to form the railway was ahead of the technology of its day, especially since it incorporated a degree of elasticity in the suspension to absorb the shock of bumping. It was followed in 1888 by

The Roberts Ruston Tractor, initially powered by steam but later by a 70 hp internal combustion engine, was far ahead of its rivals because of its unique, well-sprung suspension and steering system which gave it considerable mobility and speed across country. Initially seen by the British Army as a supply carrier or gun tower, it was also proposed, without success, as the prime mover of an AFV.

At the turn of the century the first wheeled AFVs (armored cars) put in their appearance and found limited employment in small wars.
Below: Right at the start of WW1, the Belgians and the British improvised armored cars to hold up the German advance. The Belgian Minerva was merely a touring car fitted with armor and a machine-gun.
Below right: The British Rolls-Royce of late 1914 was much more sophisticated, incorporating a naval-designed fully rotating turret which gave complete protection to the crew; and foreshadowed in shape the majority of AFVs to come.

the more practical steam-driven scheme by F W Batter of the United States, which tackled seriously the as yet unsolved problem of steering. Step by step these machines and their competitors were leading, in parallel with numerous new developments of 'footed' wheels, to the appearance in Britain in 1904 of David Roberts' advanced steam-driven, chain-track tractor, and in the United States in 1906 of Holt's conversion of a wheeled traction engine to so-called 'caterpillar tracks' for use in Louisiana wetlands and elsewhere.

Roberts, whose vehicle was built by the firm of Hornsby, was far ahead of Holt since he managed to incorporate in his machine a remarkably advanced sprung suspension and an extremely clever steering system which made it totally independent of the steerable wheels, which Holt had copied from such machines as Batter's. Indeed, the Roberts tractor, as developed by 1907 with a 70 hp liquid fuel driven engine, was a highly versatile machine capable of a speed of about 10 mph, along with excellent cross-country performance, a very small turning circle and considerable agility. The British War Office tested it extensively and successfully as a load carrier and gun tractor. A Major Donoghue, who was involved with the trials, suggested that it should be fitted with bullet-proof shields and have a gun fitted integrally. But nobody took any interest. Only one

machine was bought. So Hornsby sold the patent to Holt, who wanted to get their hands on the advanced steering system.

ARMORED CARS IN WORLD WAR I

There had been ample demonstration, prior to the European conflict which erupted in 1914, that defensive weapons overwhelmingly dominated over flesh, blood and courage in battle, and that awesome loss of life in head-on assaults [as witnessed during the Russian-Japanese War of 1904] could lead only to the exhaustion of armies. Nevertheless the Central European Powers threw themselves enthusiastically into attacks against the Allies [French, Serbian, Russian, British], who responded to the challenge with equal abandon. Within three months of the outbreak of World War I the casualty bill for both sides was enormous and the expected quick victory through offensive action was unfulfilled. At the root of the stalemate that evolved lay the ability of both sides to secure entrenched positions behind barbedwire machine-guns and artillery fire, and to withstand all but the most complicated and time-consuming assault of a pulverising siege warfare nature. By the end of October 1914 a continuous belt of trench fortifications stretched across western Europe from the North Sea to the Swiss frontier, ditches of defiance inhabited in squalor by fighting soldiers without hope of release in victory. For the only

method to hand supposed capable of breaking the deadlock was artillery. Artillery, used in mass to crush wire, trenches and their defenders and weapons would, in the months to come, be demonstrated as inadequate to the task. It would be shown, indeed [by the manner in which artillery fire churned ground into a moonscape], as a contributor to immobility and frustration.

Yet, in the opening weeks of the war, while territory and roads remained open, and unblocked by trenches, a weapon incorporating the vital potentials of firepower, mobility and survivability had been employed with telling effect. When the mass of the Germany Army entered Belgium, crushed the forts barring their way at Liège with heavy artillery and swung, via Brussels and Mons, in the direction of the political strategic objective of Paris, they protected their exposed right flank with conventional screening forces composed of cavalry formations backed up by machine-guns and light artillery. To find and check the probing German invaders, the Belgians adapted fast, open-topped Minerva sports cars, fitting them with machine-guns and, at the earliest opportunity, with steel plates. To reinforce this small force of 'mosquitos', would come fast, armed British Lanchester and Wolseley cars, also progressively improved by the addition of armor as protection for their machinery and crews. The presence of a British force carried in 50

motor buses [a brigade of Royal Marines supported by a naval air squadron] came about as the result of an initiative by Winston Churchill who, as First Lord of the Admiralty, was responsible also for the air defense of Britain. He desired not only to help the Belgians defend the port of Antwerp and relieve pressure from the Allied armies retreating to the southward, but also to prevent the establishment of German air bases within short bombing range of England and, above all, London. On 5 September, at the suggestion of Commodore Murray Sueter, he had demanded the establishment of control over an area of 100 miles radius from Dunkirk by aircraft, protected at their bases by armed motor cars of the Royal Navy operating up to 50 miles inland, under the command of the dashing Commander C R Samson.

The influence of the armored cars upon the Germans was out of all proportion to their number. They could roam freely, finding and exploiting prolific intelligence in order to ambush enemy patrols. And they could do so, moreover, with relative immunity since the only enemy weapon likely to harm them was field artillery which, with its relatively low velocities and large zone dispersal, had, at best, a 30 to 1 chance of hitting a stationary target at 300 yards – let alone one careering along at 30 mph or more. Reduced to semi-impotence from the outset of hostilities by their stark vulnerability, the decline of the German cavalry divisions was accelerated by a few armored cars which, on the reckoning of some participants in the struggle, were each in combat worth an infantry company. Never again on the Western Front would the Germans try to use mounted cavalry in mass. It would find life safer and more profitable in the wide open spaces of the Eastern Front where continuous trench lines did not exist.

Even in the east the Germans would be confronted by armored cars, for the Russian Army showed great interest in obtaining British and Belgian vehicles and in building their own. Yet this threat was virtually ignored by the Germans who, for reasons of their own as we shall see, built only 15 armored cars between 1904 and 1917 and used them only sporadically in ones and twos in Romania and on the Russian front. As a result, there are no recorded instances of 'car versus car' fights, which there might well have been at an early stage had the Central Powers [like the British, the French, the Belgians and the Italians] embraced armed motor vehicles in a big way and deployed them to the Middle East where, in open desert spaces, they enjoyed great freedom of maneuver.

British armored car units proliferated more abundantly than others, initially under the impulse of the enthusiastic handful of sailors who had held their own in combat until the entrenchments reached Nieuport during the First Battle of Ypres, thus putting an end to their mobility. The Royal Navy would contribute the nucleus of the armored car units which burgeoned in 1915 but which, at the end of the year would be transferred to the Army and incorporated in the newly created Machine Gun Corps (MGC). In fact, in the aftermath of First Ypres, the principal naval contribution to armored warfare on land would be in the realms of design and technology and in the thrusting forward of dynamic ideas of a distinctly naval character. A typical example was the Rolls Royce armored car, with its revolving turret to encase a machine-gun, which the Navy promoted towards the end of 1914.

THE 'LAND SHIPS' ARE LAUNCHED
It was in the search for ways and means of breaking the trench deadlock by the invention of a machine to cross deep and wide trenches and suppress the fire of enemy weapons, above all machine-guns, that the Navy was principally engaged. Spurred on by Winston Churchill and inspired by inventive officers from both military and civilian agencies, including naval constructors and Albert Stern, a dynamic banker of no military experience, their interest, to begin with, was far stronger than that of the Army, whose problems they were solving. Indeed from one source only – a very powerful one as it happened – did the Army, demi-officially, face up to a radical way of breaking the

impasse. Colonel Ernest Swinton of the Royal Engineers was a military historian who had seen service in the Boer War and who, as the official war correspondent at GHQ British Expeditionary Force in France, was among the first to recognise the unique problem which had developed at the front – along with the right idea for solving it. Without knowledge of the naval involvement, Swinton came to the conclusion in October 1914, as he watched trenches enclosing Ypres, that some sort of armored fighting vehicle, carried across country by a machine based on the Holt tractor he had seen before the war, would reopen the front. He appears to have been unaware, too, of the Roberts tractor, despite its official trials by the Army – probably because it had been investigated by the Army Service Corps and the dissemination of technical information throughout the Army was, to say the least, minimal. In those days, interest in mechanization was confined to a minority of military officers, who were usually regarded with disdain by the classically educated majority.

Receiving little encouragement at GHQ, Swinton discussed his idea with an old friend, Lt Col Maurice Hankey, who was Secretary to the Committee of Imperial Defence in London, as well as to the War Council. From Hankey he received encouragement and with it the stirring of genuine interest on the part of the War Office whom Hankey tackled from Cabinet level as well as urging Churchill and the Admiralty to greater involvement. The naval investigations and experiments flourished and gradually merged with studies undertaken by the War Office under the direction of the Minister for War, Lord Kitchener. The fathers of what would be the tank were talking in naval terms of 'Land Ships' while their technologists were delving into the feasibility of adopting either very large wheels or continuous tracks to carry them across country.

By the summer of 1915 exhaustive testing of tracks and suspensions – which were the most difficult technical problems to overcome – and the formulation of a military specification by Swinton were well advanced. Swinton called for a ditch-crossing capability of 8 feet (later increased to 12 feet), a speed on the flat of 4 mph, hardened steel plate to defeat armor-piercing bullets, and an armament of two machine-guns or a 2 pounder cannon. It led Stern's team to the point at which they could fix upon something like a firm design. Its power plant would be a

Little Willie was the British attempt to build a tracked AFV with a rotating turret. Eventually abandoned because it did not have the wide trench-crossing capability demanded, it nevertheless provided automotive, transmission, suspension, and track systems which were adopted for the first combat-worthy AFVs.

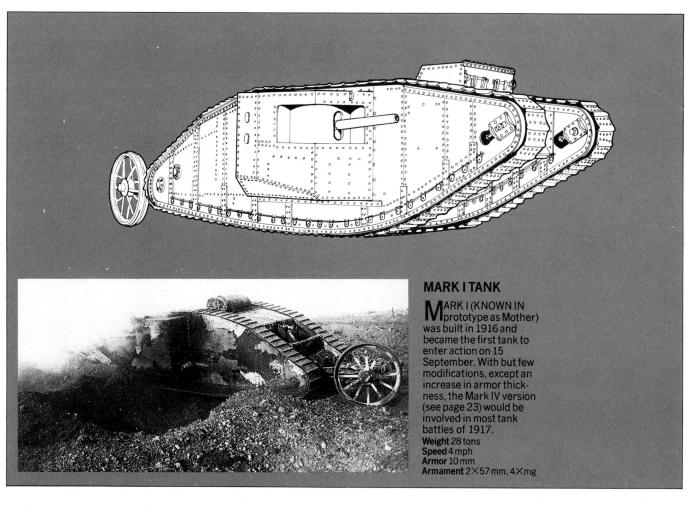

MARK I TANK

MARK I (KNOWN IN prototype as Mother) was built in 1916 and became the first tank to enter action on 15 September. With but few modifications, except an increase in armor thickness, the Mark IV version (see page 23) would be involved in most tank battles of 1917.
Weight 28 tons
Speed 4 mph
Armor 10 mm
Armament 2×57 mm, 4×mg

105 hp Daimler engine of the type currently in production to drive Holt tractors then being purchased to tow artillery. Guns and armor would come mostly from naval stocks. Wheels were rejected in favor of tracks. But none of the tracks or suspensions in existence would function in the heavy going of the trench zone. Apart from the track, the designers, to save time, improvised with existing components which could be obtained in quantity. The layout settled upon by William Tritton, of Foster and Company, resembled that of the proven Rolls Royce armored car: a steel box to hold the engine, fuel tanks, transmission and crew, surmounted by a circular rotating turret. The design of entirely original tracks was by Walter Wilson, Tritton's assistant, a highly experienced automotive engineer who was responsible for the rudimentary transmission and steering mechanism, which called for no less than four men to operate it. On 22 September, the new plate track was pronounced sound. In due course, it would carry

what was at first known as the Tritton machine, but later as Little Willie. In the meantime it had been superseded as a combat vehicle because an entirely different kind of vehicle was called for to cope with the revised requirement for the machine to cross a 12-foot wide trench.

The design which evolved was like nothing seen before or since: a rhomboidal-shaped vehicle whose tracks were carried right round the hull with a 'sponson' on each side to house the 57 mm guns and/or machine guns, with armor 10 mm thick. Known as Centipede, then as Big Willie and finally as Mother, this was the first 'tank', a generic name applied in the interests of security to persuade those not in the secret that it was merely a water cistern. The turret was abandoned, which meant that the commander, who sat in the front alongside the driver, had virtually no immediate control over the gunners in the sponsons, nor the gearsmen at the rear, when almost any sort of turn was required. The engine and track noise inside the tank drowned shouting, but there could be no attempt to install a voice communication system since nothing of the sort existed. Mother ran on her own tracks for the first time on 16 January, 1916 and within the next three weeks completed a series of secret trials to the satisfaction of her sponsors and the government. Orders for 100 of what would become known as the Mark I tank were placed in February, followed shortly by the recruitment of the first crews and their support organization. By August the first machine had been delivered and the men to crew them, drawn from all Arms of the Service, from the motor industry and straight from civilian life, had commenced training and were on the eve of being sent with their tanks to France. Awaiting was destiny, a part in the final stage of the Battle of the Somme. That had commenced in June and had made very little progress, at an immense cost in lives.

THE TANK GOES TO WAR

In August 1916 feelings of desperation pervaded at British GHQ. C in C Sir Douglas Haig's failure to break through and win a victory on the Somme prompted him to clutch at any straw and suggestions that the tanks offered something, however unpromising and if only in small quantities, could not be resisted. He demanded as many machines as possible to participate in his next major attack on 15 September, regardless of pleas from Swinton and others that a large number should be accumulated for one grand surprise blow, the consequences of which might be disastrous for the Germans. It was, indeed, a view which the French took at that very moment. Unbeknown to their allies, they too were involved secretly in the construction of a large number of tanks (chars d'assaut) with a view to using them in mass at the first big opportunity in 1917.

There was almost as much to be said for the big, delayed blow in mass against a totally unprepared enemy as there was for making empirical use of what few there were in order to test the tank's feasibility and devise battle drills. There was nothing to prove that the tactical procedures drafted by Swinton and, on 15 September, largely copied by the BEF (although Swinton's draft did not reach it) would work. Nor was there certainty that commanders at the front, invited to trust their plans and men's lives absolutely to some weird and untried weapon system would be responsible in taking such a risk. The very

existence of a blanket of secrecy is one of the best ways possible among the inherent risks of battle to pile further misunderstandings, errors and calamity one upon another. One faction assumed that enemy artillery would annihilate such large targets as they crawled forward. This was admitted by Swinton who gave that as his reason for sending tanks into action in mass in order to win through by saturation of the defenses.

On the day 32 tanks out of the 50 available reached the start line. The new weapon succeeded beyond expectation. At the same time most of the predictions, both by well-wishers and denigrators, were fulfilled. Spread out along the length of a five-mile frontage of attack, tanks which were launched tentatively into action and required to act only as auxiliaries to the infantry [who received no special instructions to vary their tactics by way of co-operation] succeeded or failed in ratio to their density of commitment. Where tanks advanced in solitary isolation and did not break down, they attracted the fire of every enemy weapon which could bear. They were overwhelmed. But where they moved forward in something like a concentrated mass, across open ground in the vicinity of the village of Flers, they made headway. At one point they overran the enemy trenches and came within sight of enemy field guns with whom they fought a duel. To Swinton's delight, they had accomplished as much as he had hoped. They had easily crushed the wire, spanned the trenches and shell holes, and helped the infantry reach their objectives with relative ease. Still more important, and not fully recognised by anybody on the British side at that moment, they had not only uplifted British morale; they had also terrified the Germans, who surrendered more readily than ever before.

Nevertheless those who decried tanks for their unreliability and vulnerability were shown to be justified. The number of breakdowns was in the region of 50 per cent after only a few thousand yards of running. The casualties inflicted by enemy field guns were also high, the gunners behind the shields of their 77 mm guns having a far better chance of seeing and hitting the monsters than had the crews inside the vehicles of replying. Yet close by Flers the first deliberate duel between tank and gun went the tank's way in a manner indicating the extreme difficulties which tank commanders endured when controlling their guns' fire. Having received information about an enemy gun and spotted its location, the commander had to leave his seat, climb back to the sponson gunners and shout instructions where to look and when to fire. Then he returned to his place, to order the driver where to go and when to stop, in theory as the target came into view of the gunners. After that, it was up to the gunners to complete the engagement.

However, artillery was found to be not the only mortal threat to the Mark I tanks on 15 September. Unbeknown to the British, the Germans in 1915 had produced a machine-gun bullet which would penetrate the steel plates increasingly being used by the Allies to protect weapon slits in the trenches. This armor-piercing (AP) bullet now proved effective against tank armor. Nevertheless, in dwindling numbers on 15 September and throughout the next few days, tanks proved their worth with several minor, local victories. These also indicated that the tank's future fortunes would depend quite as much on collaboration with other combat elements as upon its own omnipotence. This was demonstrated during a skirmish for possession of an enemy strongpoint known as the Gird Trench, when a single tank, supported by artillery fire and helped by a low-flying aircraft, succeeded in subduing the enemy to allow the following infantry to capture the trench at low cost.

It was a measure of the esteem that General Haig felt for the new weapon that, before the Somme battle ended, he had decided to give substance to its status by placing the tanks under a special headquarters of their own, which eventually would become Tank Corps Headquarters. In command Haig placed Lieutenant Colonel Hugh Elles, with Captain Giffard le Q Martel as his principal staff officer. Both were Sappers, with technical insight, and had had some connection with tanks earlier in the year. A few months later, they were joined by an infantry officer to take over as principal staff officer – Major John Frederick Charles Fuller who was blessed, along with a sardonic sense of humour and disrespect for orthodox authority, with one of the acutest military intellects of his generation.

Between the end of November and 9 April 1917, when tanks next went into action, Elles and his staff worked furiously to assimilate the lessons of the Somme and convert them to the basis of a tactical doctrine which would improve the battlefield effectiveness of the new machines and elevate them into a war-winning weapon system. As the numbers of men and machines in France were raised from the depots and factories in England, drills and training were placed on a more practical footing. Improvements to the tanks were steadily incorporated – the most important being up-armoring with 12–16 mm plates capable of defeating the armor-piercing bullet. But the 60 available Mark I and II tanks which went into action at Arras on 9 April 1917 still had the original armor and had been improved only by the removal of a pair of wheels originally fitted to the Mark Is to assist steering, but which did nothing of the sort. The latest Mark IV tank, which retained the Mark I's clumsy steering and command arrangements, would not be ready for action in any numbers until June.

Vital questions of supply, numbers and the tank's employment linked to matters of mechanical reliability and combat survivability remained. In June 1916 the British had studied the nature of the tank to succeed Mark I. They had balanced the need for an expensive, shell-proof tank against the desirability of building larger quantities of cheaper, faster tanks whose agility would be their protection. The sheer size of the manufacturing problem and the expense ruled out a 100-ton heavy tank and left the way clear for the development of the 14-ton, 8-mph Medium A tank (known as Whippet), with the same armor as the Mark IV but armed only with machine-guns. At the same time, Wilson and his fellow-designers obtained more powerful engines for Mark IV's successors and redesigned the steering system to enable one man to drive, without having to be assisted as previously.

The introduction of the British tanks at the Somme and the realization by both the French and British that they had similar thoughts about cross-country, armored fighting vehicles promoted an exchange of information and a measure of collaboration. French design had been influenced by the Holt-type track they had adopted without applying the same rigorous tests as the British. In April, at the Chemin des Dames, they would suffer troubles from this unsatisfactory suspension. The French were strongly influenced, too, by Colonel Jean Baptiste Estienne, who had been instrumental in persuading the French General Staff and industry to venture with Armored Fighting Vehicles (AFVs). As a Gunner, it was his intention to supersede the initial concept of a wire-clearing tractor with that of an armored assault gun – as were both the Schneider and the St Chamond models with a 75 mm gun fitted in the nose pointing forward. Despite their mechanical frailty, both French 'chars d'assaut' benefited from being used in relative mass [there were nearly 400 ready for the Battle of the Chemin des Dames] and from the greater simplicity of command because of the manner in which the gunner could be directed to point the 75 mm gun at pin-point targets. The fact that the Chemin des Dames battle was reduced to another massacre of French infantry owed much more to total lack of surprise over the Germans than to any inadequacy on their tanks' part, and provided further condemnation of the futility of the predominant artillery tactics.

THE GERMAN RESPONSE

The apparent ineffectiveness of Allied tanks naturally left the Germans unconvinced of their potential. A special committee (called A7V for concealment sake) was formed in October 1916 to study the subject. By Christmas, it had designed a machine based upon the Holt suspension. But it lacked such dynamic motivation as had driven the British and French sponsors and enjoyed only tepid support from the High Command. This lack of official enthusiasm was the product of several factors. From the early days of the motor vehicle, the General Staff withheld strong support – a strange attitude by leaders of the nation which had produced the first practical internal combustion engine. Prewar, the German Army had committed the bulk of its funds to rail and horse transport because both had proved perfectly adequate during the victorious European campaigns of the 1860s and 70s. There was no strong urge to change a winning combination. Yet there were many Germans who, after the collapse of their logistic system in the drive against Paris in 1914, had placed the blame on the railways for failure to repair demolished bridges and tracks in order to keep up with the advance, and on the inability of horses to maintain large enough deliveries from railheads, far in rear, to the fast-marching spearhead.

Fundamentally it was lack of a convincing military requirement, allied to mistaken forward thinking, which placed tanks low in the list of German requirements throughout 1917. While the Allies were obliged to pursue offensive action by a pressing economic and political demand to rid French and Belgian soil of the invader, the Central Powers were content – indeed compelled owing to their losses – to stand on the defensive in the West throughout 1917 while straining to overcome Russia in the East. Tanks, it was argued, had no part in the defensive battle nor in Russia, where a demoralized enemy on the verge of revolution could mount but little coordinated resistance in vast, open spaces to old-fashioned foot and horse armies. Nearly a year was wasted while the A7V Committee experimented and vacillated. Not until 1 December 1917 was an order placed for the first 100 fighting vehicles – the 30-ton A7V carried on improved Holt-type tracks. It was driven by two 100 hp Daimler engines at a top speed of 8 mph and was armed with a 57 mm gun in the nose, plus six machine-guns. Like all the other tanks then in existence, it was host to innumerable design errors and mechanical weaknesses, of which frangible armor plate was merely the most damning.

It may have been coincidence that the order for this AFV was placed at all on 1 December 1917. Undoubtedly, however, it would have been touched with a shaft of fear in the realization that the delays of the past few months might well have fatal consequences for Germany. For on 20 November on the Western Front a battle had been fought in the vicinity of Cambrai which left nobody in any nation in doubt that the tank was a deadly weapon which had come to stay.

THE OFFENSIVE AT CAMBRAI

Throughout the summer and autumn of 1917 the Allies had frittered away tanks in battles fought under the old regime. After Arras and Chemin des Dames came the capture in June of the Messines Ridge by an orthodox, siege-warfare limited assault, in which the latest Mark IV tanks made their debut in a minor but encouraging role. Then in July began what Fuller ironically termed 'The Last Great Artillery Battle', the attempt by Haig to smash his way through dense enemy defenses during the Third Battle of Ypres and to break the enemy's resistance by so-called attrition – a method which had been tried repeatedly without conclusive results since 1915. Mark IV tanks had been committed here, once more as an auxiliary sacrifice to the artillery and infantry Moloch, again without making a convincing impression but this time with calamitous results for machines. With a ground pressure of 11.6 pounds per square inch and a power to weight ratio of only 3.7 hp/ton they could not drag themselves throught the glutinous mud created by guns whose shells had wrecked the farm drainage system and churned the ground into a

THE SCHNEIDER AND ST CHAMOND M16

BASED UPON THE Holt chassis and track system, these French tanks (properly known as assault guns) had serious cross-country defects and were tactically limited due to the restricted traverse of the main armament. They nevertheless were used with some effect from April 1915 to the end of WW1 and were the fore-runners of all types of self-propelled gun in use to the present day.

Schneider M16
Weight 13.5 tons
Speed 5 mph
Frontal armor 24 mm
Armament 1×75 mm, 2×mg

St Chamond M16
Weight 23 tons
Speed 5 mph
Armor 17 mm
Armament 1×75 mm, 4×mg

morass. Many sank and provided sitting targets for German gunners. Tank Corps morale, quite literally, plumbed the depths.

The proper employment of tanks (and of men and beasts for that matter), Elles and Fuller argued, was to use them on ground compatible with their cross-country capability, terrain which was firm underfoot and relatively unbroken to allow infantry and, if possible, cavalry to keep pace with the armored advance. In June, Elles had supported a plan by Fuller to make tanks the spearhead of large-scale raids upon the enemy lines. This idea was developed shortly after Third Ypres had begun, was initially rejected but modified as Haig's main offensive stalled in the watery approaches to the Passchendaele Ridge. The sector opposite

Cambrai, preferred by Fuller, was solid chalk land upon which no serious fighting had yet taken place. Guarded on the German side by the daunting Hindenburg Line, into which they had withdrawn in March 1917, it was a seemingly impregnable position. Dense banks of barbed wire fronted a wide anti-tank ditch and row after row of well-constructed trenches, with deep dug-outs, protected the garrison from artillery bombardment. Set back in depth stood artillery with an anti-tank role. This was a sector used to rest formations which had been exhausted at Ypres; it was known by the Germans as the 'Sanatorium from Flanders'.

The abject collapse from exhaustion of Haig's offensive at Ypres provided the tanks with their first chance to show their powers in a major role in conditions suited to their use. Otherwise their emergence from the back row of the chorus might have been delayed at least another six months. But Haig badly needed a victory to compensate for the appalling defeats of the year. By the middle of October, despite his abiding conviction that tanks were too unreliable, too slow and vulnerable, and fit only for a minor role as an adjunct to infantry, he was prepared in desperation to give them their chance in the lead. More than that, he overrode the concept of a mere tank raid, or coup de main, and replaced it with a full-blooded offensive. This after-thought of an attack incorporated tank tactics devised by Fuller, as well as several tactical innovations which had been retained in the wings of experiment throughout the years. Most significantly it represented a return to the application of surprise, that supreme principle of war which had been abandoned in favour of artillery steamroller tactics which blatantly advertised every forthcoming attack.

On a front of five miles, nearly 400 tanks would be committed in the van of the assault at dawn on 20 November. Working with six

infantry divisions, they were to punch a hole through which the Cavalry Corps could break out to seize the route center of Cambrai and establish a block across the enemy lines of communication with the Arras front. In support stood batteries of machine-guns to pour a barrage of sustained fire upon key enemy positions and trenches in the forward zone. Overhead the Royal Flying Corps would, if the weather permitted, bomb enemy gun positions, supply dumps and route centers besides performing their most important task of passing back information of progress on the ground. Most important of all, concurrent with the impact of the massed tanks, would be the role of the artillery whose 1003 pieces would be precisely surveyed into their positions as a prerequisite of engaging the enemy in a totally new way. Since 1915 steady progress had been made in developng a method by which guns could be shot against targets without the prior need of 'registration' by ranging. The provision of ample ballistic and meteorological data enabled the prediction of accurate fire without warning. By handing over the wire-demolition role to tanks alone, some of them fitted with grapnels for the purpose, the guns were permitted to concentrate entirely upon the destruction of enemy emplacements and weapons, instead of wasting time and ammunition upon wire-cutting with its undesirable contribution to total loss of surprise. As an additional aid to the attack, large quantities of smoke shells were to lay a screen across dominant points and blind the enemy artillery observers, who otherwise would report and engage the advancing tanks and infantry.

The preservation of secrecy and distraction of the enemy was a lynchpin of the plan devised by HQ Tank Corps and sold to the other assault formations. Tanks, guns and men were moved quietly into position by night and camouflaged from enemy air observation which strong fighter patrols fended off by day. The story was put around that the activity was in connection with reinforcement of the Italian front, where the enemy had recently won a striking victory. As a result, although the German command did receive fragmentary intelligence of the impending attack, they took scant precautions, working chiefly on the assumption that ample warning would be given by the normal prolonged bombardment, enabling reinforcements to be moved up at leisure.

Crucial to the operation were special arrangements for breaching of the wire, the

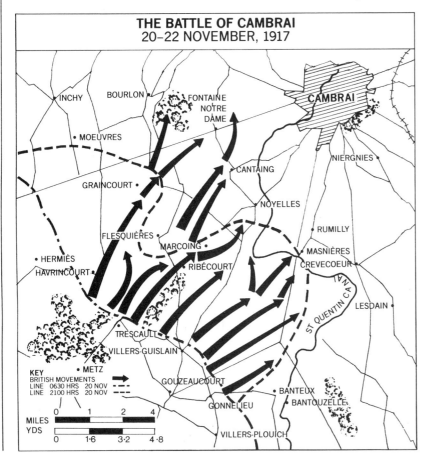

THE BATTLE OF CAMBRAI
20–22 NOVEMBER, 1917

KEY
BRITISH MOVEMENTS
LINE 0630 HRS 20 NOV
LINE 2100 HRS 20 NOV

MILES
0   1   2   4

YDS
0   1·6   3·2   4·8

anti-tank ditch and the enemy strongpoints. Vital, too was the associated need for close cooperation between tanks and infantry. In addition to crushing the vast wire barricades, many tanks carried on their noses 1¾ ton bundles of brushwood, called fascines, which they could tip into the anti-tank ditch as fillings. Once through the front line the leading wave of tanks would dominate the enemy by their presence and fire as the infantry, following in file through the gaps in the wire and supported by a second wave of tanks, would enter the defenses and mop up the survivors. That phase complete, more tanks with infantry, overtaken in due course by the cavalry, would lunge among the enemy gun and reserve positions – hoping that the enemy guns were either already destroyed by artillery fire and bombing or that the infantry and horsemen would shoot the enemy gunners at their posts.

BATTLE IS JOINED

To a remarkable extent, for so revolutionary a scheme, it worked. As the tanks started their engines and began to leave cover, all the artillery opened fire at once with a roar as the air became alive, too, with the crackle of bullets from the massed machine-guns. Instinctively the German defenders at the front went to ground and cowered in their dug-outs. To begin with, hardly a shot came back from German artillery positions. Most had previously been spotted from the air and now were struck without warning by a deluge of high explosive. Those which survived awaited orders, which did not come because, mixing with the gray mist of dawn (which severely curtailed flying), clouds of white smoke blinded the observation posts surmounting the vital high ground beyond the front line trenches. Yet poor visibility in no way prevented the tanks crawling relentlessly, on course, towards their pre-selected objectives, rolling unstoppably over the sinister banks of wire, halting only momentarily to fill the ditch with fascines and then carrying the battle ever deeper into the enemy rear. Remorselessly the overpowering ranks of machines straddled the trenches, working them over with cannon and machine-gun fire until the infantry arrived to complete the conquest with grenade and bayonet. All was achieved at astonishingly low cost, until the advance met the intermediate enemy positions where resistance at last began.

Scattered machine-gun fire from a handful of determined Germans was enough to separate tanks from infantry, for whom a speed of 3 mph across country was always unlikely, and who would advance ever more slowly when called upon to mount local attacks upon their tormentors. Inexorably the tanks on the right wing and in the center, which found themselves on an exposed forward slope in broad daylight, made what haste they could for their final objectives. These were the crossings over the Escaut Canal, which alone now barred the way to Cambrai; the crest of the Flesquières Ridge, on the left wing, which was the key to the entire battlefield; and the approaches to Bourlon Wood which commanded the vital routes leading to Bapaume and Arras.

Several tanks reached the canal two or three hours ahead of the nearest infantry. They could have crossed almost unopposed had not the only bridge capable of taking their weight been weakened by a demolition charge. It collapsed when the leading machine moved onto it. Yet tanks might still have got over if foresight and technology had made provision for assault bridges, carried on the tanks, such as would be developed in the future. But to expect anticipation of *every* eventuality in that most uncertain of environments, the battlefield, was asking too much. In any case the plan for exploitation by cavalry collapsed. Its leaders (when at last it did arrive in the afternoon, shortly after the infantry) decided that the first manifestation of reviving enemy opposition on the far bank was too stong. Apart from a single squadron of Canadian horsemen and some companies of infantry scrambling across the canal almost unopposed, the advance was allowed to come to a halt despite clear evidence that the doorway to Cambrai stood wide open.

There might also have been a breakthrough on the Flesquières Ridge, if only the infantry could have kept company with the tanks and exploited their initial success. But men on their feet enmeshed in a maze of trenches guarding this, the strongest enemy bastion, fell behind. Tanks which reached the crest had either to halt and wait or cross the skyline in full view of whatever enemy guns waited beyond. As it happened, most guns had been wrecked by the artillery fire. The few which survived were not only in bad shape (one was brought into action blocked up on timber) but also ill-prepared because they had arrived from the Russian front only the night before, were short of ammunition, and their gunners shattered to discover that the shells provided were of a new type for

MARK IV

WITH ITS 105 HP DAIMLER ENGINE, THE Mark IV tank was badly underpowered and therefore dependent on good going if it was to achieve reasonable mobility. With a crew of eight (four of whom were needed to steer it) and no inter-communication system, Mark IV was most difficult to command and control in battle over the noise of engine and guns. While the increase in frontal and side armor, to 12 mm, defeated the German armor-piercing bullet, the tank's bulk and slow speed still made it extremely vulnerable to artillery fire and very liable to catch fire when penetrated.

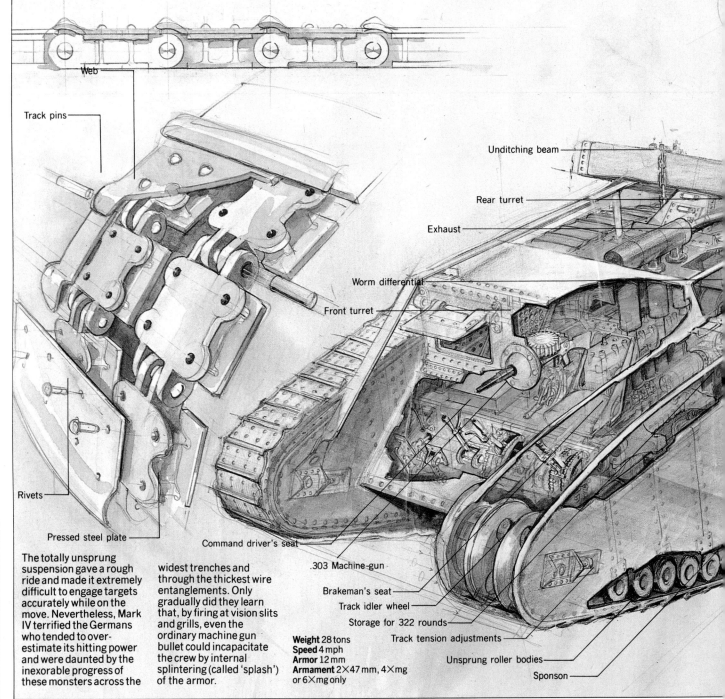

Web

Track pins

Unditching beam

Rear turret

Exhaust

Worm differential

Front turret

Rivets

Pressed steel plate

Command driver's seat

.303 Machine-gun

Brakeman's seat

Track idler wheel

Storage for 322 rounds

Track tension adjustments

Unsprung roller bodies

Sponson

The totally unsprung suspension gave a rough ride and made it extremely difficult to engage targets accurately while on the move. Nevertheless, Mark IV terrified the Germans who tended to over-estimate its hitting power and were daunted by the inexorable progress of these monsters across the widest trenches and through the thickest wire entanglements. Only gradually did they learn that, by firing at vision slits and grills, even the ordinary machine gun bullet could incapacitate the crew by internal splintering (called 'splash') of the armor.

Weight 28 tons
Speed 4 mph
Armor 12 mm
Armament 2×47 mm, 4×mg or 6×mg only

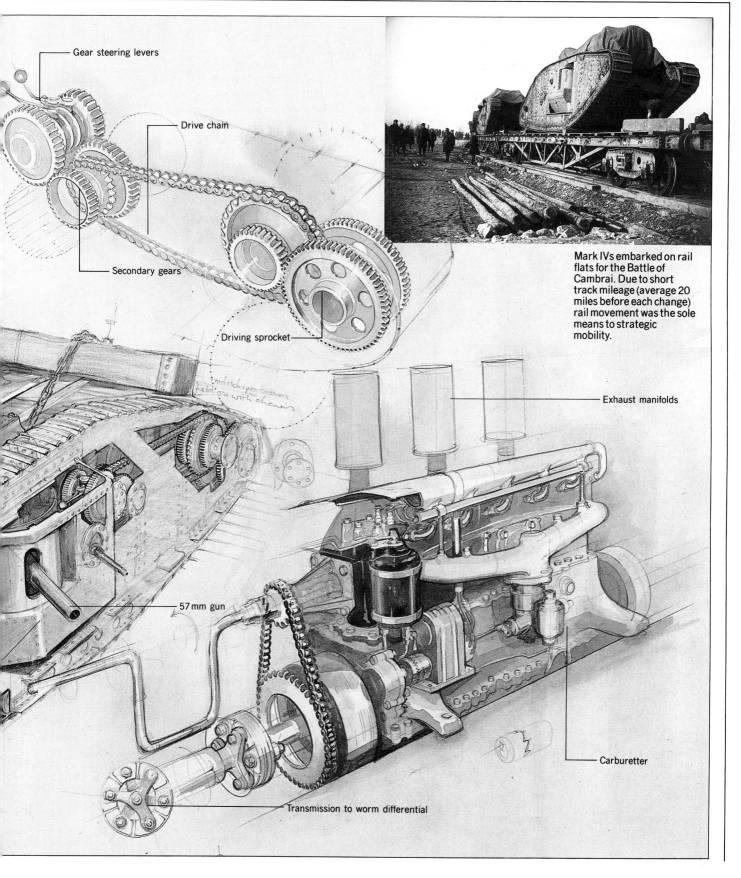

Gear steering levers

Drive chain

Secondary gears

Driving sprocket

Mark IVs embarked on rail flats for the Battle of Cambrai. Due to short track mileage (average 20 miles before each change) rail movement was the sole means to strategic mobility.

Exhaust manifolds

57 mm gun

Carburetter

Transmission to worm differential

PIONEERS OF BRITISH TANK DESIGN

WALTER WILSON

WALTER GORDON Wilson was born in 1874 and, as much as any man, designed the first tank. For a short while he was a naval officer. In 1899 he developed a light petrol engine to power a glider designed by Percy Pilcher, but Pilcher was killed in a crash. With Pilcher, too, Wilson designed a motor car. In 1904 he went to work at the Armstrong Whitworth company for whom he designed the Halford Lorry and a wheeled artillery tractor. He rejoined the Royal Navy in 1914, serving with the armored cars in Flanders before joining the tank design team. In 1915 he assisted the firm of Foster in the design of what became known as 'Little Willie', but then became the creator of its rhomboidal successor, first known as the 'Wilson', then 'Centipede', before being christened 'Big Willie', and eventually 'Mother' – the Mark I tank.

Chiefly to Wilson's credit goes Mother's transmission and, above all, the pressed-steel-plate track. Thereafter Wilson was central to British tank design and production and, as a member of the embryo Tank Corps, had a hand in all future projects. In 1917 he became Chief of Design, increasingly absorbed in the problems of transmission and steering. It was he who adopted epicyclic gears to enable the Mark V tank to be driven by one man instead of four as with Marks I to IV. And it was he who, after World War I ended, began work on self-change gearboxes for cars and tanks and on gearbox steering systems, the first of which was installed in one of the experimental Mark III medium tanks. This invention was adapted in due course for the Matilda tank, as well as the Covenanter and Crusader cruisers, and would inspire the controlled differential gearbox now used in most modern tanks.

At the outbreak of WW2 in 1939, Wilson rejoined his WW1 colleagues in designing the very heavy TOG tank – acronym for 'The Old Gang' – which failed because of, among other reasons, its inherent inability to steer! Not an easy man to work with, he had the distinction of being responsible for initiating most of the basic automotive principles of the modern tank.

PHILIP JOHNSON

PHILIP JOHNSON (born 1879) was a trained engineer who, as a civilian, helped to operate a steam railway in South Africa during the Boer War. About 1906 he joined the Fowler company to work on steamrollers and tractors intended for India. In April 1916 he enlisted in an Army Service Corps' mechanized transport company, but almost at once was sent to train drivers on the original Mark I tanks prior to seeing action with them on the Somme. He became OC of a Tank Workshop in France in March 1917 but quickly moved up to become assistant to the Tank Corps' Chief Engineer. Henceforward he plunged into design and development work. Among the innovations were specially designed tracks to help Mark IV tanks climb sea walls during a proposed (but never executed) landing in the enemy rear near Dunkirk; and, in 1918, an improvised sprung suspension to enable a modified Whippet tank to travel at nearly 20 mph – twice its designed speed. This latter project indicated the feasibility of Medium D, which Johnson was ordered to design and develop as the war ended in November 1918.

As a civilian at the Tank Design and Experimental Department, Johnson continued to work on the Medium D project, with particular emphasis upon flexible tracks and sprung suspensions. Fuller sent him to India to examine the prospects of operating tanks in the heat and in the mountains. In 1920 Johnson's reports confirmed that feasibility but went further by recommending tactics and the construction of a family of eight AFVs based on a common body – a main battle tank, a light tank, artillery carriers, a personnel carrier, and so on, in a thoroughly futuristic vein. The result was great stimulation of tank interest in the War Office and the Vickers Company after the Design Establishment and Medium D were discontinued in 1923.

Thereafter, with old colleagues from the Design Establishment, he set up the Roadless Traction Company and began the development of flexible tracks for tanks, Martel's one-man carrier, heavy guns, agricultural vehicles, half-tracked desert exploration cars and even wheelbarrows. He also designed a tracked and wheeled cradle to help launch lifeboats across beaches. Towards the end of his career he designed special large rubber tyres for use with four-wheel drive trucks and armored cars. Thus Philip Johnson always stood at the roots of the AFV business, creating vital tank elements worldwide.

J F C FULLER

JOHN FREDERICK Charles Fuller (born 1878), a light infantryman of penetrating intellect and acerbic wit was in 1916, against his desires, appointed to be General Staff Officer I of the fledgling British Tank Corps. He had seen service in the Boer War, with mobile scouts. A military genius, with technical awareness and outstanding powers of self-expression, Fuller exerted a dominant influence over the tank strategy and tactics which first blossomed as a basic doctrine at the Battle of Cambrai in 1917. Eager to demonstrate that AFVs held the key to mobility and decision, he encouraged technologists to design faster, longer-range AFVs to suit his ideas of tank-versus-tank combat and of deep penetration by armored forces. The latter concept he enshrined in Plan 1919.

Between 1919 and 1928 Fuller was extremely active in winning formal approval for a permanent British Tank Brigade as the means of experiment. Through his efforts in various key appointments, he brought about in 1927 the formation of an all-arms experimental force, the model of armored divisions to come. But he was denied its command due to his own petty obduracy over terms of reference. By 1928 an established military author, he fell from grace because of his outspokenness and the radical ideas he espoused. Yet those very ideas were taken up by far-sighted enthusiasts for tank warfare, notably by the Germans, who courted him also because of his pronounced fascist associations in Britain.

Denied further advancement in the army in the 1930s, Fuller turned to journalism and politics, while dabbling also in a little espionage against his erstwhile German 'friends'. His loyalty thought suspect by his countrymen, Fuller was denied any sort of official appointment during WW2, but became associated with the development of the very imaginative but virtually aborted CDL searchlight device. Like many a prophet, he lacked honor in his own country, but was accorded some modest recognition of his considerable achievements prior to his death.

which they did not possess the correct fuze-setting keys. It only required British infantry to advance to the crest line and shoot down the gunners to allow the tanks almost unimpeded to advance to Bourlon Wood which, almost undefended, stood in full view less than two miles distant. But the tanks were left to make their effort unaided and were picked off by the unerring aim of a few guns firing at almost point blank range whenever the tanks stuck their noses over the crest.

On the night of the 20th the Germans would withdraw of their own accord from Flesquières, but by then they had achieved their aim. They had stunned the momentum of the attack. On the 21st the British would make little progress because so many tanks were casualties. The infantry was exhausted, there were no reserves (so many men having previously fallen on other fronts or been sent as reinforcements to Italy) and the cavalry was impotent so long as a single enemy machine-gun remained in action. For the next six days, as the Germans poured in reinforcements to fill the gap torn in their defenses (one which had brought them to within a whisker of calling a massive withdrawal from Arras), the battle would revert to a familiar pattern as the number of tanks available diminished. Now it was clear that future superiority on the battle-field would depend on armored fighting vehicles, that the horse was soon to be spared the horrors of battle.

As time would show, the fight before Cambrai on 20 November had included nearly all the main innovative components of major land battles of the future – armored vehicles, unregistered artillery fire, the use of smoke and of machine-gun barrages, comprehensive air support, and the use of infantry as moppers-up instead of as the sole spearhead of attack. It was a revolution to which the Germans also were to make an original contribution on the same ground on 30 November when they retook much of that which had been lost on the 20th. For to the surprise use of unregistered artillery fire, they added revised infantry tactics in the assault, a system of infiltration of enemy positions spearheaded by special Storm Troops and ad hoc combat teams of all arms – less tanks and cavalry. Yet it was this lack of tanks which lay at the root of German vulnerability and which marked the principal difference between Cambrai and most big battles to come.

Nevertheless, even if the Germans had yet to order their own A7Vs, they did already possess a mobile anti-tank weapon system of considerable current value and immense potential – 77 mm field guns mounted as anti-aircraft guns on trucks – the successors to Ehrhardt's anti-balloon gun vehicle of 1906. It was one of these from a battery, motoring fast to Masnières from Cambrai on the 20th, which, confronted by a tank at 500 yards range, eventually destroyed its target with the expenditure of 25 rounds and lived to take part in yet another fight three days later as the British made their last throw to capture Bourlon Wood. In defense of the village of Fontaine, large numbers of these guns put five tanks out of action and were largely instrumental in bringing the advance to a final halt. Indeed, so enthusiastically did the German anti-aircraft gunners take to their new role that High Command felt compelled to issue an instruction asking them not to forget that their proper task was shooting down aircraft.

Cambrai was both a high and low water mark for British and Germans. It showed the British that they possessed an enormous advantage over the enemy, won by a technical lead which was unlikely to be overtaken in 1918: at the same time, in the knowledge that the end of hostilities in Russia would permit the Germans to send overwhelming reinforcements to the West, they realised that their weakened infantry might not in 1918 be able to withstand an opponent who fought as well as ever. For they thought that tanks in defense might have severe limitations, even though in counter-attacks at Cambrai on 1 December they had done much to stop the German counter-offensive. For their part, the Germans, shaken out of their technical and tactical lethargy by what they called 'the tank terror', were gratified that their new artillery and infantry tactics had proved as bountiful in the West as they previously had on a small scale at Riga and on a larger scale in Italy. It encouraged them to believe that what had to be their last great attempt to win the war before a flood of US reinforcements entered the field later in 1918 might just succeed – with or without tanks of their own.

They might have been a lot more worried had they realised that a man called Fuller, plunged in thought a few miles away as he studied reports of the battle as they came in to Tank Corps HQ, was already making notes on the lessons learnt. He was preparing plans which, eventually, would alter fundamentally the course of warfare besides helping to seal the Germans' fate.

CHAPTER TWO

ARMOR IN THE ASCENDANT – 1918

REACTION TO THE TANK TRIUMPH AT CAMBRAI WAS enthusiastic, yet tempered by reservations on the part of those who felt unable to push progress to a gallop – when a trot, or perhaps a canter, forward in tactical development seemed more prudent in the face of technical difficulties. Hopelessly tailed off in the armored race, the Germans, who only ever managed to build 20 A7Vs, salvaged some 40 British Mark IVs captured at Cambrai and issued them to their embryo tank units. In Italy the considerable interest which had existed in armored cars since 1912 acted as a stimulus for tank forces which, initially, looked to French models for inspiration. The Americans, whose regard for tanks had as yet been tepid, now embraced the idea, and formed a Tank Corps under Colonel S D Rockenbach. They began to design tanks and called loudly for inter-Allied tank production to win the war. In fact the Americans had no alternative because, lacking their own tanks, they depended wholly upon the French and British to equip the US units which would be ready for action under Colonel Patton late in 1918.

All attention was upon the British and the French tank forces which entered 1918 with several interesting new models to replace or supplement the machines which had carried the torch in 1917. Reaching France early in the year were the first of the British 14-ton Medium A Whippets, which had been projected in June 1916. Soon to follow would be the 29-ton Mark V, the first British one-man-drive tank, powered by a Ricardo 150 hp engine – a much improved replacement for the Mark IVs which would be wasted out in service. On the French side was a revolutionary two-man tank, the cheap Renault FT of a mere 6½ tons, armed either with a single machine-gun or with a special anti-tank cannon of 37 mm with a muzzle velocity of 388 m/sec. The Renault was the brainchild of Estienne, who demonstrated imagination by envisaging the need for a mobile, armored machine-gunner as a complement to the cannon-armed assault guns he had first sponsored.

It was the Whippets, armed only with machine-guns, and the Renaults which were the most significant innovations. Neither made any pretence at a wide trench-crossing capability, the assumption being that these would be overcome by other means after obstacles had been seized by infantry – an eventuality greatly simplified once it had been demonstrated at Cambrai how thousands of man-hours spent in excavation and construction could be nullified in a matter of minutes by fascines. The anti-tank ditch was already relegated to a mere hindrance, its place as an impediment to tanks soon to be taken by cheaper and easily laid pressure mines, improvised from shells and mortar bombs.

The main advantage of smaller and simpler machines lay in the ability of industry to build them cheaply in very large numbers (5000 Renaults were ordered in 1917), bringing closer the day when tank attacks on narrow fronts would saturate defenses by sheer mass. At the same time the Whippet promised the capability of being able to spearhead the pursuit after the heavy tanks had broken through, thus replacing horsed cavalry in its ancient role. With a far better cross-country performance than the little Renault FT, the

Whippet lacked, however, the cannon to demolish emplacements and deal effectively with enemy tanks when, as was keenly expected, they were encountered. The French made no such mistake; they ordered roughly two cannon versions of the Renault to every machine-gun type, and later replaced the 37 mm with a 50 mm gun. Upon Estienne, whom he met at the turn of the year, Fuller heaped scorn, writing in his diary, '*...An ignorant and amusing little chap. Can only think in (sic) Cannon and women and women and Cannons. Wants to fill his Tanks with 75s and his billet with chorus girls...He knows nothing of the science of war.*'

The amazing thing is that Fuller may have meant exactly what he wrote [since he repeated the slurs after the war] and was not simply indulging his caustic wit. This is a strange contradiction because already his mind was working hard on new tank tactics, including tank versus tank combat. These tactics would place far higher emphasis on the need for cannon than machine-guns.

As the ever-growing menace from the immense build-up of German forces became more apparent to the weakened Allies, a robust and, at times, vituperative debate broke out between GHQ and HQ Tank Corps as to how best to make use of tanks to counter the threat. Interwoven with British strategy and tactics were the politics related to the problems of the fading cavalry and how best to strengthen the seriously weakened infantry units. It was understandable that, faced with the need to make reductions, old-guard cavalry and infantry soldiers at GHQ (their loyalties to past tradition severely tested) strove to retain intact their long-established arms and make savings from the newest combat units, of which the Tank Corps was newest of all. Elles and Fuller found themselves in a life and death struggle for the Tank Corps, a row at whose heart lay arguments as to how best to employ tanks within the framework of a defensive strategy.

As the main plank of his measures, Fuller advocated pre-emptive tank and infantry raids of up to three divisions in strength, aimed at destroying enemy personnel and material, disrupting his arrangement and making him divert disproportionate elements to pure defense all along the front. After these ideas were rejected out of hand by GHQ, Fuller complained that the ensuing inaction on the part of the British would lead to a

The Medium A or Whippet tank which was first envisaged as a substitute for horsed cavalry.

deterioration of morale – as all too unhappily occurred. He then turned to less aggressive schemes which, nevertheless, laid down with remarkable perception, in documents omitted from his *Memoirs*, the principles upon which all future anti-tank tactics would be based.

In a letter to GHQ on 30 December 1917, Fuller wrote: '*All missile weapons may be used for destroying the Tank. They may be divided under the usual headings: Artillery, Infantry, Tanks, RFC [meaning aircraft].*

He argued that '*Mobile anti-tank defense is undoubtedly the strongest means at present obtainable. ...Tanks have a superiority over artillery in that they are petrol-driven instead of horse-drawn*'.

This initiative produced an examination of the problem by GHQ which led to a Tank Corps letter dated 15 January confirming Fuller's detailed proposals. Having defined the most likely strategic, tactical and administrative objectives of tank attacks, the type of country in which they would operate, and the methods they would employ out to ranges of two miles from their starting points, Fuller outlined the nature of tank-versus-tank combat, as he envisaged it, under two headings: (a) Individual Tanks acting as mobile batteries; (b) Tank Units co-operating

RENAULT FT

THE RENAULT FT. THIS French model was simply designed as a cheap, easily produced machine-gun carrier of poor cross-country performance to accompany infantry in the assault.

Weight 6 tons
Speed 5 mph
Frontal armor 22 mm
Armament 1×37 mm or 1×mg

with the other arms against a hostile Tank and Infantry attack '

'... *THE ACTION OF individual Tanks will be similar to that of mobile field guns. The success of their employment will depend on (a) Power of maneuver, (b) Good shooting, (c) Cooperation with the fixed and mobile defenses of the sector in which they are operating...'*

'The latter requirement entails an intimate knowledge of the defense scheme of the sector in question, as well as of the ground over which they may be called to operate.'

'If the sector is furnished with anti-Tank defenses, i.e. guns, special trenches etc (including mines), Anti-Tanks should be held in rear between these as counter-attacking units. Not only should they be stationed between *these points to beat back frontal attacks which have passed through the gaps between them, but should be so placed as to be able to take them in enfilade...'*

'The tactics to be adopted should be one of concentrating the fire of as many individual Tanks as possible on single hostile Tanks, and so destroy them one by one. Individual duels should be guarded against.'

'The main principle of action against an enemy's Tank attack followed by Infantry is – that our Anti-Tanks should work as Tank Destroyers; that is their objectives are the enemy's Tanks, not his Infantry, which should be left to our Infantry to deal with...'

'This will mean that in an important attack of Tanks and Infantry against Tanks and Infantry, command of Tank action will first have to be won before the main Infantry action can begin. This gaining of Tank superiority will probably entail a definite Tank action in advance of the Infantry, and will necessitate not only the addition of an advanced echelon of Tanks operating as Tank Destroyers, but the introduction of an extremely mobile and lightly armored Tank equipped with a pivot high velocity gun or pom-pom with all round fire. The action of such an echelon will probably be one of breaking up the enemy's line of Tanks, and enveloping one half of it, and destroying it by concentric fire, and then doing the same with the second half; in other words – applying the 'Nelson Touch' to land warfare.'

Fuller knew that with the machines at the Tank Corps' disposal these proposals could not be wholly met. He did not even bother to mention the need for radio control (which had long ago been called for by Swinton as a means of inter-communication between tanks), a technology which had been none too effectually used with 'Wireless Tanks' as advanced reporting posts at Cambrai. Nor did he touch upon a damning mechanical defect which militated against supreme mobility – the inability of tanks to move much farther than 20 miles without replacement of tracks, which wore out at about that distance, and the shortage of railway flats to move them in large numbers from one threatened part of the front to another. It was this strategic immobility which forced upon GHQ the need to spread tanks in small groups along the entire front if they were to make any immediate contribution at all; and to devise the much-reviled tactic of the 'Savage Rabbit' – that is of individual tanks dug into pits from which they would emerge, like savage

rabbits, to bite the enemy. Fuller was unfair to denigrate totally these ambush tactics without, in his *Memoirs*, also mentioning the underlying technical reasons. But he was correct in pointing out that, by so detaching machines from their logistic support facilities, they were offered as hostages to fortune in the form of breakdown and fuel shortage.

The naval allusion, even after the Royal Navy had ceased to participate in tank development in 1916, was never far from the mind of tank soldiers. As early as November 1916, Martel had written a paper proposing a 'Tank Army which would be composed entirely of fighting vehicles' – machines which he categorised as Battle Tanks, Destroyers and fast Torpedo Tanks (the latter armed with mortars to engage the enemy at 500 yards with heavy projectiles). Martel dreamed of encounters closely akin to naval warfare, with tank fleets sheltering in bases, protected by minefields and obstacles, prior to emerging to clash with opposing tank fleets. Although Fuller at first decried this image, he tended, later in 1918, to return to it – overlooking, as did everybody else who entertained such ideas, that the sea's flat plain lacked the land's topographical features which form defiles, natural cover, built-up areas and all manner of obstructions which caused the infinite number of tactical variations that were absent from naval warfare.

In stating that the imminent advent of enemy tanks would, at a stroke, seriously reduce the existing Allied superiority in armored warfare, Fuller was undeniably right. However, he was quite unaware that the Germans had been so tardy in acquiring tanks of their own and that the threat would be so very slow in emerging, and so small when at last it did appear. Not until the morning of 21 March 1918, when a five-hour unregistered artillery barrage engulfed the British lines to announce the commencement of Operation 'Michael', did every tank the Germans could scrape together roll into action – all four A7Vs and five ex-British Mark IVs. Unknown to the British command at that time, these machines achieved at St Quentin all and more than was expected of them. In 24 hours they advanced up to five miles without serious loss, and played a useful role in engineering a notable British collapse which spread far and wide along the length and depth of the British front.

Yet as the 15 days of 'Michael' ran their

A captured British Mark IV female in German employment supporting infantry with its Lewis machine gun, which is visible in the sponson. Because the Germans had been so tardy investigating the tank idea, they had mainly to depend upon British tanks captured during their counter-offensive at Cambrai in December 1917.

course, to advance the German lines up to 20 miles on a frontage of 32 miles, their tanks took no further part. For the Germans, it was the infiltration tactics of ad hoc combat teams of artillery and infantry which worked the trick. British tanks, particularly those which counter-attacked in groups, scored several successes in checking, if not throwing back, enemy penetrations. Nevertheless, it was the characteristic failure of an under-mechanized army's logistic system which eventually checked the German momentum and saved the Allies from rout. Of the hundred or so British tanks lost, the vast majority made little contribution to the defense, and fell victim in far larger numbers to breakdown and fuel starvation than to enemy fire. Individual tanks were of little effect. There are no recorded tank versus tank duels in this period. Nor would the Germans commit tanks to the next phase of the grand assault, Operation 'Georg', which hit the Allies in Flanders and, like 'Michael', came to a halt as a result of human exhaustion and logistic atrophy. Not until 24 April were tanks from both sides to indicate the true direction of armored warfare in the future.

DUEL AT VILLERS BRETONNEUX

The first tank versus tank fight of all on 24 April came about not, as supposed at the time, from a renewed major German effort to break through at the front center at Amiens, but as the by-product of a local German attack. The intention of General G von der Marwitz was to seize the commanding ground beyond the villages of Villers Bretonneux and Cachy with a view to

THE MEDIUM A WHIPPET

THE BRITISH WHIPPET WAS AN ATTEMPT to make possible the fast exploitation of tactical opportunities created when heavy tanks had broken through the enemy lines. Slightly less vulnerable than Mark IV, it was adopted instead of a 100-ton shell-proof tank because it was much easier to make in large numbers.

Its two, side-by-side, 45 hp Tyler engines each drove one track through a bevel box and cross-shaft. Steering was by a wheel which varied the speed of one engine relative to the other, although brakes could be applied to make sharper turns. Track and suspension were unsprung and subject to the same 20-mile life as Mark IV, which restricted strategic mobility. The abandonment of a very wide trench-crossing capability (which was no longer necessary once fascine-carrying Mark IV tanks had shown how easily these obstacles could be overcome) made it possible to introduce the much simpler track arrangement. This showed the way ahead to a new trend in tank design – with a revolutionary impact on tactical doctrine.

Weight 14 tons
Speed 8.3 mph
Armor 12 mm
Armament 4 mg

Twin-engine compartment

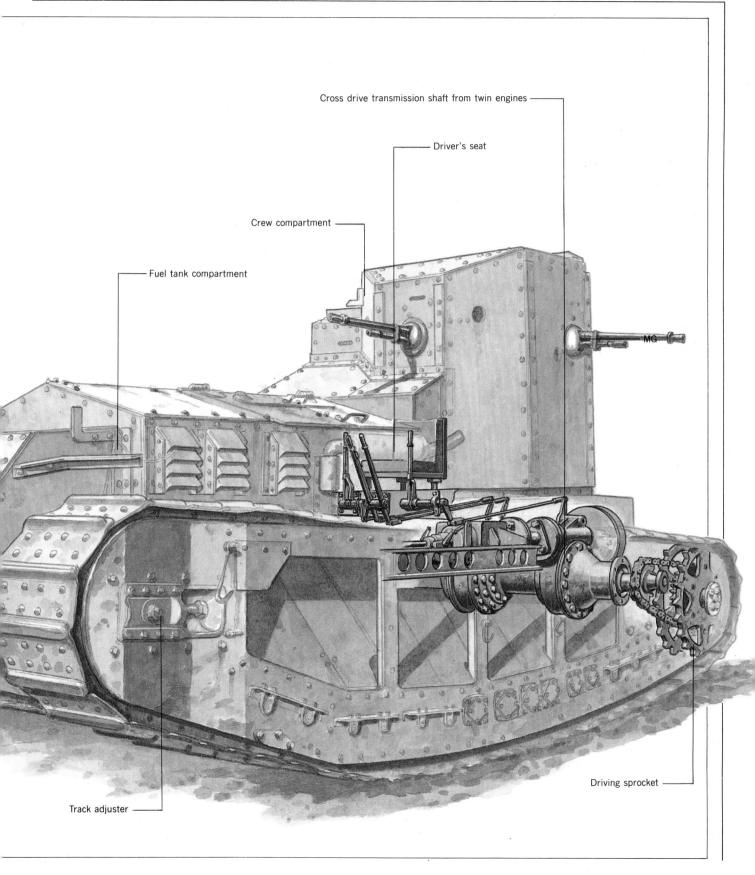

Cross drive transmission shaft from twin engines

Driver's seat

Crew compartment

Fuel tank compartment

MG

Driving sprocket

Track adjuster

Above: The female Mark V* tank was a six-foot-lengthened version of the much improved Mark V tank (see page 37). After an idea by Fuller, the intention was to carry forward, in the extra space, infantry machine-gunners to drop behind the enemy lines as a barrier against retreating enemy. In practice it failed because fumes within the hull largely incapacitated the infantry. But the idea of the Armored Personnel Carrier (APC) was born.

Right: The first tank radio sets were fitted into Mark IV tanks for use as forward message reporting centers during the Battle of Cambrai. The bulky and heavy 'spark' transmission instrument, in common use at that time, sent messages by morse code only and was therefore somewhat slow and unreliable in performance. At Cambrai radio did not come up to expectations. But the idea was henceforward worked upon with persistence both by the British and the French who already envisaged that the day would dawn when all tanks could communicate by radio with each other.

bringing the vital route center of Amiens, five miles to the east, under observed artillery fire. If, in the event, the Allied line gave way once more, well and good: 'we'll just act according to the situation', said the German Chief of Staff, General Erich Ludendorff. But with only five divisions and small reserves available for the assault by the two Corps, and an acute shortage of amunition readily to hand, the chances of a sustained exploitation were slight. Moreover, the allocation of only 15 A7Vs (the biggest concentration of tanks at one point ever achieved by the Germans) did little to enhance confidence. Indeed, as remained Allied practice, the Germans expected nothing more of their tanks than infantry support. Once through the enemy front line trenches they were to withdraw. This was an operation fraught with peril in the knowledge that serious opposition must be expected from British 18-pounder field guns, plus some tanks which had been

spotted in the woods behind Villers Bretonneux and Cachy. These positions the Germans regularly bombarded with high explosive and drenched with mustard gas in the days prior to the assault, activity which not only forewarned the British defenders, but made life extremely uncomfortable for both their gunners and the tankmen.

The ten British tanks allocated to support this sector were by no means well equipped for anti-tank warfare. Seven were C Battalion Whippets armed only with machine-guns. Two were 'female' Mark IVs, also armed only with machine-guns. Only the 'male' Mark IV, under command of 2nd Lieut Frank Mitchell, had with its two 57 mm guns the capability of penetrating the armor of the A7Vs and this machine, as the mainstay of the three Mark IV 'savage rabbits' of A Battalion under Capt FC Brown, had its crew reduced to six by gas attack before the action commenced.

In foggy conditions, made denser by gas and smoke, the Germans attacked in three groups. Group 1, consisting of three A7Vs, made straight for Villers Bretonneux; Group 2 of seven A7Vs headed for the Bois d'Aquenne with its right flank on the railway line; Group 3 with with four A7Vs drove up the slope past Bois de Hangard towards Cachy. Group 1 was entirely successful, entering Villers Bretonneux well ahead of its accompanying infantry, taking many prisoners but then having to turn about to overcome British infantry it had by-passed and who were preventing the German infantry following up. By noon Group 1 had completed its task and been sent back to its rallying point. Group 2 was almost as successful, despite more difficulties – the subtraction of one tank at the outset from breakdown; loss of direction in the fog (which hung much more thickly around the woods and Cachy than it did at Villers); two minor breakdowns in action; and the wounding of two drivers due to penetration of armor by machine-gun fire.

It was Group 3 which made history, hampered as it was by fierce enemy resistance in Bois de Hangard [which stopped the German infantry] and by the fog which made the A7Vs lose their way. Indeed, A7V *Elfriede*, under command of Leutenant Stein, wandered to the north of its course, dealt with enemy resistance but then toppled over into a quarry. Dismounting and reverting to infantry, as their training prescribed, the crew of 22 continued to hold the quarry against a British infantry counter-attack until Stein was killed and both sides decided to withdraw.

The attack commenced at 0700 hrs, British time. An hour later, Capt Brown walked forward with the local British infantry commander, Brigadier G W Grogan, to reconnoiter. As a result, German progress was ascertained but not the presence of tanks. At 0845 hrs, Brown had returned to his three Mark IVs and, in Mitchell's male tank, led the advance of his savage rabbits along the southern edge of Bois d'Aquenne (which Mitchell had previously checked out) with the two females echeloned back to the right. It was not until Brown and Mitchell reached the Cachy Switch trench they were ordered to defend, that an infantryman jumped up and shouted through an observation slit 'look out, there's Jerry tanks about'. A moment later Mitchell saw the three A7Vs of Group 3 approaching Cachy; the nearest, that of Biltz, at about 400 yards range, the other two dim in the mist to the south. He also saw advancing nearby a swarm of German infantry.

At once Brown left the male Mark IV to run across and warn the two female Mark IVs, leaving Mitchell to turn towards Biltz and open fire while still on the move. Biltz, for his part, spotted the two females, halted and opened fire as they began to turn away, hitting one without immobilizing it. Simultaneously Mitchell's gunners, having spotted the German tank through their vision slits, were taking aim through their guns' telescopes and firing ranging shots. But because Mitchell continued to zigzag on the move, preventing any continuity of shooting sequence, let alone providing a steady platform, they missed every time. Moreover the need for the gearsmen to act as loaders, while engaged also in helping steer the tank, interfered with rate of fire. Only when Mitchell at last halted at about 1020 hrs did the left sponson gunner have a real chance, scoring three hits with solid shot in quick succession on Biltz. The armor was pierced, mechanical damage inflicted, the artillery gunner killed, and two men fatally wounded, beside some minor injuries. At that Biltz ordered the evacuation of his A7V and joined up with the nearby infantry. They had no further desire to advance against the triumphant Mitchell, who now began shooting at Bitter and Muller in the distance.

Both Bitter and Muller were held up before Cachy, lacking support from their infantry who were pinned down by British fire and engaged in reorganizing for a second attempt. Simultaneously, a British aircraft had spotted them and flown back to drop a message to Capt T R Price, commanding the seven Whippets. Price at once set off for Cachy to tackle what he was led to believe was only an infantry target. Flat out, he covered the three miles to arrive on the scene at about 1100 hrs. Shaking out into line, Price charged past Cachy, over the British trenches and among the German infantry sheltering in shell holes in dead ground beyond, scattering them and disrupting their plans. But in crossing the small ridge above the dead ground, all seven Whippets came into full view of Bitter, whose gunner began to make excellent practice at 300 yards range, totally undisturbed by fire from the Whippets who were fully concentrated upon shooting and running over men. Indeed the Whippets' crews were quite unaware of the A7Vs' presence and virtually impotent against them with machine-guns, even had they spotted the German tanks through the mist. One Whippet burst into flames. The others began to zigzag, continuing to hunt enemy infantry. Then a second burst into flames, and a third was disabled. The rest turned tail over the ridge back to Cachy. There a fourth broke down within 100 yards of Mitchell, who had been an interested spectator of the entire engagement – except that he could not see the German A7V which had done most of the damage.

VILLERS BRETONNEUX, 24 APRIL 1918

THE FIRST TANK V TANK BATTLE

The encounter between British and German tanks on 24 April, 1918 was an almost accidental by-product of a conventional World War I infantry engagement. It revealed the acute limitations of the anti-tank capability of the machines available, particularly the lightly armed British Whippets.

Shown in this panorama is the moment when Bitter's A7V (foreground) is engaging the Whippets on a forward slope, even as the British crews are intent on machine-gunning and running down terrified German infantry. Already Bitter's gunner has set one Whippet ablaze and damaged another.

Map 1 (page 36) shows the opening moves on the morning of 24 April of what was to become the first tank-versus-tank encounter. The three Groups of German A7V tanks had led infantry through early morning mist, smoke and gas towards their objectives – the Bois d'Aquenne and the villages of Villers Bretonneux and Cachy. The three tanks in Group 1 were making good progress [Map 2] to subdue British infantry in Villers Bretonneux and the wood beyond,

(cont.)

CACHY

MITCHELL

BOIS D' HANGARD

NORTH

VIEWPOINT

VILLERS BRETONNEUX

THE FIRST TANK V TANK BATTLE (continued)

before being compelled to turn about to help their own infantry caught by the British still holding out in the village. Group 2, however, had problems. One of its seven A7Vs had broken down; some were veering off course in the fog; and two had suffered minor damage. Yet this Group also managed to reach its objectives without further serious incident.

Map 2 also shows Group 3 groping past Bois de Hangard towards Cachy. Like the others, it was well ahead of the infantry it was supporting. But on this flank Lieutenant Mitchell's Mark IV 'male' tank emerged from its hide in Bois L'Abbé to engage the advancing enemy and give 57 mm gun support to the two accompanying machine-gun armed 'female' Mark IVs. The time was about 0945 hrs and the range, in improving visibility, some 400 m when Mitchell and his Section commander, Captain Brown, saw two German tanks, one of which was commanded by Leutnant Biltz. As Brown departed on foot to contact and send back the out-gunned machine-gun tanks Biltz opened fire, damaging one of them; while Mitchell maneuvered to engage Biltz without at first scoring. Not until 1020 hrs did Mitchell halt to give his left sponson gunner a reasonable chance of crippling Biltz's tank with three rounds of AP solid shot. This crippled the A7V and led to its evacuation, with two men left dead inside. A few minutes later Mitchell managed also to get the A7Vs commanded by Leutnants Muller and Bitter in his sights, but without noticeable effect.

Meanwhile, as can be seen in Map 2, Captain Price's seven Whippets, alerted by air-dropped message, were advancing upon Cachy intending to engage what they believed were enemy infantry only, trying to enter the village. Mitchell (see Map 3), patrolling to the northward, is a spectator of the retreat of the Whippets. The Whippets' leader, Price, remains quite unaware that his losses have been caused by an enemy tank and not, as he reported, a field gun.

The main action ended at midday with the Germans secure in Villers-Bretonneux but frustrated outside Cachy by the well-timed British tank attack. As Group 2 retired, Mitchell encouraged their departure at 1000 m range with a few optimistic and errant rounds of 57 mm shot before, at 1245 hrs, breaking a track. At 1430, just prior to

the mutual retirement of both sides, Bitter and Muller tried once more to seize Cachy but were thwarted because their infantry were cowed by the battle going on around them. The battlefield was left to broken machines, many of their crews having dismounted and fought as infantry.

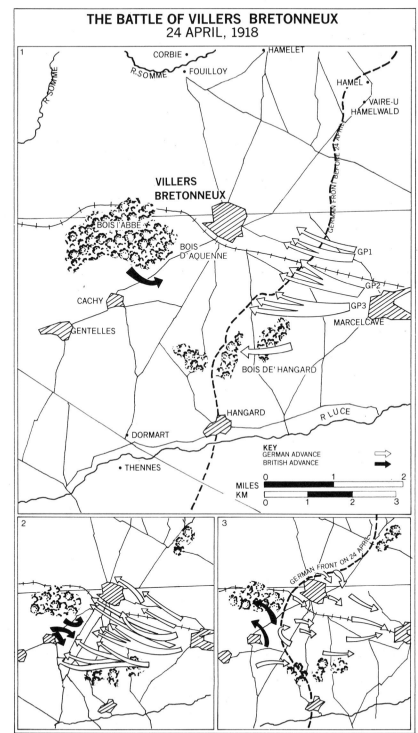

THE BATTLE OF VILLERS BRETONNEUX
24 APRIL, 1918

LESSONS OF THE ENCOUNTER

The main battle was over. Mitchell would continue to patrol the Cachy Switch, speculatively engaging at 1000 m some A7Vs of Group 2 withdrawing from Villers Bretonneux, but having a track wear out and break at 1245 hrs. About 1430 hrs, while arranging the evacuation of his wounded, he was to see Bitter and Muller advance once more to shell Cachy, but then retire for good because the German infantry declined to follow. It was Mitchell's conclusion that it was a great day for the German tanks. They had, indeed, had the best of the tank-versus-tank encounter and done all, and more, that the infantry expected of them. Mitchell overstated a little by calling it 'their Cambrai'. There was a wealth of difference between a massed attack which had achieved most of its objectives and a localised affair (albeit one that captured 2000 prisoners) which failed in its main aim.

The lessons of Villers–Bretonneux were, however, highly important, even if only the tank men of both sides drew profound conclusions from it. German convictions about the need for tanks were strengthened, along with the validity of their technique of shooting at the halt. At HQ Tank Corps it was appreciated that this was but the first of many such similar events to come, one which indicated a need to develop and practice techniques for shooting accurately on the move and which made it highly desirable that

as soon as possible all tanks should be given an anti-tank weapon. They began at once by replacing on as many female tanks as possible one machine-gun sponson with a 6-pounder gun sponson, thus producing what became known as the 'hermaphrodite tank'. At the same time, the Germans, in particular, began the development of special, low profile anti-tank guns, varying in caliber from 13 mm to 37 mm, to offset a disparity in tank numbers they had no hope of rectifying.

In the months to come, as the number of tanks available to the Germans grew no greater, those pouring from British and French factories amounted to thousands. In the wake of Operation 'Georg', successive German blows against the French, as they in turn were brought to a halt, were riposted by immediate tank counterstrokes of terrifyingly increasing dimensions. Renault FTs, which appeared in battle by the dozen in May, were being launched to attack by the hundred in July, by which time the latest British Mark V tank was joining the Whippets in making a devastating impact. Soon these local tactical moves were to be raised onto the strategic plane as the result of an imaginative paper written by Fuller in January 1918 in which he envisaged deep penetrations of enemy defenses by all arms forces. Fuller proposed to develop the role of the Mark V tank, by giving it the capability to act as an armored personnel carrier (APC) in addition to its primary role as a fighting tank. His

The male Mark V, seen here with infantry in the advance in 1918, was an improvement on the Mark IV if for no other reason than it had a good, new 150 hp engine and needed only one man to drive it. Along with Whippet, it was the mainstay of the British Tank Corps in 1918.
Weight 29 tons
Speed 5 mph
Frontal armor 12 mm
Armament 2×57 mm, 4×mg

GERMAN A7V

THE A7V WAS GERMANY'S FIRST AND only production tank; only 20 were made in time for battle in 1918. With a suspension based on the pre-war Holt design, this clumsy AFV was an attempt to incorporate a combat team of anything up to 20 men in a single vehicle – with artillerymen to man the gun, infantrymen to serve the machine-guns, and somewhat despised mechanics to drive and maintain it.

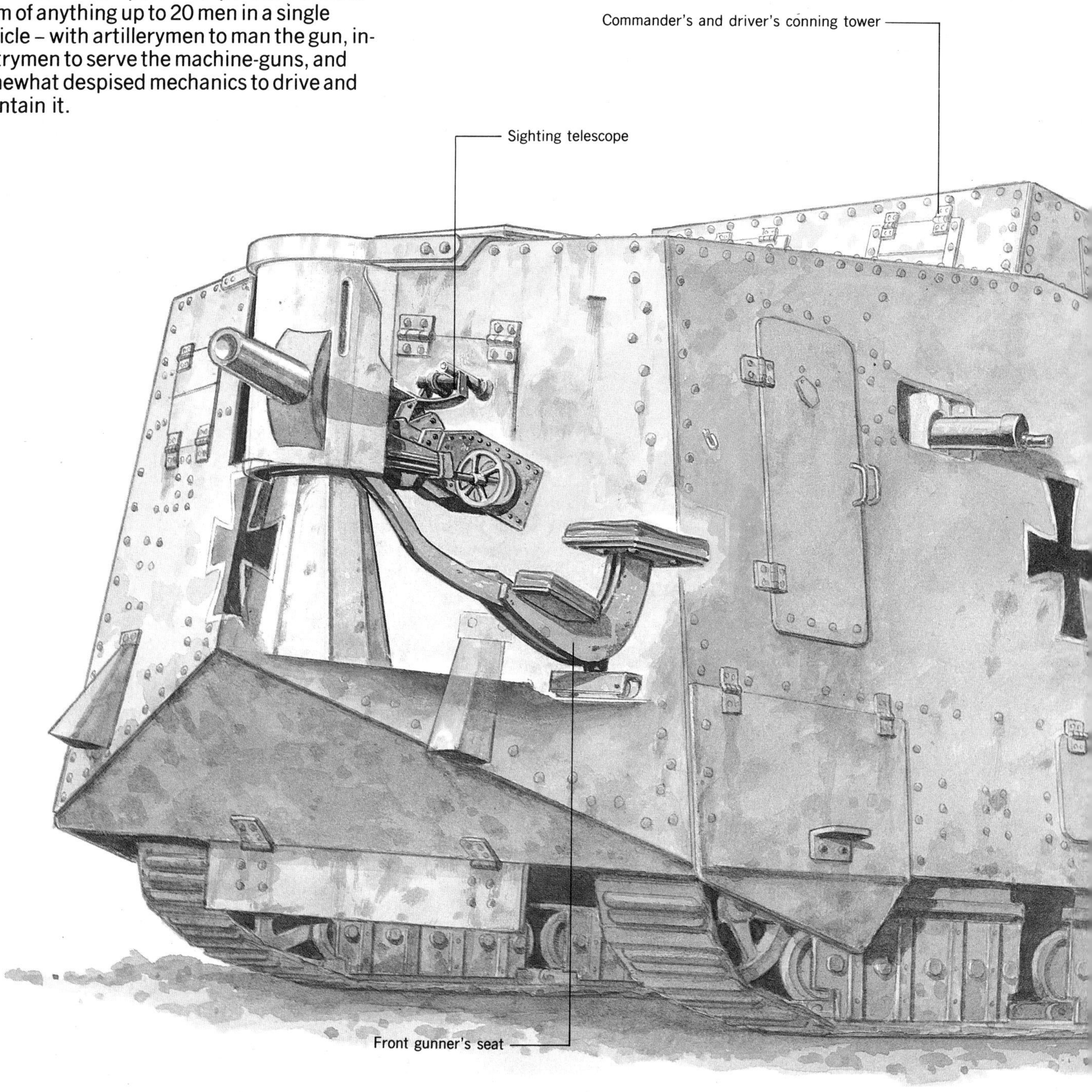

Commander's and driver's conning tower

Sighting telescope

Front gunner's seat

Two Daimler 100 hp engines powered the vehicle over a 20-mile radius. The suspension was unsprung. Yet for all its defects, it proved reasonably reliable and successful in action, if not too popular with its crews, some of whom preferred the captured British Mark IVs.
Weight 32 tons
Speed 5 mph
Frontal armor 30 mm
Armament 1×57 mm, 6×mg

Exhaust pipe from engine

Driving sprocket

suggestion was to insert a six-foot center section to provide room for 25 infantry machine-gunners (or stores), making it possible to exploit armor protection to deposit safely the machine-gunners in the sensitive enemy rear with promising psychological effects.

That was the genesis of the Mark V* which was ready for action in time for the Battle of Amiens of 8 August, when no fewer than 288 Mark Vs, 72 Mark V*, 96 Whippets, 12 Austin armored cars and 90 French Renaults crashed through the German lines on a 25-mile frontage to a depth of nine miles in a single day. This blow, to the accompaniment of massive surrenders and a collapse of German morale, tolled the death knell of the already exhausted Central Powers – and also that of horsed cavalry as the arm of exploitation and pursuit. For, once more offered the wide gap they demanded, the cavalry were unable to live up to their promise and ride through. It was the Whippets and the armored cars, moving fast into open spaces created by the heavy tanks and infantry, that performed whatever exploitation was achieved. Not once were they impeded by the German tank arm, which was neither in position nor with the strength to do so if it had chosen. At Amiens it was tank versus gun in the armored exchanges, with tanks suffering badly but usually, with infantry help, coming out on top.

The psychological effect of the overwhelming numerical strength of the Allied tank forces upon both sides was pronounced. Perniciously it was assumed by both sides that every tank seen in action *must* belong to the Allies. At Fremicourt near Bapaume, on 31 August, when the local German troops were placed on alert because several British tanks had been spotted advancing against

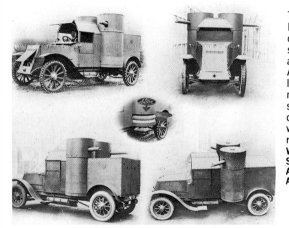

The Austin armored car. Based in 1917 on a truck chassis, it was used with success in a breakthrough at the Battle of Amiens in August 1918. Of only limited combat value, its mobility was severely restricted by its two-wheel drive and narrow wheels which virtually made it road-bound.
Weight 4.5 tons
Speed 35 mph on road
Armor 8 mm
Armament 2 mg

Vaulx-Vraucourt, five German A7Vs sent to counter-attack were engaged by their own artillery with the loss of two machines. Had this not happened it is very likely that the Germans, who were less than 2000 yards from the flank of the British attack, would have engaged the British Mark IVs from a position of considerable advantage. But a few weeks later at Niergnies, on the outskirts of Cambrai, the boot was on the other foot.

THE BATTLE OF NIERGNIES
Throughout August and September the Germans had fallen back, using their tanks but little until 7 October. Then it was they managed to concentrate ten Mark IVs (formed into so-called 'captured battalions') to the south of Cambrai in an endeavor to check an impending British offensive which was intended to envelope the city next day. Six lay in wait at Awoingt and four at Wambaix until the axis of the British thrusts towards Niergnies and Serainville was disclosed. In the half light of dawn the Germans headed for the smoke-enshrouded combat zone where enemy tanks and infantry were reported to be following up their artillery barrage. Unavoidably they confronted eight Mark IV tanks of 12th Battalion, four allocated to lead against each of the villages. At Serainville, after two German Mark IVs were knocked out by artillery fire, the others pulled back, amazingly unseen by the four British tanks even though they were within close range of each other. In blissful ignorance, one of the female British tanks con- tinued to advance, veering to its left through the village and making for Niergnies via Forenville.

At Niergnies, however, there was no question of the converging tank groups avoiding each other in the battle gloom. Each saw the other at the same time, but while the Germans deliberately withheld their fire, the British copied them in the belief that, by some miracle, the four tanks of C Company advancing from Serainville, had already arrived! The range was down to 50 yards before Capt Rowe, in tank L16, realised that he was facing an enemy machine. His first shot penetrated but only disabled the target a moment before the German shot back, wounding Rowe and killing his driver. Bailing out and then contacting L19, nearby, Rowe led it towards the enemy. But L19 was full of wounded and without gunners to fire the 57 mm guns. This tank also was hit twice and set alight, as was L12, when it blundered into the fight, its commander still in the belief that the enemy tanks belonged to C Company. And finally the fourth tank, L8, commanded by Lt Martel, dropped out of the running due to loss of coolant through a leaking radiator. Yet it was Martel who, nevertheless, stopped the rot. He joined forces with an artillery observation officer and they turned a captured enemy field gun against the Germans, knocking out two tanks at short range. At this moment the female tank from C Company put in an appearance. It was quite unable with its machine guns to penetrate the surviving four enemy tanks, but sufficient by

Mark V tanks go into action in 1918 with infantry in support. Notice the wide dispersion between tanks, and also the oak beams carried on rails for attachment to the tracks for un-ditching if the tank became bogged.

its presence to persuade the disheartened, though victorious, Germans that this was the cue to depart.

By a twist of fate neither the French nor the American tank troops were ever exposed to tank-versus-tank combat in World War I, mainly because the Germans were in the habit, for mechanical reasons, of withdrawing their tanks from the forward areas once they had completed their task in support of an attack. As a result, when the Americans, for example, used the 174 Renaults of their 304th Tank Brigade in the assault on the St Miheil salient on 12 September, it was to hit an opponent who was already in the process of withdrawal and without a tank in place. Preserved from the German experience of repeated exposure to overwhelming onslaughts by hundreds of tanks at once, none of the British, American or French troops came fully to sense what was too horrifyingly real to the Germans – that the multiple effects of mass along with mobility, firepower and protection added up to 'Tank Terror' in a battle- and war-winning way. It was ignorance of reality on the Allied part that was to create, by default, consequences of dire peril by underestimating the true threat of armor just as dread of the Terror sometimes led the Germans to overrate it; although usually this awareness guided the Germans along the course, leading to the day when their armored fighting vehicles and formations would become dominant weapon systems in any engagement undertaken on land.

The encounters at Villers Bretonneux and Niergnies had, however, established the

pattern, in microcosm, of the majority of subsequent tank-versus-tank engagements, besides teaching vital lessons. Among the latter was the need for the commander completely to command his gunner from a revolving turret, in order to eliminate the need to maneuver the tank into a firing position. Another lesson was that the gunner must be taught special techniques to obtain the best from much-improved armament.

CHAPTER THREE

THE EXPERIMENTAL DECADES

IN THE IMMEDIATE AFTERMATH OF THE WAR THE TANK'S prospects hung in the balance, threatened in some quarters by the danger of extinction at the hands of those who chose, from self-interested prejudice, to regard the tank as a freak. A sufficient number of thinking soldiers who realised that the horse must, eventually, be superseded by mechanization, rallied to its side. But the support accorded and the solutions proposed to questions of organization, method and technology varied widely, conditioned by national circumstances and the opinions of revered senior field commanders now entrenched in the Ministries of War.

Russia, racked by revolution and civil war, had to make do with such tanks as the British and French supplied to the White Armies and which, in due course, fell into Red Army hands. She possessed no tanks or tank policy of her own. Germany, forbidden tanks by the peace settlement of the Treaty of Versailles, briefly experimented with copies of captured British machines, and even projected a 150-ton monster before being compelled to abandon these experiments and secretly concentrate on plans for the future. The United States, tending to revert to isolationism, merely retained large numbers of the Renault type and of the heavy Mark VIII tank she had been building in collaboration with the British at the end of the war. The US Army, at the will of General John Pershing and by Act of Congress, abolished the Tank Corps, handing over all tactical and technical developments to the Infantry corps – a fate which virtually brought innovation to a halt. For several years the only genuinely imaginative work in the United States would be carried out by a maverick inventor named J Walter Christie. In line with his belief in high mobility, Christie produced in 1921 the prototype of an amphibious tank which had a profound effect on amphibious warfare.

France, as the world's pre-eminent military power, also felt convinced that tanks were of value only as auxiliaries to infantry. Under the direction of General Petain, the Army placed tanks under infantry control with the result that such technical innovations as were attempted in the next decade were strictly subordinated to infantry doctrine. The concept of the one-man turreted Renault was conserved while minor resources were apportioned to development of a 70-ton monster, design of which had started in 1916. Above all, suggestions by Estienne that a start should be made with the formation of a mobile force in which the cavalry would play a prominent part, were rejected.

THE BRITISH EXAMPLE
In Britain it was different. For one thing, in 1919 Britain was at war with Afghanistan and anticipating prolonged trouble in that region, including India. Here armored cars demonstrated that they had a limited role but tanks, which had sufficed in the confines of Europe and Palestine, were of no use in the vast area of the Indian sub-continent. Fatefully, the enthusiasm of Elles and Fuller was strong enough to win decisive support for a program of experiments with armored vehicles and warfare, and to overcome those in the hierarchy who did everything in their power to belittle the new arm. Most significant of all, Fuller managed to have inserted in the Tank Corps' terms of reference a requirement to explore the so-called 'independent role' in addition to that of infantry support.

The independent role had its roots, of course, in the tactics Fuller had worked out in January 1918 for the Mark V* tank but which he had amplified most dramatically in May of that year when the tactical significance of a project for the Medium D tank dawned upon him. Medium D, the fourth in the series of medium tanks which had been born in June 1916, as the result of the technologist vision of a 'cavalry' tank, was ahead of its time – a 20-ton amphibious machine with a speed of 20 mph, a sprung suspension, a range of 200 miles, and a 300 hp engine transmitting power through an epicyclic geabox designed by Walter Wilson. Technically feasible, it eventually had to be abandoned in 1921 due to expense, complexity and unsolved mechanical problems. But, using Medium D as the catalyst on the assumption it would be in service in 1919, Fuller had envisaged in his famous Plan 1919 the concept of fast tanks breaking through the enemy lines and, supported by mobile infantry and artillery and by air power, ranging far, wide and disruptively deep in the enemy rear while heavy tanks broke down the by-passed enemy main defenses. The war ended before it could be tried in practice using the new Medium C tank.

The demise of Medium D and of the Government Tank Design Department in 1923 simply acted as a spur to the British War Office who asked the firm of Vickers Ltd to step in and produce a tank which would fulfill the requirements of deep penetration and satisfy the none too clearly formulated demands of the Indian Army for a tank suitable to conditions in its spheres of responsibility. In 1921 the War Office had asked Vickers to build a light tank, a machine capable of operating almost anywhere in the world, which might be suitable for the short-range infantry support role in addition to the long-range independent one, and which could be the workhorse of the trials already called for. To begin with, Vickers, who had to acquire tank construction experience as they went along, tried to improve upon the Medium B tank which Foster and Co had built in 1918, but whose speed of 8 mph and range of 140 miles fell well short of the operational requirement. Vickers initially discovered that tank construction, with small plates, was different from shipbuilding, with large ones. The sprung suspension was inadequate and there were numerous other defects awaiting solution. The adoption of a fully rotating turret fitted with a 47 mm gun,

in accordance with Tank Corps specifications, was to become the most significant feature of their next offering, the Vickers Light Infantry Tank.

As a rule, throughout the 1920s, such AFV design as was attempted fell under the rule of a universal doctrine declaring that the tank's role was subjugation of enemy machine-guns by its own machine-guns, that cross-country speed need not be much in excess of 10 mph, and that armor protection of about 14 mm only need be provided as a protection against shell splinters and armor-piercing bullets. The absence of the immediate threat of a major war, allied to severe budget restraints, imposed a policy of economic simplicity. Despite the emergence in 1918 of several high-velocity anti-tank guns, a revival of the concept of a super heavy tank capable [like Stern's 1916 double-skinned 100-ton Flying Elephant] of deflecting direct hits from such weapons as well as field artillery fire, was squashed. Cheap light tanks in the 6-ton range with, perhaps, a sprinkling of medium tanks of 20 to 30 tons were to be the order of the day. When the Vickers Light Infantry Tank with its ridiculous 8 mm armor turned out at 12 tons it was retitled Medium Tank. It went into production in 1923.

The Vickers Medium tank, for all the inadequacy of its armor, its top speed of 15 mph and its 150-mile radius of action, nevertheless took tank design a long step forward. Vitally, it incorporated what the British had learned from recent history in that its armament, unlike those of French tanks, had a specific anti-tank purpose. Nearly all matters of tank design within the parameters of size, weight and cost to fit a fighting vehicle for its role are subject to a compromise.

THE GUNNERY PROBLEM

The designers of the Medium, instructed to create a turret layout of maximum efficiency in which the commander could directly control the gunner to maintain rapid and effective application of fire, opted for a three-man arrangement which, in due course, would become standard to most turrets. Compelled, by restrictions of space and weight, to dispense with the good 57 mm gun in current use in the heavy tanks, the smaller, lighter 47 mm gun was adopted as main armament. With a muzzle velocity of 533 m/sec, it penetrated armor quite as well as its predecessor, using either solid shot or armor-piercing high explosive shell (APHE).

APHE, however, lacked good destructive power against field works and anti-tank guns, a shortcoming which was accepted by the Tank Corps because it was content to spray fire from machine-guns, no less than three such guns being provided in turret and hull mountings.

Although the grouping in the turret of commander, gunner and loader (who, in due course would also be radio operator) solved the fire control difficulties which had plagued the Foster tanks, this arrangement prevented the commander from controlling the driver. The eventual introduction of the laringuaphone system proved little better than shouting at or kicking the unfortunate man in his front seat below and forward of the turret. Nor was an improvement of firing accuraly assured by the new turret layout. For one thing, hand-operated, geared elevation and traversing mechanisms were cumbersome and useless if employed while on the move. Yet accurate fire on the move against pin-point targets was the declared aim of the Tank Corps gunnery experts in the 1920s. It was a technique which they developed in the Medium tank as well as in the unique 31-ton heavy tank, built for experimental purposes by Vickers in 1926 and called the Independent.

When Colonel Charles Broad transferred from the Royal Artillery to the Royal Tank Corps in 1923 he was almost at once appointed to command the Gunnery School, tasked to develop shooting techniques and technology and to link them with new tactics. Special gun drills had to be worked out to achieve high rates of fire; a method developed of acquiring targets and indicating them quickly and with certainty to the gunner; and practical shooting techniques evolved to help the gunner hit the target with the maximum speed and the minimum use of ammunition – although the stowage for 100 47 mm rounds in the Medium tank was ample for most purposes.

Prior to action, the loader would open the breech of the main armament, push a round in and close the breech behind it – a procedure made necessary with the non-semi-automatic 47 mm gun but eradicated later when semi-automatic pieces came into service, whose breeches closed automatically on loading and remained open after the gun had been fired and the cartridge case automatically ejected. The loader would then tap the gunner's arm to tell him loading was complete. Target acquisition, as evolved throughout the 1920s and 30s, depended upon the commander spotting the prey, judging its range and ordering the gunner to traverse in that direction as fast as possible – a rate of rotation which speeded up considerably when manual cranking was replaced by electric or hydraulic mechanisms. Lining up a 'blade vane sight', the commander would shout 'steady', as it came near the outer edge of the target and 'on' when it was accurately aligned. At that moment, the gunner, once he identified the target, would also shout 'on'. In the meantime, if there was time, the commander would announce the range and description of the target. A special jargon was employed – a tank was called a 'Hornet'; machine-guns were 'Maggies'; anti-tank guns 'Ants'; infantry 'Men', and soft-skinned vehicles 'Transport.' So the sequence of an order would be:

Commander: *'Three pounder! Traverse right. 800 hundred (yards). Hornet. Steady...On'.*
Gunner: *'On'* or, *'Not observed'.*
[In which case the commander would give supplementary instructions such as relating the location of the target to a nearby lone tree.]

EXPERIMENTAL AFVs OF THE 1920s

Right: The Vickers Light Infantry Tank based on Medium C, had sprung suspension and represented an attempt to encourage private industry to set up tank design facilities.
Weight 13 tons
Speed 15 mph
Frontal armor 12 mm
Armament 1×47 mm, 1×mg

Far right: A Medium C tank fitted with experimental wire radio aerial arrays. Only a few Medium Cs, which would have played leading roles in Fuller's Plan 1919 if WW1 had continued, were built.
Weight 20 tons
Speed 8 mph
Frontal armor 12 mm
Armament 4×mg

Commander: *'Fire!'*

Whereupon the gunner, after making proper allowance for range, laid the telescope's sighting graticule centrally on a static target (or at the leading edge if the target was moving), and having also taken account of his own vehicle's movement if it was not stationary, would squeeze the trigger. The gun would leap back on recoil, slide forward on run-out, and the loader would then open the breech, automatically ejecting the spent cartridge case, before once more going through the loading sequence. Meanwhile commander and gunner studied the flight of shot by its tracer and observed its point of impact – in full expectation that, unless there was a miracle or the range was point-blank, it would miss.

The factors making a first-round hit unlikely were many and various. Inequalities in ammunition performance, slack gun control mechanisms, indifferent optics and rough and ready zeroing of the gun to the telescope graticule, were but some of ever present technical anomalies. But human error, quite apart from traumas injected by stress of battle, made accurate shooting at the halt, let alone on the move, an inevitable matter of chance. The missing of even the easiest of targets could be blamed chiefly on poor judgement of range in varying conditions of light, allied to variable standards of crew training and practice. Within a relatively short distance of leaving the gun muzzle, a projectile begins to drop below the line of sight. With the 47 mm gun this meant that, at ranges above 200 or 300 meters, an increasing angle of elevation had to be applied in order to compensate for the shot's reaction to gravity. Practice in judging distance, no matter how frequent, could never be perfect. So the gunner would expect to miss with the first round and was trained, in cooperation with the commander, to spot fall of shot, shift the telescope graticule to that point, relay the gun to target center and fire again. In theory a hit would then be obtained and on the test ranges this was occasionally achieved. But usually, even in a stationary tank, it took several rounds to hit a static target: while if either was in motion, the chances of a hit fell off dramatically to the point of fluke.

Yet these were the methods which the British Royal Tank Corps and all the other

Left: The Vickers Independent. Only one of these was built as a heavy tank project, but it proved too expensive. As a practical test-bed it was invaluable in establishing new transmission systems, suspensions, and tracks, besides contributing to the development of efficient fighting compartment and armament arrangements.
Weight 31.5 tons
Speed 25 mph
Frontal armor 29 mm
Armament 1×47 mm, 4×mg including one AA

Also in this picture can be seen three examples of the two-ton light one- or two-man AFVs which acted as the prototypes of larger turretted light tanks, and also as open-topped infantry weapon-carriers. Extreme left and right are Carden Loyd designs; in the distance the Martel machine.

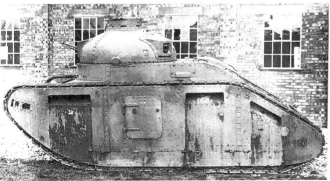

Horizontal line Upper Flag; Vertical line Lower Flag:	FORMATION	DIRECTION	MOVEMENT	ATTACK	MISCELLANEOUS	PROTECTION
R ·—	Ground Impassable	Tanks RIGHT INCLINE	ADVANCE	OPEN ORDER or ATTACK	CONFORM	Protection FRONT
W ·——	Form LINE AHEAD	Enemy in Sight	HALT	SINGLE FLANK ATTACK	Do Not CONFORM	Protection RIGHT
T —	Form COLUMN	Tanks LEFT INCLINE	2nd Bn. A.Coy. Light Sec.	DOUBLE FLANK ATTACK		Protection LEFT
I ··	Form TRIDENT	Change Direction RIGHT	DECELERATE	3rd Bn. B.Coy. Medium Sec.		Protection REAR
N —·	Form TWO UP	Change Direction LEFT	EXTEND	CLOSE ORDER	5th Bn. C.Coy.	Tanks take COVER unit comd'rs to report.
K —·—	Form LINE	Tanks ABOUT TURN	CLOSE			Light Bn. Close Support Section.

The Flag Signal card was devised to enable orders to be passed by this method from tank to tank during the exercises of 1931. In battle such methods were unreliable. (See page 53 for an example of its use.)

tank crews of armies throughout the world were to adopt until well into the 1940s when the heat of war made radical improvements vital. In the meantime, Broad's introduction of advanced training methods, using mock-up turrets [which rolled, yawed and pitched] and firing sub-caliber ammunition on indoor ranges, were the first steps in raising tank gunnery above the level of accuracy which previously had been acceptable in the 'target area' dispersion of conventional artillery. Measures such as these, linked to the gradual appearance in small numbers of motorized equipment, including a few examples of 1-ton, two-man 'tankettes', designed by Martel and by Sir John Carden, were being grafted onto changing tank tactics as pressure from progressive radicals to introduce Fuller's ideas proved irresistible.

For one thing, a turreted tank was shown to have a distinct tactical advantage over the sponson design. It could engage the enemy without complete exposure to enemy fire. A commander searching for targets would try first to position his tank so that only his head out of the cupola was above a crest line, thus taking up what was called a turre-down position. He might then order the gunner to traverse in the direction of the target before advancing a few yards to allow only the gun and the telescope to be visible prior to firing: this was called hull-down.

THE FIRST MECHANIZED FORCE
Of far greater significance were the series of tactical trials in Britain, to comply with the charter of 1920 to explore all forms of armored, mechanized warfare. Their start had long been delayed, due as much to lack of suitable vehicles and finance as to inertia by those in charge at the War Office. Not until 1927 was it possible to assemble a hotchpotch of modern, cross-country vehicles to represent what, in later parlance, would be termed a mobile Battle Group – the experimental Mechanized Force of all arms which was to

VICKERS MEDIUM TANK

THE SO-CALLED MEDIUM TANK (DESIGN-ed in 1922 as a Light) performed as the principal AFV in the British mobility experiments of the 1920s and 30s. In fighting compartment and general layout it was far ahead of anything else at that time, particularly in respect of its radius of 150 miles and reasonable reliability – providing the crews worked hard at maintenance.

Sprung suspension contributed to its high speed but low track life was a great handicap. Starting was mechanically and magneto assisted. The gear box gave eight forward gears, while the Rackham steering mechanism of clutches, incorporated with epicyclic gears, was another advance on the direction of systems which were easier to operate and much less wasteful of power. Its 47 mm gun reflected the need for a specialized high-velocity anti-tank weapon, leaving machine-guns to deal with other kinds of target.

Weight 12 tons
Speed 15 mph
Frontal armor 8 mm (which was derisory)
Armament 1×47 mm, 6×mg

Track unit

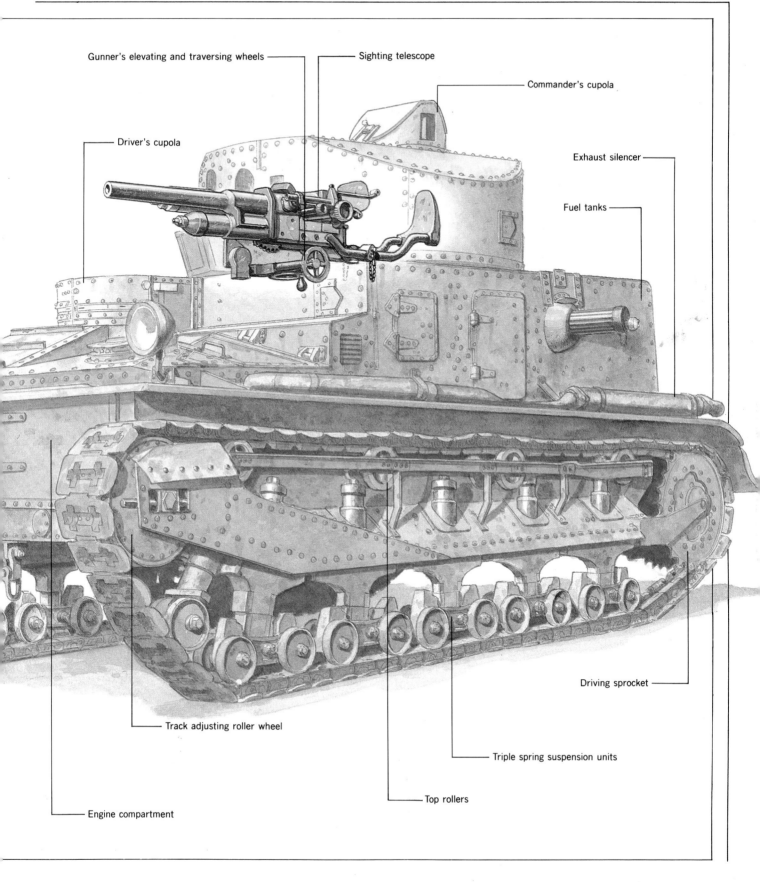

Gunner's elevating and traversing wheels

Sighting telescope

Commander's cupola

Driver's cupola

Exhaust silencer

Fuel tanks

Driving sprocket

Track adjusting roller wheel

Triple spring suspension units

Top rollers

Engine compartment

The special Command Tank based on the Medium tank for use by the British Army in the 1931 voice radio experiments. (Compare the, by now, standard rod aerials with those shown on page 44.) The sets in use were crystal-controlled and therefore easy to tune to one another, quite reliable, and of immense value since they permitted commanders rapidly to converse directly instead of wasting much time in morse telegraphic communication. But natural crystals were in worldwide shortage (their supply was soon to be monopolised by the United States) and so other, less accurate methods such as heterodyne tuning, had to be devised.

In attendance are Vickers Light Mark II tanks. These were often used for reconnaissance but, in this instance, carry liaison officers tasked to take the Brigade commander's detailed instructions to battalion and company commanders, or to accompanying units of other arms.

Weight 4.5 tons
Speed 30 mph
Frontal armor 10 mm
Armament 1×mg

be pitted in exercises against a larger conventional force of cavalry and infantry. The outcome was to provide a shock and an inspiration, not only to the participants but to the military world at large. A battalion of just over 50 tanks (only four of them with radio), a reconnaissance battalion of armored cars and 'tankettes', a machine-gun battalion mounted in half-track and six-wheeled trucks, five mechanized artillery batteries, a motorized field company of Royal Engineers and about two squadrons of aircraft managed, by untrammelled maneuver, to paralyze an 'enemy' infantry division and cavalry brigade. Lacking tanks themselves, the outmoded 'enemy' felt compelled to shelter from the armored force in villages and copses, permitting their fast-moving tormentors to rove much as they chose. Short of adequate radio communications the Mechanized Force was unable to disseminate information and orders flexibly. However, this did not prevent the main body maneuvering with a deftness and security that was itself shattering to defenders who were first distracted and then systematically neutralized.

Because the 'enemy' was denied tanks in the main exercises, there were no tank versus tank engagments, although it was obvious that, if they had been present on both sides, clashes of that kind would have been inevitable. In his comments on the exercises, Broad (by now working for General Sir George Milne, the Chief of the Imperial General Staff, who had been instrumental in initiating the experiment) noted that the gun in the tank was most important because it gave a *'Forward gun in support of infantry, and that it was essential against other*

AFVs, against houses and strong points; and there was its moral effect.'

He also referred to Armor which *'Must not be sacrificed to speed to detriment of protection. If it is the moral (sic) of the RTC will go after the first battle.'*

THE RADIO REVOLUTION
Broad was to be the spur in Milne's flank, pouring Fuller's and his own ideas into the mind of a CIGS who was only too happy to experiment with all manner of new ideas and machines and push ahead with a gradual policy of modernization. This policy was restricted by shortage of money and by lack of public enthusiasm for anything military at a period when it was hoped, and by some assumed, that the last Great War had been fought. Broad wrote the vital training manuals setting out the lessons learnt from the experiments, called for in 1919, which had at last begun in 1927 and would continue as a series until 1931. Closest of all to his heart was the desire to fit out an entire armed force with modern radios capable of speech transmission instead of slow morse code. As with almost everything else in the technical field, radio communication was undergoing a revolution. The large and heavy 'unquenched' radio sets of World War I were being replaced by the first generation of small, robust, 'quenched' sets working in the high-frequency range. Manual tuning was being supplemented and gradually replaced by crystal tuning. Leading the field were the Germans, followed by the Americans and the British. The latter were experimenting in 1928 with the latest RT (radio telephone)

crystal sets and by 1930 had sufficient to equip a considerable number of tanks. By 1931 there would be enough sets for Broad, commanding an improvised Tank Brigade of three battalions of medium and light machines, to maneuver the entire force by radio telephone from his command tank.

The spectacular feat of 1931, rightly judged as crucial to the propagation and development of armored formations, was preceded in the summer of 1930 by a far more significant but less publicised radio-controlled tactical exercise by the three tank battalions concerned. These Salisbury Plain maneuvers were embryos of most armored force combats to come, comprising battles between mixed forces in which the tanks of both sides frequently clashed against each other. The supporting arms, relegated as auxiliaries to tanks, did what they could but the decision was won by the armored monsters in their midst. For exercise purposes, the Tank Brigade under Brigadier Kenneth Laird, consisting of 2nd, 3rd and 5th Bns RTC each equipped with a mixture of medium and light tanks, was often divided to provide the opposing cavalry and infantry force with a protective tank element. Thus it was that during an exercise in which the Tank Brigade was ordered to move 22 miles from Perham Down to cover occupation by friendly infantry of bridgeheads to the east of the River Avon, only the 2nd and 5th were retained within the Brigade while the 3rd fought for the 'enemy'.

THE TEST OF THE TANKS

Led by a screen of light tanks, stiffened by a few mediums, 5th RTC moved off from Perham Down at 0800 hrs followed at an interval by Brigade headquarters and 2nd RTC. Three hours later, after covering 20 miles, the light tank patrols had taken up a line of observation on a wide front just outside Imber. As a rule, a tank column, moving unopposed, could travel at 8 mph by day, or at 5-6 mph without lights on a moonless night. Fragile as the Medium tanks' tracks were, and uncertain their other mechanical components, breakdowns were reduced to a minimum by frequent halts for inspection and maintenance. It was not unknown for the brigade to advance 150 miles in three days, including one major action; or 70 miles in a single day prior to a battle that same day.

On this occasion the light tanks were in time to spot the 'enemy' advancing in three columns across the wide open undulating arena of Salisbury Plain, leapfrogging from village to village and from copse to copse. At once the radio reports began to flow from the light tanks to RHQ 5th RTC, who relayed them through their rear link set to Brigade headquarters which was thus kept constantly in touch with news of the enemy advance. This advance was repeatedly assessed by the umpires to be checked by harassment from the light tanks and a few Mediums sent forward by CO 5th RTC. Within the space of an hour they successfully engaged enemy cavalry moving out of Imber, infantry moving along the Chitterne to Tilshead road, and a force of mechanized infantry and tanks swinging round the northern flank through Urchfont.

This contact in the north led to a tank-versus-tank confrontation. Having ambushed and stopped the leading enemy forces on the Plain, Brigadier Laird opted for a major effort against the strong enemy force outflanking him through Urchfont. Pulling back 5th RTC Mediums, he sent them northward to occupy the commanding ground along the Ridge Way escarpment up which the enemy were thought likely to climb to carry out their task. Due to insufficient time for maintenance, this move caused breakdowns, but a sizeable blocking presence was, nevertheless, created in time – a wasted effort, as it turned out, since the enemy had no intention of directing tanks up so steep a slope.

When the tank clash did at last take place it was on open ground favorable to both sides, each group preceding their infantry and artillery while light tanks scouted ahead and to the flanks, searching for the enemy positions or thrust lines. Inevitably the light tanks drew enemy fire. Yet their radio reports from the front built up a distinct image of the evolving situation – even if at times those reports mislead both battalion and brigade comanders. Dramatically the Medium tanks were thrust into a head-on, shifting encounter, from turret-down observation to hull-down fire positions. Regrettably, neither side tried seriously to out-flank the other, even though this was expected of them. Still more unfortunately, Laird retained 5th RTC a good five miles apart from the attacking 2nd RTC, with the result that when the Second became heavily engaged, the Fifth were unable to intervene within the necessary five minutes [such was the pace of maneuver] to outflank and overwhelm 3rd RTC's opposition before that unit had time to withdraw in good order.

SALISBURY PLAIN, ENGLAND, SUMMER 1930

REVOLUTION OF RT CONTROL

The revolution in tank warfare inherent in the development of RT control was brilliantly demonstrated during the British exercises of 1930. Although such exercises often tended to be unrealistically engineered and at the mercy of controllers and umpires whose limited understanding of the new type of armored warfare was well known, the clear meaning of this first example of the ability of direct voice-radio control to accelerate the movement of mobile forces was dynamic. Warfare would not be the same again.

The panorama shows Medium tanks of the 2nd Battalion RTC in hull-down position among the scouting Loyd carriers. They are engaging 'enemy' cavalry and infantry which had debouched from the woods. Also visible are the tanks of the 3rd Battalion which are trying to pin down the 2nd by fire while developing a flank attack through dead ground, to the right of the scene. Already the 2nd is blocking this avenue and both sides are now engaged in an unprofitable head-on confrontation.

(cont.)

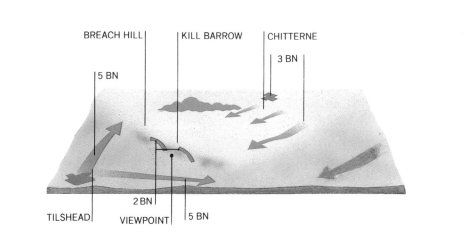

BREACH HILL   KILL BARROW   CHITTERNE

5 BN   3 BN

TILSHEAD   2 BN   VIEWPOINT   5 BN

REVOLUTION OF RT CONTROL (continued)

The 'battle of Tilshead' had begun with three 'enemy' columns composed of horsed cavalry, mechanized and marching infantry, supported by artillery and the 3rd Bn RTC, advancing eastward to secure crossings over the River Avon. However, the Medium Armoured Brigade (composed of 2nd Bn and 5th Bn RTC) had advanced 20 miles from Perham Down (to the eastward) and by 1100 hrs had established Loyd carrier patrols overlooking the axes of enemy advance. Meanwhile the 2nd and 5th concentrated in the vicinity of Tilshead to counter the main enemy thrust wherever it was disclosed.

At 1122 hrs the patrol overlooking Imber reported by RT: 'One squadron cavalry moving out of Imber' – the first of a series of reports describing, over the next hour or more, the build-up and engagement of this column and the one appearing from Chitterne. Realistically the umpires gave judgement in favor of the armored patrols which, with their machine-guns and mobility, well out-matched men and horses in the open. Then, at 1230 hrs, the patrol overlooking Urchfont reported strong mechanized infantry advancing east and attempting to climb the escarpment to take the defenders in flank. Air reports also seemed to confirm that this was a main enemy thrust. Again the umpires judged that the fire power of the defenders was too much for the infantry's wheeled and half-tracked vehicles struggling slowly up the steep slope. Yet Brigadier Laird, in directing the majority of 5th RTC's Medium tanks to block this northern thrust, acted prematurely to weaken his central reserve. For the main enemy thrust, the tank force of 3rd Bn RTC was about to erupt from cover at Chitterne to attempt a swift breakthrough to Tilshead through to the Avon crossings in the Medium Armoured Brigade's rear.

Laird moved fast as air and ground scouts reported this new and deadly threat. Short sharp orders by radio telephone [RT which in the old days would have taken far longer to transmit either by messenger or morse code] launched 2nd Bn RTC within minutes to occupy Breach Hill and Kill Barrow, thus dominating 3rd Bn's axis. Then ensued the action as depicted in the panorama.

Laird was well-informed by a steady stream of reports, yet delayed over-long

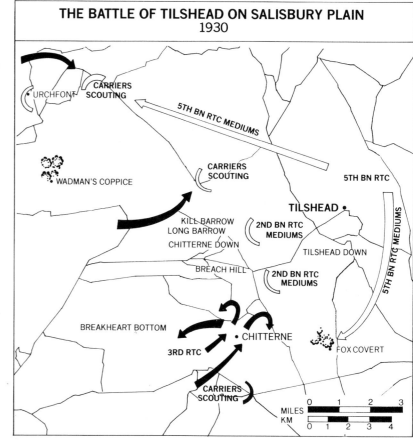

THE BATTLE OF TILSHEAD ON SALISBURY PLAIN
1930

before committing his remaining elements of 5th Bn RTC. Consequentially, his belated attempt to outflank the 3rd Bn RTC, via Fox Covert and Chitterne Barn, was thwarted by a wary opponent also well provided with information of this threat from the 3rd's Loyd carriers screening the southern flank of the attack.

The dynamism inherent in improved radio communication can be detected in the account of another contemporary exercise when the 5th clashed with the 2nd in the open. Before battle was joined, the 2nd's direction of attack was discovered and reported to Force HQ over the radio rear link. By the same means, Force HQ also monitored 5th RTC's orders for attack against the 2nd – a thrust which went in at top speed, even as the Force Commander, located well forward to keep in touch with developments, was shrewdly repositioning 3rd RTC from reserve for timely support of the 5th. Moreover, so slick were the communications, that the results of the battle were broadcast by the umpires within five minutes of its conclusion.

Above: A Vickers Medium whose commander is sending orders by flag display. (See code system on page 46.) Two-man Carden Loyd carriers can be seen acting as a tactical screen ahead of the Medium.

Left: A rare picture of an unusual event of the 1930s when amphibious trials were being carried out with AFVs landing from an experimental Mechanized Landing Craft, the forerunner of many such craft to come in the 1940s. The AFV is a Dragon, based on the Vickers Medium tank chassis and normally employed for towing wheeled artillery – the British gunners, like those of other nations, having set their faces against self-propelled guns. Like the landing craft, it had many defects, but both taught valuable lessons as mechanized war loomed over the horizon.

TRENDS OF AFV REARMAMENT

These British experiments with mechanization took place against a background of international preparations for disarmament talks and as the clouds of the Great Financial Blizzard of the 1930s were gathering. Yet they happened also to harmonize with an underlying deterioration in international relations which initiated programs of rearmament of ever-mounting scale and complexity. These programs, in the minds of many responsible politicians and economists, were thought likely to revive faltering national economies. Despite the strong tendency of most people to regard armies as likely to be of far less importance in future warfare than air forces, the attention of the world's major powers was caught and held by the armored tactics displayed on Salisbury Plain. This led in rapid succession to diffuse ways of emulation by different armies with a corresponding spin-off in technological growth.

No one nation precisely copied another, although Britain and France were regarded as the trend-setters in organization, method and technology. They exported not only techniques, but also machines and technology to other interested nations, who used them as models for their own evolving fighting vehicle industries. The upsurge of interest in AFVs coincided with a fundamental change in tank philosophy. The advent of very accurate anti-tank guns of between 20 mm and 47 mm with caliber velocities of about 700 m/sec (2300 ft/sec), put an end to the delusion that machines with a mere 14 mm armor could survive or that speed and mobility alone were adequate protection. By 1930 25 mm armor was the minimum considered acceptable, a thickness increased to 70 mm just three years later for the protection of the slower machines which the French and British were dedicating to the task of close infantry support. Already, quite logically, the cheap yet vulnerable 'tankettes' which depended entirely on inconspicuousness for survival and which could never possess an anti-tank capacity had been relegated to the role of infantry machine-gun carriers. Light tanks for reconnaissance, henceforward, would be armed with guns up to 20 mm, with armor of between 14 mm and 30 mm, and would reach weights of 10 tons. Medium tanks, regarded as main battle tanks in high-mobility, deep-penetration forces, usually were given 30 mm armor and armed with a 37 mm, 40 mm or 47 mm gun; they would weigh in at around 16 to 20 tons with speeds up to 25 mph. Already the need for a weapon larger than 47 mm for firing effective high explosive and smoke shells was recognised, creating a demand for so-called Close Support tanks in which a low-velocity gun of about 75 mm replaced the high-velocity weapon.

There was a price to pay. Increases in the size of weapons called for larger turrets and wider hulls to mount them. Wider hulls introduced problems of transportation with an upper limit to permit transport over long distances by rail. With each increase in size arose a need for more powerful engines along with better suspensions and wider tracks for adequate cross-country performance. And influencing every factor were escalating costs, particularly in response to calls for better armor capable of defeating ever more powerful anti-tank guns.

Each nation proceeded according to its ambitions and circumstances. The Japanese,

J WALTER CHRISTIE

Above: J Walter Christie with a later model of one of his unique inventions, endeavoring to persuade prospective, but sceptical, American buyers.

CHRISTIE WAS BORN IN 1865. He learned engineering from the shop floor, but came late to the design of AFVs, in 1915, when he conceived a self-propelled howitzer with a big-wheeled suspension. As an inventor who built models before converting them to blueprints from the disassembled pieces, Christie was far more concerned with ideas than with production. The failure of his Front Drive Motor Company's front-wheel-drive racing car was followed in 1912 by the largest production order he ever received – 186 fire engines, based on one of his tractor designs. But it was the United States' entry into WW1 in 1917 which prompted him to design a light tank, the M1919, which had sloped armor and a suspension which enabled it to move on wheels or tracks – the basis of many future projects.

whose aggressive intentions against China and in the eastern Pacific triggered a new arms race, felt no requirement for deep penetration. Therefore they settled for light and medium machines, mostly based on Vickers' designs, for conventional infantry support in amphibious operations. The French, for whom infantry support, with their own designs of thickly armored AFVs, remained paramount, nevertheless gave considerable attention to the development of a good medium tank (the 20-ton SOMUA). They grouped the SOMUAs into an all-arms formation, the Division Légère Mécanique, whose role was similar to that of old-fashioned cavalry divisions, but whose organization resembled what the British and the Germans called 'armored divisions'. The British General Staff also tended to give far greater emphasis to well-armored infantry support tanks rather than to the high-speed, deep-penetration machines which Fuller and

Broad had sponsored with such zeal. But when it came to spending money, they put far more of it on light 6-ton machines, which had a role in Imperial policing, than on powerful main battle tanks for Europe, whether they be the latest 16-ton medium tank or the heavy infantry types.

From US private enterprise, at a time when the US Army was at its nadir during the worst of the Depression when isolationist policies took a firmer grip than ever, there came shafts of light in the design of Christie's latest offerings. In 1928 he displayed a very fast, 8-ton vehicle which could drive either on its tracks or its large road wheels and could reach a speed on its wheels of 70 mph. Little more than a project study, it was further developed by Christie in 1931 as a 10-ton tank with a 37 mm gun and sloped frontal armor. It was a vehicle with many engineering defects but which exhibited military characteristics of balanced mobility, speed, armament and

After WW1 Christie perceived that future AFVs must be capable of moving on water and being lifted by air, in addition to having a good road and cross country performance. In 1921 he announced an improved M1919 with sprung suspension, and in 1922 the first of four amphibious vehicles which would later be developed by others into the Landing Vehicles (Tracked) (LVT) which from 1942 spearheaded many Allied invasions. But it was his 1928 fast tank, with its road speed of 70 mph on wheels and 42 mph on tracks, which was the great trendsetter. For from the interest created by this model came orders from the US Army to develop a medium tank of smaller characteristics, with sloped armor (the significance of which he first realised) and a rotating turret – the T3 powered by a Liberty aero engine of 338 bhp. But as usual Christie delayed production and infuriated his sponsors with fresh proposals for even faster, airborne tanks. The US Army abandoned Christie, but by then the Russians (and in due course the British) had taken up his ideas and

were intent on production.
Once more his sponsors found Cristie in person extremely difficult; it was Christie's ideas that were worth pursuing as the basis of a practical machine. Although the Russian BT2 looked very like T3, it was completely redesigned by US and Russian engineers. Likewise the British firm of

Nuffield discovered to its cost that only the big wheel suspension had real value. Yet the basic idea behind the Russian BT tanks and the later T34s, T54s, T55s and T62s, besides the British Cruisers Mark III to Mark VII, many of which exist in front-line service in the 1980s, remained Christie's.

THE 1931 CHRISTIE T3 TANK

FEW WERE MADE, BUT its combination of sloped armor, round turret, and big-wheel suspension were to have a profound influence on Russian and, to a lesser extent, British design. The power came from an ex-aircraft 338 hp Liberty engine. The T3 had a crew of three, although Christie gave small consideration to the arrangement of fighting compartments since his attention was mostly on the automotive aspects of design.
Weight 10 tons
Speed 26 mph on tracks
Frontal armor 22 mm sloped
Armament 1×37 mm, 1×mg

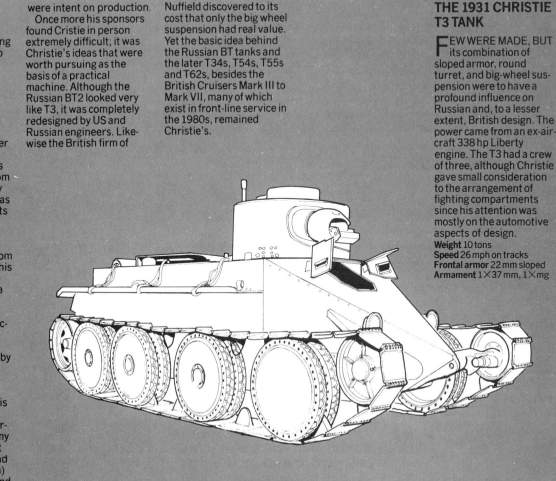

M2A3 Light tank of the US Army, which was among the few new pre-1940 tanks produced in any numbers by that country, was fit for little else but reconnaissance, infantry support and experimental exercises. It was, nevertheless, the test bed for a very sound suspension system and the first rubber-pad tracks.
Weight 13 tons
Speed 40 mph
Frontal armor 17.5 mm
Armament 1×.5 inch mg, 3×mg

protection that set definitive standards. Finally rejected by the Americans, whose Army at that time desired and could afford little better than a light tank with machine-guns, the Christie basic idea was to be adopted by the British and the Russians as the basis of their future tanks in the independent role – and for much else besides.

As for the Russians, they were embarking upon a program of rearmament to which was committed a far higher proportion of national investment than in any other country. With such vast resources, they could try out everything that was on offer from abroad as a basis for their own concepts and designs. Rejecting French tank designs at an early stage, they not only copied British Vickers designs of light and medium tanks, as well as purchasing Christie's 1931 model, but set their own designers, along with British and American engineers, to develop far more sophisticated and battleworthy AFVs. Adopting a high-velocity gun of 76 mm caliber and armor of 75 mm, they had by the late 1930s begun to overtake their rivals in the design of powerful medium and heavy tanks, the latter weighing over 40 tons. They were also forming large armored units and formations assigned to every acknowledged kind of AFV usage as tried by the British, the French and, most recently, the Germans.

The Germans, inspired by Colonel Heinz Guderian, had at first secretly copied the British, taking for their tactical model the writings and experience of Fuller and Broad. Though they participated clandestinely with the Swedes and Russians in technical experiments, it was to a Vickers' design that their first secretly built tanks of the early 1930s were built – but it was their own home-designed models which eventually went into service. Severely restricted by economic and

industrial constraints, the Germans concentrated on only two types of tank which Guderian perceived as the dominant weapons, provided they were used in close collaboration with all arms (except for horsed cavalry). He would have preferred heavy tanks for infantry support, but went without because they were too expensive. Therefore he opted for 10-ton light tanks along with two medium machines of about 20 tons – a close support model (Mark IV), with a low-velocity 75 mm gun, and a tank-killer (Mark III) with a 37 mm gun. The Germans concentrated all these AFVs in formations, the celebrated Panzer divisions, intended to operate effectively in every phase of war, on most kinds of terrain.

At first sight the German organizations looked very similar to those under consideration by France and Britain. It was only later that it became clear to what extent German doctrine differed in vital respects. For while there was universal agreement that tank units were sure to be involved in tank-versus-tank combat, there were fundamental differences of opinion as to how this would come about and where the emphasis would be. Later, it was to be seen that AFVs of the Panzer division were perfectly capable of cooperating with infantry and artillery in attack and defense. The division was also prepared to launch out independently in the British manner, to seize vital ground for infantry occupation, or to lie back in defense against attacking enemy armor. But whereas the British and French tended to envisage tanks maneuvering like fleets at sea for line-of-battle duels, the Germans [copying Fuller's original dictum of 1918] were inclined to avoid this if possible. They preferred to hand over the defense of vital ground, which had previously been seized by tanks and infantry, to anti-tank guns. Thus they reserved the tanks for further action in counter-penetration or in carefully integrated flank leverage and counter-attacks against a disorganized opponent. They deprecated cavalry-type charges against emplaced opposition, rightly fearful of the costly and perhaps irreplaceable losses that would be incurred. Above all, the Germans were fiercely determined to use their armor in concentrated mass to achieve its maximum shock effect, and to resist (as others could not) the temptation to split it up like the 'Savage Rabbits' of 1918 in defense of a dispersed line of infantry.

Nobody really possessed sufficient evidence or practical experience with which

FIRST STEPS TO A PANZER FORCE

PzKw IID was the standard German light reconnaissance tank, with a gun which had some anti-tank capability against light AFVs. It was very reliable and was frequently used in main combat in 1939 and 1940.
Weight 10 tons
Speed 35 mph
Frontal armor 30 mm
Armament 1×20 mm, 1×mg

PzKw IV C was the first German medium tank. Its short 75 mm low velocity gun, fired only high explosive and smoke rounds – and therefore was of little use in the anti-tank role. A fairly reliable machine, its greatest potential lay in its room for development, which progressed throughout WW2.
Weight 18 tons
Speed 25 mph
Frontal armor 30 mm
Armament 1×75 mm 40 cals, 2×mg

to judge whose doctrine was correct. Prolonged debates centered upon theory, as factions jockeyed for positions and the cavalry protagonists still fought [notably in Britain, Germany and the United States] for the retention of their mounts, Scientific operational analysis was virtually untapped. Exercises were subjectively controlled by umpires who often were ignorant of the real potential of armored, mechanized forces; as a result, spurious decisions were often made and false conclusions drawn. The few actual campaigns fought in the 1930s were also misleading since in none were sound combinations of the latest machines, communication systems and techniques attempted.

Right: BT7 was the ultimate Russian derivation of Christie's 1931 model. Vulnerable though it would later prove, this tank had many advanced features, along with the remarkable range of 375 miles. With BT2, BT5 and T26, it was produced in very large numbers, but was regarded as a light tank.
Weight 14 tons
Speed 33 mph
Frontal armor 20 mm
Armament 1×45 mm, 3×mg

Above: T26B, here in service with Government troops during the Spanish Civil War, was a development of the 1930 Vickers six-ton light tank. Like the BTs, it was produced in large numbers and used in the Manchurian, Polish, and Finnish campaigns of 1939/40. Reasonably reliable and helped by the good, British-invented manganese steel track, its gun proved perfectly adequate against Japanese tanks and sufficient against all European tanks of its kind.
Weight 9.5 tons
Speed 17 mph
Frontal armor 15 mph
Armament 1×45 mm, 2×mg

CAMPAIGNS OF THE 1930s

The fact that Italian tankettes did tolerably well against primitively armed Abyssinian forces in 1935 did nothing to advance the debate surrounding tank effectiveness. If an enemy lacks anti-tank weapons, even of the simplest kind, thin-skinned vehicles of poor armament are likely to survive.

Much more might have been learnt between 1936 and 1939 from the Spanish Civil War if the contenders had been equipped with the latest medium tanks fitted with comprehensive radio communications, and if they had been better trained and led imaginatively. As it was, in Spain only the Republican Government armies fielded AFVs that were armed with anything bigger than a heavy machine-gun and even their tanks were only

categorised as light – the Russian-built 9-ton T26Bs of Vickers derivation with 37 mm and 45 mm guns, and the 10-ton BT5s of Christie origin with a 45 mm piece. Moreover, their commander, General Pavlov, was unable to handle them in independent operations, partly due to lack of technique, largely through poor communications, and also because the tank brigades tended to be too independent and did not combine with artillery and infantry who launched attacks along predictable axes of advance. The Fascist opposition, meanwhile, under the influence of their leader General Franco, preferred to employ what AFVs they possessed only in close infantry support. This was not so stupid since Franco's German 6-ton PzKw I tanks and Italian 3-ton CV3 tankettes were barely combat-worthy and quite incapable of withstanding the smallest anti-tank gun. Russian T26Bs and BT5s frequently dealt with them at stand-off ranges. Indeed, Colonel von Thoma, who commanded the German tank troops, paid a reward to Spanish infantry who went out to capture several dozen enemy T26Bs, a far superior substitute for his own feeble AFVs.

The first tank-versus-tank action, on 24 October 1936 between three Republican T26Bs and three Fascist CV3s, set the pattern of clashes to come. The T26s, advancing against infantry, were charged by the CV3s, one of which overturned. One T26 was also hit on a track and immobilized but continued to fight. A CV3 armed with a flamethrower

then optimistically tried to stalk the T26s at almost point blank range! The Russian gunners simply let it come close before shooting it to pieces. Fascist artillery now joined in, scoring a direct hit on a T26 whose entire crew was killed.

It was understandable, therefore, that both the participants and observers of a war which produced numerous tank versus tank skirmishes, but no great tank battles, and in which the tank played only a subsidiary role, should have concluded that what a number of pundits were already declaring was correct. This was that the small, field-mounted anti-tank gun, augmented by field artillery along with minefields, had mastered light and medium tanks in the independent role; and that only thickly armored infantry tanks might prevail in the future. So depressed was von Thoma that, to Guderian's wrath, he went so far as to recommend that there was no need to waste precious resources on a radio set in each tank.

There was much more to be learned from an encounter in another confrontation zone. A fierce, large-scale frontier 'incident' between the Russian and Japanese armies took place along the Manchurian frontier in the summer of 1939. Hereabouts the Japanese had been harassing the Russians for a year or more and, in May, had pushed forward three infantry divisions on a 10-mile front towards the River Khalkhin, supported by 180 tanks, 500 guns and 450 aircraft. In past confrontations there had been several head-on col-

lisions between tanks of both sides, but always within the framework of a conventional infantry/artillery battle. This time it was the mixture as before to begin with, except that the new Russian commander, General Georgi Zhukov, took the opportunity to retain about 100 of his 498 AFVs as an independent force (6th Tank Brigade) for counter-attack. When Zhukov's counter-attack against the two forward Japanese divisions began on a broad front at the end of August, it was preceded by a conventional heavy artillery bombardment in support of the infantry, who were aided by T26 tanks. This led to a series of encounters all along the front. The shock for the Japanese was the sudden eruption of 6th Tank Brigade through guarded sectors on the flanks, and the inter-position of its latest BT5 and BT7 Christie tanks, with 45 mm guns, across their lines of communication. This classic double envelopment was to be mirrored a day or two later by the Germans in Poland.

The outcome was a shattering encirclement of the Japanese who lost some 40 000 men to the Russians' 10 000 – a lesson the former were to take to heart in their care to avoid further provoking the Russians. The key to the Russian victory was Zhukov's rapid reinforcement of his tank spearheads with mounted infantry and mechanized artillery, thus sparing his tanks severe penalties in unsupported confrontations with the retreating Japanese machines. For he also compelled the escaping Japanese tanks to attack em-

Left: M89 was a standard Japanese infantry support tank derived from a Vickers design of 1929. It had little to recommend it, except as support for infantry. Indeed it came to symbolise the lukewarm attitude of the Japanese to all AFVs, which were subjugated to infantry requirements in the difficult, under-developed terrain Japanese forces largely fought over.
Weight 12 tons
Speed 15 mph
Frontal armor 17 mm
Armament 1×57 mm, 2×mg

The Battle of the River Khalkhin in 1939 was a classical example of double envelopment. The Russians enveloped the Japanese, with surprise attacks via flanks and rear, while the main Japanese force, relatively immobile, was held in place by frontal assaults.

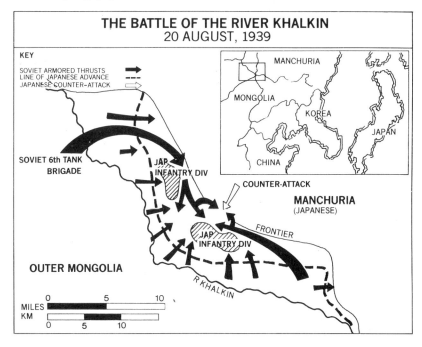

THE BATTLE OF THE RIVER KHALKIN
20 AUGUST, 1939

KEY

SOVIET ARMORED THRUSTS
LINE OF JAPANESE ADVANCE
JAPANESE COUNTER-ATTACK

MANCHURIA

MONGOLIA

KOREA

JAPAN

CHINA

SOVIET 6th TANK BRIGADE

JAP INFANTRY DIV

COUNTER-ATTACK

MANCHURIA
(JAPANESE)

FRONTIER

JAP INFANTRY DIV

OUTER MONGOLIA

R KHALKHIN

MILES
0   5   10
KM
0   5   10

placed guns and eventually to succumb to superior force and logistic strangulation, the epitome of the methods which the Germans were about to demonstrate in a manner originally pioneered by the British. Ironically, indeed, the sheer magnitude of the German triumph in Poland in September 1939 was to overshadow completely what had already been achieved in August by the Russians – with historic consequences.

THE POLISH CAMPAIGN, 1939

When Germany invaded Poland on 1 September 1939 the assault was preceded by air attacks on communication systems and spearheaded on the ground by six Panzer Divisions, four so-called Light Divisions of low tank content and several mechanized infantry divisions. In all the German tanks committed amounted to about 3200 of which half were the highly vulnerable PzKw I light tanks (built originally only for training

purposes) and a mere 309 good medium tanks – 98 PzKw IIIs and 211 Close Support PzKw IVs. Against this formidable host, the Poles could pit just 190 modern light tanks with 37 mm guns, of French Renault or British Vickers origin, plus 470 feeble tankettes and 90 armored cars.

Outclassed from the start, the Polish armored troops compounded their initial weakness by unreadiness for action and by largely dispersing among the infantry those tanks which were prepared. Moreover, those which were retained in reserve, as will be seen, achieved nothing. For the German armored formations, rolling forward rapidly in concentration within hours had by-passed or brushed aside troops holding linear positions, and within a few days were plunging deep into the Polish hinterland. Here was a double shock for everybody who studied these events – be they uninitiated Germans, shaken Poles or sceptical French, British,

GERMAN ARMORED OFFENSIVES, 1939

THE ORGANIZATION OF a German Panzer Division of 1939, showing the interrelated mix of mechanized reconnaissance, tank, infantry, artillery, engineer, and logistic units.

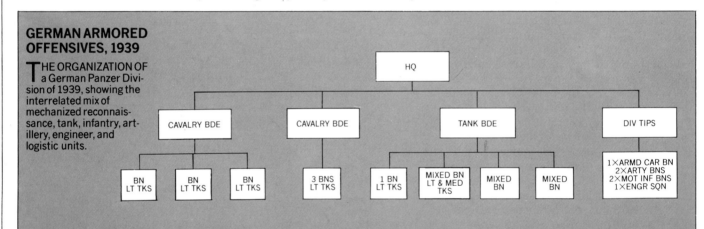

HEINZ GUDERIAN

HEINZ WILHELM Guderian (born 1888) was a light infantryman who became a radio specialist, with clear insight into technology in addition to his charismatic talent as a leader and organizer within the Great German General Staff. Selected in 1922 to work for Motorized Troops, Guderian was among the élite who formulated the shape and philosophy of the German forces which went to war in 1939. It was he who founded the Panzertruppe with the tank as

the dominant weapon, working in close conjunction with the other arms, as an offensive formation. Enthused by the ideas of Fuller and the British tank experiments in the 1920s and early 1930s, Guderian pressed hard for panzer divisions, (influencing Hitler in the process) and in 1935 took command of one himself, rising to command of an Army Corps in 1938 (in which appointment he took part in the occupation of Austria and the Sudetenland) before becoming Chief of Mobile Troops at the end of 1938.

It was, however, as a Mechanized Corps Commander in 1939 that he made his name with tanks in action in Poland, then winning public acclaim and the devotion of his troops at the head of the dramatic thrusts to the Channel and the Swiss frontier in 1940. Again, during the invasion of Russia, his dash and willingness to take a calculated risk won striking victories, triumphs which consolidated a reputation for hotheadedness that led to his dismissal for disobeying orders before Moscow in December.

Recalled to become Inspector-General of Armored Troops in February 1943, he spent the next two years

struggling to repair the damage inflicted on the Panzertruppe in battle and by neglect in their re-equipment and training. Such successes as his men enjoyed in the struggles from 1943 to 1945 were to his credit. But when Guderian was appointed Army Chief of Staff in July 1944, with responsibility for the Eastern Front, the hopeless situation was beyond the capacity of any man. Bravely defying Hitler as he did in the closing months of WW2, he was fortunate to escape with his life into American custody at the war's end.

Russian and American pundits. Not only had the armor moved fast but it had maintained momentum, thus disposing of the myth that mechanized formations would soon grind to a halt from collapse of logistic support. The German supply organization, tried and tested in exercises and during the unopposed take-overs of Austria and Czechoslovakia, kept the flow of supplies moving without once letting down the triumphant mechanized columns as they advanced at average speeds in excess of 11 miles per day over a nine-day period. Within 15 days the Polish air force had been annihilated and Polish ground forces thrown into disorder and largely immobilized, except where they held out for a further fortnight in tank-proof localities, notably in Warsaw which was grimly defended.

It was not only the sheer violence of the German attacks which overwhelmed the Poles, who fought with the utmost tenacity and courage wherever and whenever they could. It was the rapidity and direction of the thrusts which did the trick, by far out-distancing Polish counter-measures, to leave their best mobile troops high and dry, mostly uncommitted to battle. The battalion of useful French Renault R35 tanks, held back in concentrated reserve, never fired a shot and eventually made their escape into internment in Romania. Another unit, moving by rail to block Guderian's mechanized corps as it swept down upon Brest Litovsk, far to the east of Warsaw, was captured entrained and intact in railroad sidings. What few tank-versus-tank battles occured, and there are few clearly recorded, were mere skirmishes amid a debacle, and of no importance except as symbols of resistance. Nearly all the 217 tanks lost by the Germans in the month-long campaign fell to bravely served artillery and anti-tank guns – and the vast majority of these were light tanks with scanty armor.

THE RUSSO-FINNISH WAR

How far behind German practice one of its chief future opponents had fallen [despite its good showing in Manchuria] was revealed to the world in up to 50 degrees of winter frost when Russia chose to invade Finland in November 1939. With hardly any tanks of her own and only 112 37 mm anti-tank guns, Finland was not expected to hold out for long. That the Finns did so for three gruelling months of combat against immensely strong Russian forces, with several hundred light and heavy tanks to the fore, was due not only to the difficulty of the terrain and the arctic

weather but also to mechanical and human deficiencies. In the appalling conditions vehicles broke down in large numbers. Often they had to be abandoned because untreated fuel froze and the already ramshackle Soviet logistic organization starved the fighting troops of vital supplies. It needed but a stiff defense by patriotic Finns, fighting on their own ground, to wreak havoc with the enemy armored forces, blunt their initial offensive, and expose inept Russian generalship which attempted, with fatal results, to launch tank attacks without infantry and artillery support.

The Russians [as will later be explained in more detail] at once began to take steps to put matters right by copying the German system. Yet the lessons of the Finnish campaign seemed once more to cloud the situation by demonstrating that field anti-tank guns alone, properly handled, *could* master tanks.

The Polish campaign, September 1939. Fast-moving German mechanized spearheads penetrated deeply into the hinterland through static Polish defenses which only once managed a serious, but ineffective, counter-stroke with mobile troops.

CHAPTER FOUR

ANTI-CLIMAX TO CLIMAX IN 1940

THE LULL OF THE SIX-MONTH 'PHONEY WAR' WHICH elapsed between the end of the Polish campaign and the start of the German invasion of Denmark and Norway in April 1940 was a period spent by the armored forces of France and Britain, on the one hand, and Germany on the other, in expansion and reorganization. Not that these changes had much impact upon what happened in Scandinavia. The German conquest of Denmark was almost bloodless and the land fighting in Norway, though prolonged for two months, was a contest between infantry among mountains and fjords where AFVs could play but a limited role. Indeed, many of the German tanks despatched to Scandinavia were sunk in transit.

On the eve of the German offensive against Holland, Belgium and France on 10 May, the French had ready for action about 3000 modern tanks, some 500 of the new 20-ton SOMUA and about 320 32-ton Char Bs, along with large numbers of H35 and R35 light tanks. Each of these had guns capable of penetrating all types of tanks and were largely immune to the German field- and tank-mounted 37 mm gun. It was in doctrine, organization and faith in themselves that the French were defective. Their methods were outmoded and their gunnery inferior, inequalities which placed their tanks at a severe disadvantage to the Germans in almost any confrontation. Doctrine implied that the three Divisions Légères Mécaniques (DLMs) in the Cavalry Corps, under General R Prioux, were merely horsed cavalry that happened to have been mechanized. So those divisions, each with 174 tanks, were to fan out as a covering force for the main Allied armies designated to move to the support of Holland and Belgium in the event of a German invasion. Having made contact, they were then to withdraw under pressure to the Allied line of defense on the River Dyle and enter reserve, poised to counter-attack enemy penetrations prior to rolling him back in a grand counter-offensive. Similarly, five so-called Light Cavalry Divisions, each of which actually did include a brigade of horsemen in addition to its light Motorized Brigade of armored cars, H35 tanks and mechanized infantry, were to screen various sectors, including the reputedly tank-proof terrain of the Ardennes.

Dispersed across a wide frontage, the tanks, infantry and guns of these formations were to be committed in small packets or as individuals, their opportunities for mutual cooperation further diminished by inherently poor communication systems. Yet even if they could have been used concentrated against the German armor, each tank commander, [whose tasks included directing his crew, in most instances loading the gun, acquiring targets and estimating their range, taking up a fire position by directing the driver, aiming the gun, firing, and reloading] would have been completely out-fought by the German tanks whose two-or three-man turret crews enjoyed an infinitely better state of efficiency. A German tank commander could concentrate on the command function, leaving the shooting to his specialist gunner.

The attempt by the French army to form divisions for concentrated offensive operations, long delayed prewar by the old guard but given life in the aftermath of events in Poland, took shape with four so-called Divisions Cuirassées Rapide (DCR). Each comprised two battalions of Char Bs (60 heavy tanks) and two battalions comprising

Left: A PzKw II, in company with a Czech-built 38t, engages the enemy. Though these were only light tanks, the Germans (being short of PzKw IIIs) were compelled to use both for tank-versus-tank combat in the Medium role.

38t
Weight 10 tons
Speed 26 mph
Frontal armor 25 mm
Armament 1×37 mm, 2×mg

Below: A 38t at speed.

Below left: A PzKw IV giving close high-explosive support, in lieu of artillery.

78 of the latest light H39 tanks. However, only a single battalion of mechanized infantry and two battalions of artillery were included in each division which was like the German panzer divisions neither in shape nor in outlook. Moreover, only three DCRs had been formed before the Germans struck (the fourth being still in course of assembly); none had yet trained to the techniques demanded by fluid operations; and every tank suffered from the same gunnery limitations as afflicted the rest of the French armored forces.

As for the British, they arrived in France in 1939 with a mass of light tanks and only 50 heavy Infantry tanks, not one of which was armed with an anti-tank cannon. By May 1940, this parlous inadequacy had been increased merely by more light tanks and a single additional battalion of Infantry tanks, which included 23 of the latest heavy Matilda IIs with a 40 mm gun. Not until the Germans attacked were elements of an armored division, with a few score cruiser tanks capable of engaging in anti-tank action, shipped across to France.

Against the German force of ten panzer divisions (the four light divisions had been up-rated and recategorized), most of which included a far higher percentage of PzKw III and IV tanks than in 1939, an Allied defeat was a certainty despite their superiority in numbers and in guns and armor protection. And this disparity worsened with the appearance in the German order of battle of self-propelled assault guns with main armament of limited traverse – a configuration not unlike the French St Chamond AFV of 1916. Adapting the chassis of obsolete PzKw I light tanks and also converting several PzKw IIIs, the Germans produced turretless AFVs which lacked the tactical flexibility of the tank, but were easy and cheap to build. These AFVs could make superior use of 47 mm and short 75 mm guns which otherwise would have found a less effective assault role with the infantry. The German infantry had been found wanting in thrust in Poland, a shortcoming correctly ascribed to lack of some kind of AFV in close

Right: French R35 light tanks grinding through the mud, watched by an officer from his half-track car. Though designed mainly for infantry support, battle duties involved this light tank in many different tasks.
Weight 10 tons
Speed 13 mph
Frontal armor 45 mm
Armament 1×37 mm, 1×mg

Below right: The German 37 mm infantry anti-tank gun which, though easy to manhandle and conceal, had great difficulty penetrating Allied medium and heavy tanks except at point-blank range. (See tables of performance.) After 1940 it was called 'the door knocker' by the Germans and largely replaced by the superior 50 mm 60 cals weapon.

support. The mass of German armor nevertheless remained with the panzer divisions which, for the most part were combined along with mechanized infantry divisions in special, 'fast corps' in groups as an élite striking force.

THE BATTLES OF THE FRONTIERS, MAY 1940

The German plan to conquer Holland, Belgium and France in one swift campaign is celebrated in history for its brilliant concept and execution; it would have been impossible without the complementary use of air power and mechanized forces. The Dutch, who had virtually no AFVs of their own and whose terrain was not considered suitable for their use, would be crushed in four days by an airborne landing in rear linking up with the swift advance of infantry columns and a single panzer division. Belgium and Luxembourg would be invaded along the length of their frontier with Germany, the four panzer corps involved striking hard in the north towards Brussels, via the Maastricht appendix, towards Dinant in the center; and in greatest strength, in the south towards Monthermé and Sedan. Yet ironically, and perhaps significantly, it was the two corps committed to the southern axis, and upon which the famous 'Sichelschnitt plan' with its intention of scything through the Allied defenses was founded, which saw the least amount of tank-versus-tank fighting in a campaign dominated by tanks.

Principally, the southern sweep's freedom from intense tank confrontations was to begin with, due to the French having committed only a few AFVs in a sector where they depended upon the Ardennes acting as a choke, and upon the Maginot Line fortifications to stop any direct attack. Also the bulk of their DLMS were pushed into Belgium while the DCRs were held back in reserve, behind the River Meuse. Driving across the Meuse and into the tortuous Ardennes countryside (through which they nevertheless had little difficulty in travelling) the French DLCs with their infantry, horses and handful of H35 tanks bumped into the standard covering forces of panzer divisions advancing to contact – reconnaissance patrols of armored cars and motor cycle troops, backed up by advanced guards of infantry and anti-tank guns closely supported by artillery with tanks on call if required. Against these well-integrated, experienced and highly aggressive combat teams the

French, whose mission was to scout out the land and inflict what delay they could on tentative enemy probes, backed off in haste. Here was a strength and violence they had not been told to expect. Infantry and cavalry were no match for the lightest of enemy AFVs; the H35 tanks were easily wrecked by 37 mm anti-tank guns if they stayed to fight, the ranges of engagement being rarely more than 200 m. Occasionally the appearance of heavier German tanks injected a contagious panic which was to spread back among the already retreating French troops who were often mixed up inextricably with a mass of civilians fleeing the invasion. Tank Terror, which the French had never experienced in World War I, but which had already been too well known by the Germans, began to infect French morale even before its ramifications were manifested in strength.

On the evening of 10 May, air reconnaissance had made plain to the Allied high command that a mass of enemy mechanized forces was advancing through the Ardennes, as well as across the Maastricht appendix to cross the Meuse past the Belgium fortress of Eban Emael which already had been conquered by an airborne coup de main operation. By the evening of the 12th the leading German elements had arrived within sight of the Meuse between Dinant and Sedan, while beyond Eban Emael they were in fierce contact with Prioux's Cavalry Corps.

Only briefly held by the Belgiums on the Meuse and Albert Canal, Lieut General Erich Hoeppner's XVI Corps, including 3rd and 4th Panzer Divisions, bypassed the Belgian infantry and thrust towards the River Dyle on 11 May. Meanwhile Prioux's Cavalry Corps, with 2nd and 3rd DLMs, had discovered upon arrival at the Dyle that the prepared defenses they had expected for their planned main covering position to the eastward at the Gembloux gap were more in name than substance. Seeing this, Prioux appreciated that a prolonged delaying action was unlikely and that the scheme for defense of the Dyle lay in jeopardy, particularly since the main French armies had delayed their approach march for fear of air attacks. These attacks did not materialise because nothing suited the Germans better than that the Allies should be lured forward unopposed while their principal thrust developed through the Ardennes to encircle an unsuspecting enemy from flank and rear.

Hoeppner's XVI Corps made contact with elements of Prioux's Cavalry Corps in the neighbourhood of Hannut on 12 May. At first it was an affair of light forces. Vedettes from the DLMs, spread thinly, encountered the strong panzer divisions' screen. Skirmishes took place between armored cars, motor cyclists and a few French 25 mm anti-tank guns, the latter reporting by radio, 'shooting and then scooting' as formidable German combat teams put in an appearance. Delay was inflicted on the Germans at each ambush or as they came to identify and then deploy against successive temporary stop lines, shielding the main Cavalry Corps covering position centred on Gembloux. Progessively the fighting intensified. At the same time both sides began to gauge each other's prowess, strengths and weaknesses, forming notions which were to shape tank tactics and technology in the future.

Although the strong infantry elements of the DLMs were emplaced along the forward stop lines and were the initial keystone of the Gembloux position, it was upon their AFVs that attention became fixed, with each side paying most respect to the opposing bigger machines. The Germans had little trouble dealing with the small H35s, but the SOMUA was impervious to their 37 mm shot unless they closed the range and maneuvered to shoot from the flank against the thinner armor and the ventilation grills. Fortunately for them, French techniques and tactics permitted this.

The French tanks rarely maneuvered, seeing it in the nature of their role (encouraged by thick armor) to fight from static positions and engage in the kind of duels which honor demanded and which Fuller had deprecated in 1917. In any case, the tactics of immobility were forced upon them by lack of radio communication at the lower levels. Battle plans were issued verbally in advance of action; sub-units had to congregate and stop to receive fresh detailed orders; and most commands in battle were relayed by flag signal – which frequently were invisible among dispersed positions and through mist or battle smoke. Against such an inflexible opponent, the Germans could maneuver at will and fluently, controlled by radio at all levels. Moreover they learnt how to do so with relative immunity from fire once it was noticed that not only were the French tanks shooting very slowly, but also were hitting only occasionally. Repeatedly the over-burdened French commander/gunners failed to estimate range and aim-off against moving German targets which made excellent use of ground.

Yet throughout the 14th, the French gave ground only slowly, the SOMUAs dominating proceedings when confronting enemy combat teams. German tank losses, though not crippling, were disturbing and thought-provoking. Yet already the Germans had noted the lack of French cohesion, the way they fought in loose formation, uncoordinated among themselves and with supporting arms, and how they made little use of concentrated numbers. Fight hard as did individual French tanks and small groups, they had no permanent answer to the thrust of well-knit all-arms teams which broke through at Merdop and thrust for Gembloux, only to be checked by an anti-tank obstacle at Perwez and by local Cavalry Corps counter-attacks. By this time the main Allied armies were becoming firmly established along the Dyle line and beginning not only to support the Cavalry Corps but also, perniciously, to seize possession of its tanks instead of releasing them into a counter-stroke reserve as Prioux's orders prescribed.

German XVI Corps on this front was checked by an enemy force amounting to 81 infantry battalions with strong artillery, and no fewer than 800 tanks belonging to the armored formations and separate tank battalions allocated to close support. In dismay Prioux would complain of the infantry commanders: '*THEY HAVE ALready begun to dismember the Cavalry Corps, and are distributing the tanks along the line*'.

This was a natural reaction among leaders who clung to the SOMUA, a far superior weapon system to the older and lighter tanks already allocated to them. The tally of losses among the two DLMs told their own story; out of 160 SOMUA only 30 had been lost, several of those abandoned when they ran out of fuel; but of a similar number of H35s no fewer than 70 were missing. Lower though the German losses were, they had mounted up, allowing the Cavalry Corps to achieve its aim before being dismembered. Nevertheless the halting of XVI Corps by the French was only a transient phase, and one which, unrealised by the French command, was a distraction, diverting their attention from the real menace – the mechanized mass thundering through the Ardennes. Moreover, not only had the DLMs been badly shot-up prior to dispersal, but their crews' morale had also

CHAR B

CHAR B WAS THE BEST FRENCH HEAVY tank with which the so-called DCR armored divisions were chiefly equipped. It was conceived as a project for infantry support in the 1920s, but not until 1935 was a production model settled upon. Although the one-man turret followed current defective French practice, hampering fire by the useful 47 mm gun, the hull-mounted short 75 mm close support gun had some merit.

75 mm ammunition

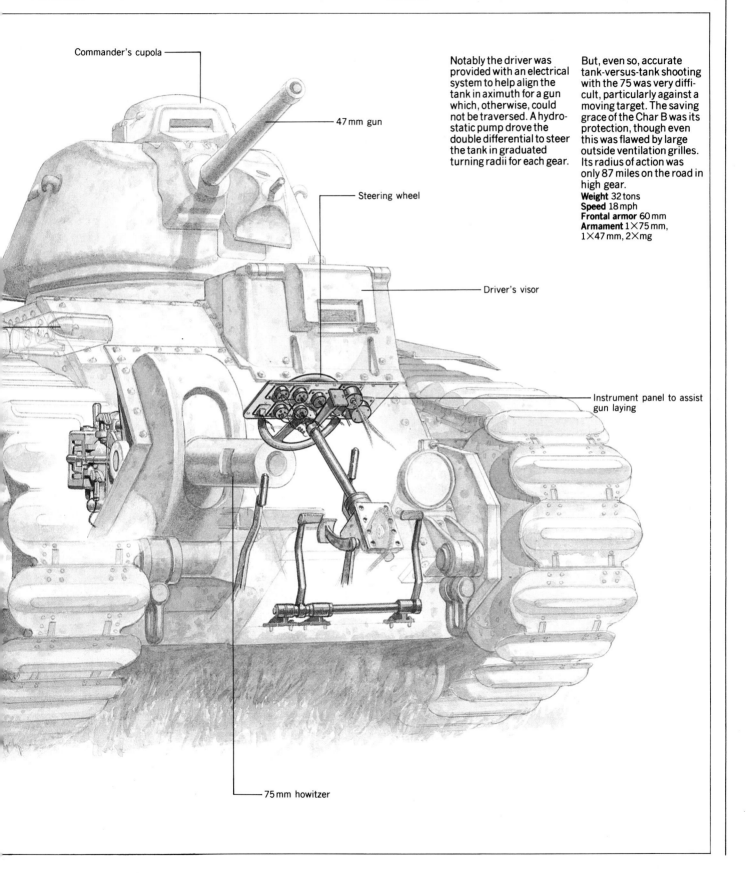

Commander's cupola

47 mm gun

Steering wheel

Driver's visor

Instrument panel to assist gun laying

75 mm howitzer

Notably the driver was provided with an electrical system to help align the tank in aximuth for a gun which, otherwise, could not be traversed. A hydrostatic pump drove the double differential to steer the tank in graduated turning radii for each gear.

But, even so, accurate tank-versus-tank shooting with the 75 was very difficult, particularly against a moving target. The saving grace of the Char B was its protection, though even this was flawed by large outside ventilation grilles. Its radius of action was only 87 miles on the road in high gear.
Weight 32 tons
Speed 18 mph
Frontal armor 60 mm
Armament 1×75 mm, 1×47 mm, 2×mg

suffered. Never again would they fight with such determination against German tanks. Henceforward, those AFVs Prioux would at last recover personally by appeal to the highest authority would fight tentatively and in dread of German tanks.

FATE OF THE DCRs

When the menace of the German thrust through the Ardennes became more evident on 11 May, the French began sending the 1st, 2nd and 3rd DCRs from their locations in the vicinity of Reims to meet the threat. Meanwhile the 4th DCR, under Brigadier General Charles de Gaulle [which was still in the process of forming from a collection of unrelated units] began a hurried improvization to fit itself for battle. In fact none of the DCRs was fully equipped. Each was deficient in liaison vehicles and most signal units, quite apart from being psychologically unprepared for the task. Initially the Char B battalions had been trained for infantry support. They were neither mentally prepared for the concept of the 'Rapide' part of their role in the so-called DCRs, nor equipped with suitable tanks. The Char B was not so very rapide, being fundamentally a heavy infantry

support AFV of relatively short range – a mere 140 km compared with the 175 and 200 km, respectively, of the German PzKw IIIs and IVs.

The 1st DCR, commanded by General Bruneau, was sent by rail on the 10th to Charleroi to intervene in the Gembloux gap if required. Its journey had been chaotic. A warning order was followed by two distinct counter-orders, leading to confusion. The early arrivals detrained from their rail flats on the 12th, the day upon which Lieut General Hermann Hoth's XV Corps, with 5th and 7th Panzer divisions in the van, were taking their first look at the Meuse, to the north of Dinant. The Germans had arrived on the river's east bank poised for a quick crossing, having already overcome several lesser obstacles on the way. Belgian troops, reinforced by the French 1st and 4th DLCs, had put up quite stiff resistance among the demolitions and defiles of the intricate Ardennes. Yet their efforts were insufficient to disrupt XV Corps' plan.

While 1st DCR's supporting units and supply echelon were threading their way to Charleroi through the jam of terrified refugees who increasingly clogged the roads,

SOMUA S35

LIGHTER THAN CHAR B, this French medium tank was the main equipment of the panzer division-like DLMs. It was developed from a series of enlarged light Renault types, dating back to the 1920s. Handicapped by the one-man turret, it proved ineffectual in combat, despite its good armor.
Weight 20 tons
Speed 25 mph
Frontal armor 55 mm
Armament 1×47 mm, 1×mg

its tanks settled in around the city and spent 13 May doing nothing while in the small hours the Germans crossed the river on a wide front and began building up their strength on the west bank. The first flights of anti-tank guns were soon across to deal effectively with the initial local counter-attacks by French infantry support tanks. The leading German tanks were held back until the night of the 13th/14th until heavy bridges had been constructed. But by dawn they were advancing with deadly purpose.

It was the sight of tanks belonging to 7th Panzer Division (Major General Erwin Rommel) thrusting beyond the river on the morning of the 14th which inspired orders at 1330 hours to General Bruneau, instructing him to move to Stave, Corenne, Flavion and Ermeton to counter the threat. This move of a mere 23 miles took all of 14 hours to complete, choked by the crowds of fleeing civilians and demoralised soldiery in flight from the front. Crawling along in low gear by fits and starts, the leading B demi Brigade reached its concentration area between Ermeton and Flavion at 0300 hrs on the 15th. It was short of fuel, with no chance of topping up immediately since the petrol trucks had been positioned in rear of the column and were badly delayed. H demi Brigade and the two artillery battalions sent to Corenne were little better off for fuel. They were further reduced to a single artillery battery when the other five were sent to the rear because Bruneau concluded that the attack he was meant to carry out at dawn was impossible. Heavy dive-bombing attacks now peppered the French assembly areas, further delaying refuelling and shaking troops who were totally unprepared for such treatment. Bruneau failed to radiate energy, in part because he had no indication of the unprecedented speed of the German advance, an ignorance compounded by poor communications with units at the front and his own failure to establish a protective reconnaissance screen. It came as an appalling shock when, at 0830 hrs during refuelling, the B demi Brigade detected a phalanx of unidentified tanks approaching from the diretion of Anthée fanning out into a wedge-shaped formation and directing a hail of fire upon surprised Char Bs and H39s standing nakedly exposed in open fields.

66th Panzer Battalion had begun crossing the Meuse on the morning of the 14th to reinforce those units of Colonel Rothenburg's 25th Panzer Regiment which was already heavily engaged in the vicinity of Onaye. Its Commanding Officer, Lt Col Rudolf Sieckenius, resisted sending his tanks forward piecemeal, managing to convince Rothenburg that they must operate concentrated. Nevertheless, by mid-afternoon the complete battalion had pushed through a defile in the woods to seize Anthée. Simultaneously, echeloned back to its right, the leading tanks of 5th Panzer Division also were putting in an appearance. To a rehearsed drill, the reconnaissance elements of each division probed ahead during the night amidst the feverish tremors of a locally defeated enemy. Soon they found the B demi Brigade and reported by radio the French refuelling areas. At once a battle group consisting of 66th Panzer Battalion, augmented by 37 mm anti-tank guns and supported by field artillery, thundered down the road to Flavion, ready for what Rommel and Sieckenius called 'sea battle' formation.

Directing operations at the head of his battalion, Sieckenius ordered two leading companies, each composed of light 38ts and PzKw IIs, backed up by PzKw IVs, to deploy into wedge and fire broadsides while the third companies extended the wedge to the flanks and systematically overlapped the French concentration area. Meanwhile the attached 37 mm anti-tank gun unlimbered and joined in as the field artillery brought down fire among enemy trucks and men. It cannot be said that the German shooting was of pin-point accuracy or capable of penetrating the Char B's armor until at extremely close range, Gunners, whose practice shooting had been curtailed by ammunition shortage blazed off vast quantities of shot of which the great majority missed. The French tanks, caught napping and making little effort to escape, were shot to pieces bit by bit (some German gunners specialising in breaking tracks) until at last their crews' morale collapsed. Nineteen Char Bs (all those present) and 14 H39s were knocked out or captured at hardly any cost to the 66th Battalion. Attempts by French crews, distracted by the plethora of assailants, to swing the Char Bs to bring the hull-mounted 75 mm gun on line were ineffectual and simply exposed their thinner sides to fire. The baffled commander/gunners in the rotating turret did no better than had their counterparts in the SOMUAs. Not once did the French coordinate their defense since the batteries of their inadequate radios had run flat.

FLAVION, FRANCE, 15 MAY 1940

PANZERS DESTROY 1ST DCR

Trapped in a debacle of their own choosing, the Char B and H39 tanks of the French 1st DCR are easy prey for the German Panzer guns. Their destruction, in what was one of the relatively few large scale tank-versus-tank battles of the 1940 campaign, gave notice not only of superior German command and control methods, but also emphasized the importance of speed and surprise in the execution of such encounters. It showed, too, how out-classed were tanks armed only with the obsolete 37 mm gun against heavily armored opponents. As a result, the gun-versus-armor race accelerated from this moment.

The arrival of the Char B and H39 tanks of the French 1st DCR in the region of Ermeton, Flavion and Corenne throughout the early hours of 15 May had been anything but orderly due to the difficulties of the road march from Charleroi along routes jammed with refugee and military traffic. Confusion and panic were rife. Both B and H demi Brigades reached their harbor areas extremely short of fuel after a 23-mile low gear journey in 14 hours. Despite continuous German air action, no attempt was made to hide among nearby trees and hedges. The tanks sat in the open, quite unaware of their immediate peril because no attempt was made to deploy a reconnaissance screen to the eastward.   (cont.)

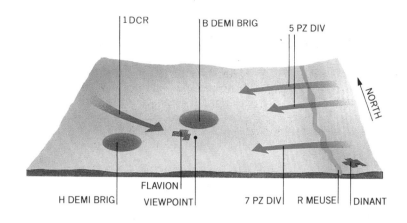

1 DCR   B DEMI BRIG   5 PZ DIV

NORTH

FLAVION

H DEMI BRIG   VIEWPOINT   7 PZ DIV   R MEUSE   DINANT

PANZERS DESTROY 1ST DCR (continued)

Lt Col Sieckenius's 66th Panzer Battalion, spearheading the advance of 25th Panzer Regiment in the direction of Flavion, took no such liberties. Scouting armored cars and motor cyclists of 7th Panzer Division found B demi Brigade and reported its position by radio to Sieckenius who adopted what the divisional commander, Major General Rommel, called 'sea battle formation'. The picture he received was of enemy heavy tanks immobilized, engaged in filling up from fuel trucks – the supply echelon having at last arrived piecemeal, shortly after lunch, following a frustrating journey. The enemy's extraordinary laxity was scarcely imaginable to the eager Sieckenius. Rapidly he deployed his tanks and 37 mm anti-tank guns into wedge formation. Leading from the front, he confirmed from personal observation the truth of the reconnaissance reports and smoothly directed the two leading tank companies into fire positions.

The panorama depicts the action at its height. German 38t tanks are firing their 37 mm guns from 200 m or less – into the thinner sides and ventilation grilles of the Char Bs. The PzKw IVs are bringing down 75 mm fire against trucks and dismounted crews, their low velocity high explosive shells almost harmless against the thick French armor.

Also coming into action from nearby cover, their crews crouched behind armored shields, are field 37 mm anti-tank guns. Closing to the sound of battle from the north are more tanks, those of 5th Panzer Division which, informed of easy pickings, is eager to share the feast. But they are not so fortunate as Sieckenius's unit. A reception is prepared by the French by this enemy who is not suffering from complete surprise: 5th Panzer Division's tank losses are far heavier than those of the 7th. Meanwhile Rommel, to whom the Flavion encounter is but a segment of a mosaic of destruction of a demoralized enemy, is urging the rest of 25th Panzer Regiment to press on towards Philippeville, soon overrunning H demi brigade at Corenne, thus reducing 1st DCR to a mere 50 tanks which themselves have only a few hours' service remaining. The destruction is complete.

THE ATTACK ON THE FRENCH 1 DCR BY 7 AND 5 PZ DIVS
15 MAY, 1940

KEY
GERMAN ADVANCE
FRENCH POSITIONS

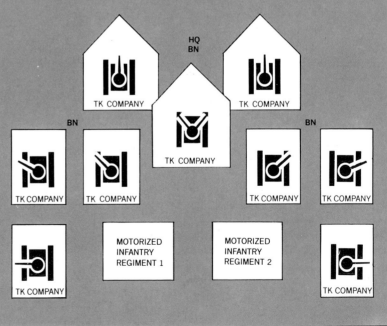

SEA BATTLE FORMATION

THE LAYOUT OF THE 'sea battle' formation adopted by 66th Panzer Battalion as it attacked 1st DCR at Flavion. The tank 'wedges' drive like arrowheads towards the enemy while each company's guns are traversed to cover flanks, front, and rear. Commanders ride at the front, basing their decisions on swiftly occurring changes in situation and transmitting orders by radio. The infantry, with their anti-tank guns, are tucked in behind while the artillery brings up the rear, leap-frogging from one fire position to the next. Meanwhile armored cars probe ahead and cover the flanks.

THE ASSAULT CONTINUES

In a subsequent fight, the French did better although the rest of B demi Brigade was dismembered with equal violence at Ermeton by Colonel Werner's 31st Panzer Brigade. However, the French did manage to inflict heavier losses. The first one of the Char B Company commanders knew of the German presence was a hit on his left side armor, which he at first assumed to be by accident from one of his own side. Wildly he loosed off five rounds of 47 mm in the general direction of the enemy and then advanced. All at once his driver spotted a tank in a wood at which he could fire the hull 75 mm simply because it happened to be bearing in that direction. Nearby a German tank burned, its men bailing out. But only now he saw that his left flank was thronged by big German tanks, some of which appeared to be on fire.

'...*My RADIATORS ARE THEMSELVES smashed in; my 75 is hit on the side of the muzzle, and remains jammed at maximum recoil: I continue with the 47.*'

Seeking a safer fire position to the south, he came under heavy 105 mm field gun fire as the German artillery joined in to harass the French, whose losses mounted. '*From a distance, I can make out the "Gard", the door of whose turret is open...on my right a knocked-out tank of the 28th; the line of German tanks forms a semi-circle which I estimate at between 50 and 60. I order my company to retire..."Ourcq" and "Yser" withdraw slowly, while I see "Hérault" burning...*'

Nothing the French could do had the slightest chance of stopping either 5th or 7th Panzer. Treating the victory at Flavion as a minor incident, Rommel thrust towards Philippeville, bypassing H demi Brigade at Corenne and overrunning French infantry in panic. By nightfall 1st DCR was reduced to 50 tanks of which several intact Char Bs were being taken along by the Germans as prizes. Next morning, as a result of mechanical breakdown and fuel shortage, that number had dwindled to 17, which on the night of the 16th were finally eliminated by Rommel to the south of Avesnes.

The dissolution of the remaining DCRs was every bit due to combined enemy pressure and French incompetence as had been that of the 1st. On 13 May the tanks of 2nd DCR were sent to Charleroi by rail but then diverted to St Quentin. Then they were dispersed to Hirson and scattered to act as pill boxes along the River Oise standing against the five panzer divisions in General Ewald von Kleist's group as they advanced apace from Monthermé and Sedan. 2nd DCR's supply echelons went by road to Guise and Rethel where they were struck by the advancing Germans on 15 May. Piecemeal the division deployed: piecemeal it was destroyed. Never did it concentrate. As for 3rd DCR, its destiny awaited it at Chéméry where it arrived early on the 14th to counter Guderian's XIX Corps (operating on the left of the Kleist Group) in its initial phase of breakout from the Sedan bridgehead. Instructed to attack off the line of march at 1100 hrs, there was never the slightest hope that it would. Its operational procedures were antiquated. Vital warning orders were not issued, refuelling was ponderously slow, deployment drills related to the pace of battle in 1918. Not until 1600 hrs had the leading tanks reached the start line. Yet already the corps commander had called off the attack and reverted to defense, telling 3rd DCR to form strong points to deal with Guderian's battle groups advancing south. But suddenly those battle groups swung west, exposing their flank to counter-attack. It was another 12 hours before an order to make such an attack was given, demanding a further 12 hours' preparation, followed by successive postponements as the divisional command system wallowed in a morass of inefficiency and defeatism. The opportunity for a concentrated blow was lost. All the individual units, sub-units and tanks could do was strike a few haphazard blows against German infantry, who were by now in quickly prepared positions which were secured by anti-tank guns and assault guns.

Finally there was de Gaulle's 4th DCR, the least prepared DCR of that misdirected quartet, which pestered Guderian's southern flank as he thrust westward. Occasionally it attempted dramatic (and later well-publicised) nips at the Germans, but rarely to much effect. Finally it was launched headlong against German infantry bridgeheads south of the River Somme near Abbeville and, in company with the cruiser and light tanks of the British 1st Armoured Division, was smashed by 37 mm anti-tank guns and 88 mm dual-purpose guns. Of intense tank-versus-tank combat it experienced virtually none.

The dismemberment of the DLMs and the

destruction of the DCRs sealed the fate of the Allied armies by eliminating their mobile, armored striking arm. The thin, tactically outmoded 'stop-lines' which the French desperately ordered in the path of the German advance were quite incapable of stopping tanks in mass. Sometimes German tank leaders broke through or bypassed them without being aware of the event – although infantry following in the wake and encountering a resurrected defense were not so fortunate. The fact remained that the best antidote to a fast armored mobile force was one of similar characteristics. But only once throughout the entire campaign were the Germans faced with anything remotely resembling that.

THE ARRAS COUNTER-STROKE

This happened at Arras shortly after Guderian's XIX Corps had reached the Channel coast at Abbeville on 20 May. The passage of XIX Corps, in parallel with General Georg-Hans Reinhardt's XLI Corps, as they spearheaded the Kleist Group, had been swift and barely checked once the break-out from the Meuse bridgeheads had been accomplished on the 14th/15th. French stop lines meant nothing to them, and minor harassment from uncoordinated French tanks and guns hardly deterred them. Not

once did their logistic system fail throughout a six-day advance of 150 miles to the sea. And even though their tank strength declined to 50 per cent, this was mostly as the result of mechanical failures, not enemy action – and was not nearly as serious as the losses through unreliability suffered by the British, for example, which amounted to 75 per cent. In any case, fluctuations in strengths were of only minor account to an army so long as it could recover and repair equipment. This the Germans were managing while they advanced, at the same time as the retreating Allies were being permanently deprived of their immobilised machines. Only on 21 May did Allied armor advance in a coordinated manner to challenge German tanks and in so doing demonstrated the true significance of an armored counter-stroke.

It had become obvious, to soldiers and civilians alike, that the German corridor thrusting like a neck beyond the infantry body was vulnerable to the chop. The plan of the newly-appointed General Maxim Weygand had this as its intention, but Weygand was permitted neither the time nor opportunity to assemble the necessary Allied forces. Instead there occurred a local improvization largely activated by British insistence as the German mechanized flood tide threatened Arras, the main base of the British Expeditionary Force which had entered Belgium along with the French and was about to be cut off from its supplies. As Kleist's Group rolled past Arras's southern environs on the 20th, Rommel's 7th Panzer Division, heading Hoth's XV Corps, reached the city's outskirts that afternoon and was vigorously rebuffed by a reinforced infantry garrison. This check gave just sufficient time for the Allies to react.

Already scanty elements of Prioux's Cavalry Corps – about half the 3rd DLM with a few scraps from 1st DLM – had assembled on Vimy Ridge. That night they were joined by 58 British Matilda I Infantry tanks and 16 of the tough Matilda IIs belonging to 1st Army Tank Brigade. Short of intelligence about the enemy, devoid of air cover and racked by indecision among their senior commanders, these armored units were reinforced by infantry and guns of the British 50th Infantry Division and ordered on 21 May to form three columns to attack the Germans south of Arras. Planning was extremely hurried. The infantry arrived at the very last moment in an exhausted state, having been forced to march all night along roads choked

The Allied counter-stroke at Arras on 21 May 1940, showing the collision of concentric encirclements by the opposing forces. Notice in particular how both the Allied and the German tank units largely, and by accident, avoided each other. But see how each fell foul, with dire losses, of emplaced guns.

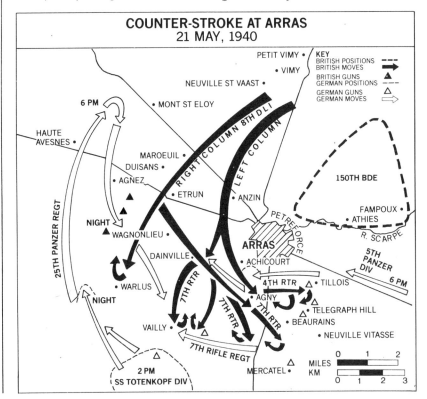

COUNTER-STROKE AT ARRAS
21 MAY, 1940

by fugitives. Virtually none of the radios were working properly, there were hardly any maps available, and from the outset the field artillery was unable to play its full role due to communication troubles. Moreover the plan was misconceived since it involved the three columns executing a wheel round Arras to the start line. This meant that the inner column of 4th RTR's Matildas had a far shorter distance to travel than the center column of 7th RTR's Matildas and even less than the outer column of 3rd DLM's SOMUAs and H35s. Cohesion was impossible. In any case the supporting infantry were quite unable, on foot, to keep pace with the tanks and only the inner 4th RTR column was able to comply with its orders. 7th RTR got lost on its way to its distant start line and disintegrated into unrelated packets which approached the enemy in disorder, out of control and thus deprived of mutual support. 3rd DLM, instead of covering the right flank, chose to follow in the British wake, probably because they had heard of the presence of a massed German tank formation moving simultaneously on a reciprocal course to the intended center line to themselves. Shaken at Gembloux by the accurate German tank fire, for them discretion became the better part of valour.

The German tank force they had detected was Colonel Rothenburg's 25th Panzer Regiment spearheading Rommel's 7th Panzer Division in its wide right wheel towards Acq. The Germans whom 4th RTR encountered in the southern environs of Arras were from the Reconnaissance Battalion and the 6th Rifle Regiment, screening the panzer division's right flank, and protected only by 37 mm anti-tank guns. Against these the Matildas had little to fear, the German shot bouncing harmlessly off armor 65 to 80 mm thick. The tanks' machine-guns killed gun crews, set soft vehicles alight and put panic-stricken infantry to flight. As 7th RTR appeared, this rot spread to 7th Rifle Regiment advancing in the wake of 25th Panzer Regiment through the village of Vailly. Terror of tanks was not exclusive to the French. Rommel himself became involved in organizing the defence at Vailly, relying upon intensive fire, even from 20 mm anti-aircraft guns against the tanks of 7th RTR and 3rd DLM as they arrived by dribs and drabs in the vicinity of the village. He might well have been overwhelmed if this right wing of the Allied attack had been controlled and concentrated and had even a modicum of artillery fire been directed in support. As it was, a check was imposed as the British and French tanks, far ahead of their infantry, began to lose confidence and momentum. Time was granted the Germans. Far too tardily, due to a command failure and too close involvement in the fight, Rommel ordered 25th Panzer Regiment back to the maelstrom.

Meanwhile 4th RTR was continuing its triumphant progress among the shattered 6th Rifle Regiment, emerging upon open ground in the vicinity of Beaurains with only the artillery of 7th Panzer Division between it and the final objectives at Mercatel and Neuville Vitasse. But unbeknown to the Matilda crews, there lurked in Mercatel a weapon they had not heard of – a few 88 mm guns, posted for anti-aircraft defense among the 105 mm howitzers, and which now assumed the role of prime tank killers. Opening fire at a range of about 1000 m, the 88s and 105s between them put a stop to the British rampage, a drizzle of speculative British artillery fire falling in their vicinity far too late to neutralize the guns and save the unsupported tanks. For although the shells from the German 105s inflicted cumulative damage of an eventually fatal nature, the 20 pound kinetic energy of a shot arriving from an 88 at 820 m/sec (2690 ft/sec) was an instant kill. It could actually knock off a Matilda's turret. In a matter of minutes 4th RTR's attack was crushed by extremely accurate gunnery. Had they been able to neutralize or destroy the vulnerable enemy guns, the Matildas might have advanced farther, in which case they would have collided head-on with the advancing tanks of 5th Panzer Division racing up the road to 7th Panzer's rescue. As it was, only a minor brush took place between tanks in this sector as night fell and as both sides decided to call off the fight.

25th Panzer Regiment was less fortunate after it had been compelled to forego an early supper at Acq and race southwestward in the direction of Vailly. Suddenly in the twilight it found itself under heavy fire from a line of guns covering the villages of Duisans and Agnez – 40 mm pieces emplaced by 50th Division as a flank guard and fortuitously reinforced by reluctant SOMUAs and H35s of 3rd DLM. There was no time here to deploy into elaborate 'sea battle' formations. In any case, the close nature of the ground proscribed such tactics, and the urgency of joining the harassed infantry stood paramount in Rothenburg's mind. Sheer weight of numbers carried the Germans through to the outskirts of Warlus where a separate, furious infantry-style battle flared up during the evening. Around the approaches between that village and Agnez lay 20 destroyed German tanks, several of which had fallen to SOMUAs at close range. Nevertheless, in a battle which had been dominated by tanks and in which 7th Panzer suffered its highest losses of the campaign [89 killed, 116 wounded and 173 missing, plus casualties inflicted on the SS Totenkopf Division] it is noteworthy that this was the only important

tank-versus-tank incident of the day. The vast majority of tank losses (48 of them British) were either inflicted by field anti-gun fire or caused by mechanical failure.

THE CONQUEST OF FRANCE

After Arras there were no more concentrated tank-versus-tank battles. The Allies were about to be deployed in action against guns or in scattered encounters with what little survived of their armored forces. What remained of 4th DCR and the major portion of British 1st Armoured Division, equipped with a mixture of 15-ton Cruiser tanks Marks I, II and III, plus many light tanks, would be consumed by 37 mm and 88 mm guns between 24 and 27 May in the set-piece attacks against the Somme bridgeheads near Abbeville. On two other occasions – along the slopes of Vimy Ridge on 23 May and in fighting across the Lys canal on the 27th – Matildas of 1st Army Tank Brigade checked 7th Panzer Division and momentarily deflected it from its purpose. However, at Calais, where a battalion of British cruisers and light tanks had been put ashore to help hold the port and attack Guderian's flank, the aggressive inland move of the armor ran into tanks and guns of 2nd Panzer Division at Guines and, at close range in light rain, the British lost 13 tanks without reply. Thereafter they concentrated their attention upon evacuating troops from Dunkirk, leaving all their equipment behind. In due course, what was left of the encircled French armored formations surrendered away to the east.

Once the Germans had regrouped their forces and replaced the relatively few of their tanks destroyed in battle, there was virtually no Allied mobile arm to stop them when they struck southward on 5 June. Latching their defenses to hastily prepared positions in depth, the Allied armies could merely impose delay, albeit with notable local successes. Their troops fought better than they had in the opening bouts of the renewed contest, at a time when they had been best equipped to do so. Here and there German tank losses from well-served French guns were high. But once the main defensive zone had been penetrated, the panzer and motorized divisions roamed at will, creating ample space even for marching infantry formations to enjoy what limited mobility they possessed.

As for the British on the left flank, while the French crumbled, they raced for the ports on their unceremonious way home across the Channel, leaving all but seven cruisers and

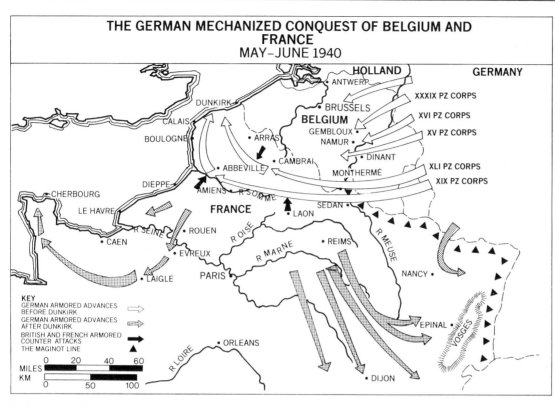

THE GERMAN MECHANIZED CONQUEST OF BELGIUM AND FRANCE
MAY–JUNE 1940

The sweep of the German Army, spearheaded by the fast, mechanized formations, as they engulf western Europe in May/June 1940. Note the close concentration of the panzer corps as they move with ever-increasing momentum across the frontier, penetrate the densest enemy defenses, and then go full-tilt to the Channel coast and, in due course, deep into France. Note, too, how few are the counter-attacks, with only the one at Arras making any impression.

light tanks from 1st Armoured Division in enemy hands. The memory of defeat would be a chilling one. Of their armor, only the heavy Matildas had made a deep impression, indicating that armor of at least 80 mm must in future protect main battle tanks. Gunnery lessons also made it plain that existing techniques left much to be desired. Cruisers of 1st Armoured Division provided one instance of what was amiss when taking 40 shots with 40 mm guns starting at 1000 m to knock out two approaching German medium tanks.

Both sides, indeed, completed the campaign with their minds filled with anxieties and good resolves aimed at improving their AFVs. How well they could implement their keenest desires would be at the whim of High Commands – bodies inundated by long lists of ambitions and inhibitions from every military arm, and plagued by rivalries, ignorance, technical deficiencies and manufacturing limitations.

THE GUN-ARMOR COMPETITION
As the result of battle experience in France and Belgium, planners abandoned any hope of sustaining the policy which had imposed on the Germans cheap thinly armored tanks armed mainly with 37 mm guns. The British, whose shores were now in imminent danger

of invasion, were convinced that the 40 mm gun too must be replaced by something bigger and better.

The Germans already had in production two kinds of 50 mm piece. These were the 'short' L42 42-caliber version, with a muzzle velocity of 685 m/sec (2247 ft/sec), and the 'long' L60 60-caliber with a muzzle velocity of 823 m/sec (2700 ft/sec); both of which could fire a none-too-devastating high explosive shell in addition to shot. There would have been no difficulty fitting the more powerful L60 gun to both the PzKw III and the IV since the hulls of these AFVs at, respectively 2.91 m (9.5 ft) and 2.96 m, (9.7 ft), were wide enough to accommodate a turret of sufficient diameter to mount them, along with their larger recoil mechanism. In the event, and to the disgust of specialists like Guderian, it was decided to give the L60 to the infantry and the L42 to the tanks, fitting it only in the PzKw III – thus leaving the PzKw IV in its close-support role with the 'short' L24 75 mm gun. Production problems dictated this solution, as did a Hitlerian policy decision, related to a conviction that the war was already won, to limit new weapon developments as much as possible in order to avoid over-taxing the German economy. At the same time the military requirement [influenced by evidence that there had been far more anti-tank-gun-versus-tank engagements than tank-versus-tank fights] gave priority to the strengthening of the infantry whose morale might suffer if they felt neglected – as had happened, for example, at Arras. After all, it was argued, there had been numerous occasions when tanks had been adequately supported by 37 mm, 105 mm and 88 mm guns in both offensive and defensive situations. So the tank was not necessarily the key anti-tank weapon and would be better employed as a battlefield bully and arbiter in deep penetration mobile operations. Indeed there arose a chorus from those who argued that the much cheaper and more easily built self-propelled gun, of limited traverse, was sufficient for most combat tasks.

For the British, the upgrading of their armored forces was bedevilled by the aftermath of defeat and the fact that, in July 1940, they possessed but 200 modern tanks to guard their island. It was vital, therefore, that they should increase quantity, regardless of quality: better to have some outmoded tanks rather than no tanks at all as a result of delays in setting up new models and production facilities. The same applied to armament. While the Germans had conceived the need for the 50 mm gun before the war, and had such guns ready in 1940, the British, who had stated a requirement for the 57 mm (6-pounder) gun in 1938, had been dilatory. Not until January 1940 was approval given, with the result that production was delayed until 1941 and still further deferred because, in the crisis of 1940, increased production of

PZKW IIIE

RATED A MEDIUM TANK BY THE Germans, the PzKw IIIE still fulfilled a principal role as tank-killer with its short 50 mm gun. (However, see performance tables.) Powered by a Daimler-Benz 300 hp engine, it developed into a reliable AFV and was well-liked by its crews.

Radio aerial

Engine

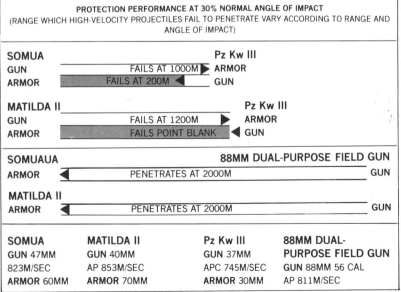

GUN VERSUS ARMOR–I
PROTECTION PERFORMANCE AT 30% NORMAL ANGLE OF IMPACT
(RANGE WHICH HIGH-VELOCITY PROJECTILES FAIL TO PENETRATE VARY ACCORDING TO RANGE AND ANGLE OF IMPACT)

SOMUA   Pz Kw III
GUN   FAILS AT 1000M ▶ ARMOR
ARMOR   FAILS AT 200M ◀ GUN

MATILDA II   Pz Kw III
GUN   FAILS AT 1200M ▶ ARMOR
ARMOR   FAILS POINT BLANK ◀ GUN

SOMUAUA   88MM DUAL-PURPOSE FIELD GUN
ARMOR ◀ PENETRATES AT 2000M   GUN

MATILDA II
ARMOR ◀ PENETRATES AT 2000M   GUN

SOMUA	MATILDA II	Pz Kw III	88MM DUAL-PURPOSE FIELD GUN
GUN 47MM	**GUN** 40MM	**GUN** 37MM	
823M/SEC	AP 853M/SEC	APC 745M/SEC	**GUN** 88MM 56 CAL
ARMOR 60MM	**ARMOR** 70MM	**ARMOR** 30MM	AP 811M/SEC

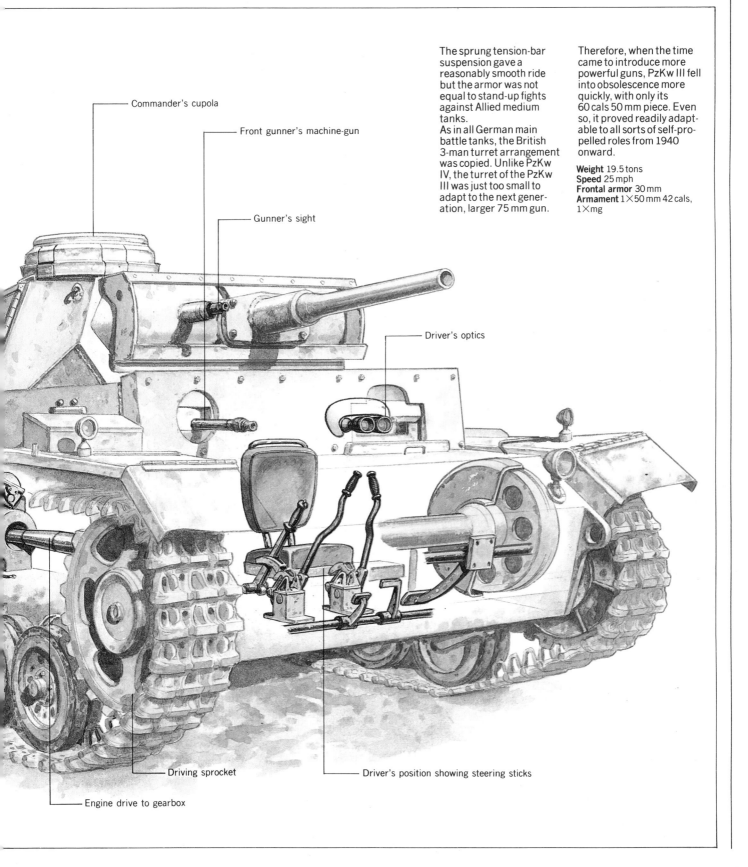

Commander's cupola

Front gunner's machine-gun

Gunner's sight

Driver's optics

Driving sprocket

Engine drive to gearbox

Driver's position showing steering sticks

The sprung tension-bar suspension gave a reasonably smooth ride but the armor was not equal to stand-up fights against Allied medium tanks.

As in all German main battle tanks, the British 3-man turret arrangement was copied. Unlike PzKw IV, the turret of the PzKw III was just too small to adapt to the next generation, larger 75 mm gun.

Therefore, when the time came to introduce more powerful guns, PzKw III fell into obsolescence more quickly, with only its 60 cals 50 mm piece. Even so, it proved readily adaptable to all sorts of self-propelled roles from 1940 onward.

Weight 19.5 tons
Speed 25 mph
Frontal armor 30 mm
Armament 1×50 mm 42 cals, 1×mg

the existing 40 mm (2-pounder) had to take precedence, again because something obsolete was better than nothing at all. British selection of the 'right gun' had been founded upon the criteria of their own tanks' armor and not by the need to defeat what the enemy had or might soon have. And in 1940, although the thickest German armour was only 30 mm, it was not realised that it was face-hardened, tending to cause plain 40 mm armor-piercing shot to break up on impact.

When it came to fitting the 57 mm gun to British tanks it was realised that the hulls of existing machines (unlike those of the Germans) were too narrow to mount a turret ring of sufficient diameter. Prewar it had been accepted that tanks of dubious track reliability would have to be carried by rail on longer journeys, particularly since road tank transporters were not available. British rail gauge was narrower then the German. Vehicle width was restricted because nobody tried to find a way round the problem. This meant that Cruisers Mark I to Mark V and Infantry tanks Mark I and Mark II [the Matildas] were unable to accept the bigger gun, while Cruiser Mark VI [Crusader] and Infantry tank Mark III [Valentine] proved unsatisfactory with the large gun mounted in a very cramped turret and with reduced ammunition capacity.

These shortcomings would not at once be serious for Britain and could have been overcome if, by 1942, a reliable tank to the specifications laid down after Dunkirk had been produced. What was needed was one with 80 mm armor and a good 57 mm gun, with the capability of being fitted with a 75 or 76 mm gun when the time was ripe. How effective the existing AFVs could be if properly handled by shrewd commanders was to be demonstrated at the year's end in conditions totally different from those of France.

DESERT WAR AND ITALIAN DEBACLE

Italy's entry into the war on Germany's side in June 1940 brought the Italians face to face with the British in East and North Africa – in the latter region mainly along the coastal strip of Libya, Cyrenaica and Egypt. Here in the desert a unique form of warfare, with AFVs predominant, held sway. Yet, to begin with, there was little in the way of tank-versus-tank action, chiefly because the Tenth Italian Army in Cyrenaica was equipped with 200 of the L3 carriers, [which had been so out-classed in Spain] reinforced by 60 extremely poor 11-ton 37 mm self-propelled M11/39 guns, neither of which were a match for the cruiser tanks of British Western Desert Force under Lieut-Gen Richard O'Connor. As a

WEAK LINKS IN THE BRITISH ARMOR

Right: A British Light tank Mk VI in bivouac in the Western Desert. This six-ton machine was fit only for reconnaissance. With its twin machine-gun armament and meagre 14 mm armor, it was a failure in combat in France in 1940.

Below right: Cruiser III was the British adaptation of the 1932 Christie design, of which only the big-wheel suspension survived. Chronically unreliable, with weak tracks, it eventually was phased out of service in 1941, to be replaced by Cruisers V (Covenanter) and VI (Crusader) – which were not much better.
Weight 14 tons
Speed 30 mph
Frontal armor 30 mm
Armament 1×40 mm, 1×mg

result, throughout June, July and August of 1940, British AFVs did much as they pleased while the less mobile Italian Army could move only slowly from one fortified place to another, trusting in artillery and anti-tank guns to protect its vital and exposed lines of communication. While the Italians anchored themselves defensively to mined topographical features, the British indulged in the sort of aggressive 'naval' warfare they had learnt on the open (but somewhat more cluttered) spaces of Salisbury Plain. In so doing they tended, at times, to underrate the tactical importance of vital ground.

In September 1940 the Italians invaded Egypt in strength, making the British withdraw to their forward base at Mersa Matruh. There were no important tank encounters, the British concentrating on inflicting delay by waspish attacks from the desert flank and on preserving their small armored force for the future. At the same time they managed to build a moral superiority over the Italians who never felt secure or confident in the sandy and rocky wastes. When the Western Desert Force chose to attack the fortified Italian camps on 9 December it achieved total surprise, the light and cruiser tanks of 7th Armoured Division cutting off the camps by scything round their flanks while infantry, led by a

single battalion of Matilda IIs, entered the camps by the rear unmined entrances and systematically overwhelmed the entire Italian defensive system. The very few tank-versus-tank engagements inevitably ended with British victory since the Matilda's 40 mm gun could penetrate the M11/39's 29 mm armor at any range while the M11/39's 37 mm gun made no impression on 80 mm armor. One by one the Italian lodgements in Egypt were wiped out. The way to an invasion of Cyrenaica was opened, leading to the siege and capture in turn of the ports of Bardia and Tobruk – with scarcely one tank ever firing at another on a battlefield dominated by AFVs and artillery.

Not until 24 January, when a few light tanks and three cruisers of the 7th Hussars were advancing on Derna, was a serious tank challenge mounted by the Italians. Unexpectedly the British found themselves confronted by 12 M13/40 tanks of the Babini Armored Brigade and were forced to retreat by an adversary whose 47 mm gun and 40 mm armor were not to be despised. Running for their lives and firing on the move, the cruisers managed to hit one M13 out of 55 shots, but were feeling fairly desperate until they enticed the Italians onto a line of stationary 2nd RTR cruisers. In an ambush at 400 m range, seven skylined M13s were knocked out

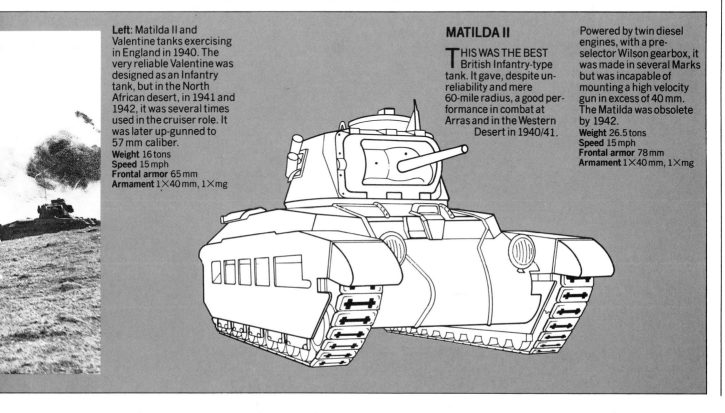

Left: Matilda II and Valentine tanks exercising in England in 1940. The very reliable Valentine was designed as an Infantry tank, but in the North African desert, in 1941 and 1942, it was several times used in the cruiser role. It was later up-gunned to 57 mm caliber.
Weight 16 tons
Speed 15 mph
Frontal armor 65 mm
Armament 1×40 mm, 1×mg

MATILDA II

THIS WAS THE BEST British Infantry-type tank. It gave, despite unreliability and mere 60-mile radius, a good performance in combat at Arras and in the Western Desert in 1940/41.

Powered by twin diesel engines, with a pre-selector Wilson gearbox, it was made in several Marks but was incapable of mounting a high velocity gun in excess of 40 mm. The Matilda was obsolete by 1942.
Weight 26.5 tons
Speed 15 mph
Frontal armor 78 mm
Armament 1×40 mm, 1×mg

Italian M 13/40 medium tanks. For most of their service in the Western Desert, these tanks were outclassed. Designed as an infantry support AFV, the armor was too thin, the two-man turret somewhat inefficient, and the obsolete Vickers-based suspension hardly compatible with the desert terrain over which the tank was required to operate.
Weight 14 tons
Speed 18 mph
Frontal armor 40 mm
Armament 1×47 mm, 4×mg

in a matter of minutes. After that, the Italians resumed their strategic withdrawal to Benghazi.

A culminating moment arrived on the afternoon of 5 February when armored cars of the 11th Hussars, supported by infantry and anti-tank guns, set up a road block near Beda Fomm, across the Italian escape route from Benghazi. They had taken a short cut across the rocky desert from Mechili, a master-stroke which could pay off only if 4th Armoured Brigade, with a mere 15 25-pounder guns and four under-strength tank battalions with 32 cruisers, could overwhelm the mass of the retreating enemy army which still possessed 50 M13s. Fortunately for the British, the astonished Italians either gave up easily when fired upon or tried

initially to overcome the block by small-scale attacks, all of which failed. As the British light tanks harried the telescoped enemy column from the flank, 2nd RTR's cruisers prepared a reception on 6 February for the first attempt by ten M13s to drive them off. At a range of 600 m, the M13s were struck and at once eight were either disabled or in flames. Throughout that day and on until midday the 7th, the British tanks, gradually reinforced and most flexibly controlled by radio, held the enemy armor at bay while the closely attendant artillery and anti-tank guns took a full share of the spoils whenever enemy forces attempted to overrun the 11th Hussar road block. Jockeying from one fire position to another behind ridges which ran parallel to the road, the British were able to inflict heavy casualties at little cost to themselves.

There is no recorded instance of a British tank being knocked out by a M13, most of their losses being caused by shellfire or breakdown. In fact the last five M13s knocked out fell to a single anti-tank gun with five shots at point blank range. Indeed the major British problem throughout was logistic – how to haul forward or capture enough fuel to sustain their mobility and how to find enough ammunition to replenish their constantly dwindling stocks. As for the Italians, their tanks might have functioned far better had they benefited from radio control. Even so the British would never have it so easy again.

The British offensive in the Western Desert, December 1940 to February 1941. The British infantry, with Matilda IIs, destroyed the fortifications thrown up by the Italians in Egypt, while the 7th Armoured Division cut off the flying enemy, successively isolating the ports of Bardia and Tobruk for eventual capture. Finally came the race to Beda Fomm with the culminating and complete destruction of Tenth Italian Army.

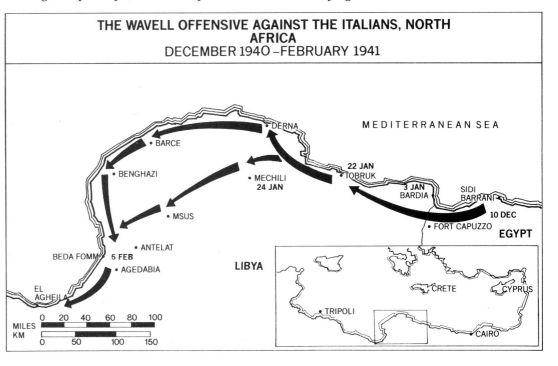

THE WAVELL OFFENSIVE AGAINST THE ITALIANS, NORTH AFRICA
DECEMBER 1940 – FEBRUARY 1941

MEDITERRANEAN SEA

DERNA
BARCE
BENGHAZI
MECHILI 24 JAN
MSUS
ANTELAT
BEDA FOMM 5 FEB
AGEDABIA
EL AGHEILA

22 JAN TOBRUK
3 JAN BARDIA
SIDI BARRANI
10 DEC
FORT CAPUZZO
EGYPT

LIBYA

MILES 0 20 40 60 80 100
KM 0 50 100 150

TRIPOLI
CRETE
CYPRUS
CAIRO

CHAPTER FIVE

THE CLASH OF HORDES

WHILE TENTATIVELY PLANNING, IN JULY 1940, TO invade Britain (before aborting the attempt in September) Hitler was setting in motion his most grandiose scheme of all – the conquest of Soviet Russia. Throughout the ensuing winter and spring, the vast project matured, though never with total commitment of relatively limited resources. Inevitably some forces had to be kept in the West to confront the British. Repeatedly, in February and March, it became necessary to divert large German armies to the Mediterranean war zone; to shore up the crumbling Italian position in North Africa, to Albania (where the Greeks had thrust back the Italian army after its invasion of their country in October), and to conquer Yugoslavia after an uprising against German infiltration there in March.

In North Africa, the desert war took a new turn. Against weakened British forces left holding Cyrenaica after the victory at Beda Fomm a highly mobile German Africa Corps, commanded by Lieut-Gen Erwin Rommel, managed in April with 5th Light Division (consisting of a mere 150 tanks, only 80 of them the good PzKw IIIs and PzKw IVs) to advance to the Egyptian frontier. Faced, to begin with, by only 22 British cruisers and 25 light tanks (which broke down in the ratio of one for every ten miles run) Rommel's tank crews had it all their own way and rarely needed to shoot at an enemy tank until they were stopped dead by the defenses of the encircled port of Tobruk and decisively counter-attacked by an assortment of British cruisers and Matildas.

Throughout May and June, Rommel, reinforced by 15th Panzer Division, would wrestle with reinforced British armored forces at Tobruk and along the frontier. These encounters were limited, on the German side, by endemic logistic shortages and on the British by ignorance of how to make the best use of their superiority in tank numbers against skilfully handled German guns and anti-tank guns.

Time without number, British AFVs found themselves involved in suicidal attacks against emplaced guns (including the 88 mm) while lacking guns of their own to fire HE or smoke in direct support, or sufficient help from affiliated artillery to neutralize the enemy artillery.

Across the rolling desert wastes both sides indulged in the sort of naval tactics rehearsed on Salisbury Plain by the British in the 1930s and practiced by Rommel and Sieckenius at Flavion in May 1940. Yet on the several occasions when tanks did come face to face at ranges of between 1000 and 100 m or less, the results were anything but impressive, no matter how spectacular a battle raged amid thick dust clouds. At much beyond 500 m range, neither side stood much chance of penetrating the other's armor even if they happened to score a hit. Below that distance, engagements tended to be sporadic as a result of bad ground or poor visibility in heat-shimmer or dust clouds. Judging distance in mobile conditions could be extremely difficult in the open desert.

Here, even more than in other campaigns, emplaced anti-tank gunners, given time to measure the range, held the advantage; they did the most damage. Yet, as always, most tank losses were due to the problem of mechanical failure.

It was of considerable importance to the Allied cause that these early desert confrontations, in their ebb and flow, at last provided the British with examples of captured German tanks to take away and investigate. After nearly two years of war, they discovered the German secrets, particularly that of face-hardened armor plate.

INTO RUSSIA – FIRST PHASE

In addition to up-gunning PzKw III tanks and the infantry anti-tank gun (earlier described), the Germans radically changed the composition of their panzer divisions while increasing the number of self-propelled assault guns available to infantry formations. After September 1940 each panzer division would have only one panzer regiment (either of two or three tank battalions) and two infantry regiments (each of two motorized battalions) plus a motor cycle battalion, the usual reconnaissance unit, artillery and engineers. Though regretted by some, the reduced AFV content did assist with handling, quite apart from doubling the tally of panzer divisions and increasing the number of mechanized infantry units.

The Russians were also in process of transition. In the aftermath of their misleading experience in the Spanish Civil War they had tended to create smaller infantry support and reconnaissance units, but were now reverting to tank corps. Each corps would consist of Tank Divisions and Mechanized Rifle Divisions, the former with two tank and one motorized infantry regiments, the latter with one tank and two motorized infantry regiments. This vast reshuffle coincided with a program of re-equipment. The obsolete Vickers-derived heavy T28 and light T26, and the Christie-type BT light tanks, were gradually being replaced by vastly superior heavy KV1s and medium T34/76s. So much change at once not only overloaded the apparatus of organization, but, at a time when many of the most experienced officers had been purged by Stalin for political reasons, brought decay. Training fell to such a low ebb that unit tank strengths were often lower than 35 per cent fit for action. Thus the Russian strength of some 17 000 AFVs was far more apparent than real. Communications equipment was poor and command and control systems rudimentary and unpracticed. Few even of the best commanders had the knowledge or the facilities to match the sophisticated and flexible German experts.

Large as was the German invading force which entered Russia on 22 June, 1941 it could not cover every mile of territory conquered. Wide gaps always opened between the fast mechanized columns spear-heading the mass of marching cavalry and infantry, spaces which had to be patrolled by aircraft and ground reconnaissance troops when seeking enemy concentrations and providing warning of hostile reactions. But as had been the case in Western Europe, in the desert and in the Balkans, the sheer speed and coordinated dash of the German onslaught completely overwhelmed and stunned opposition which, numerically, was greater. Although forewarned of the enemy menace, Josef Stalin, as supreme Soviet commander, refused, until it was too late, to permit an alert. Indeed, there is current speculation that Stalin was on the eve of launching a spoiling attack of his own against the Germans. Be that as it may, the surprised Soviet army and air force were knocked off balance at the outset, and found it impossible to recover their equilibrium before immense damage was inflicted upon them.

So far as the armored struggle was concerned, the Germans with over 5000 tanks had overall superiority. The PzKw IIIs and IVs were technically better in every respect than the T28s, T26s and BTs and were able by splendid coordination of all arms to out-match enemy formations which rarely concentrated fully or managed to work as part of a team. Many Russian tanks were swept up in the initial rush having fired hardly a shot. Those which a few days later appeared in hastily assembled brigade groups were invariably massacred, or cut off and deprived of fuel until they surrendered or were abandoned. The overrunning of the Russian Baltic Front by General Hoeppner's 4th Panzer Group; of the Central Front by General Hoth's 3rd and General Guderian's 2nd Panzer Groups; and of the Southern Front by General von Kleist's 1st Panzer Group were operations of a similar pattern – a series of all-embracing encirclements which consumed entire armies within the first month's campaigning. Take the operations of Hoth and Guderian as examples: by 29 June the large garrison at Brest Litovsk had been obliterated, six divisions netted at Bialystock, six more at Volkovsk and a further fifteen bagged in the Novogrudok pocket, when the pincers of the two panzer groups closed at Minsk after advancing against opposition some 200 miles or more in a single week. Numerous tank-versus-tank actions there were, but almost always ending in a German victory. Key to the German success was, as usual, excellent radio control while the Russian control was either erratic or totally non-existent below battalion or company level. Brain power defeated brute strength and ignorance: it was as basic as that!

Inexorably the Germans stormed on. When their armies' jaws closed on 12 Russian divisions at Smolensk on 16 July, bringing the capture of 3100 guns and 3200 tanks after a three weeks' squeeze, the High Command triumphantly called it a success 'of unparalleled historical significance' in the 'time, space and the fierceness of the engagements'. Yet, ominously, there were reasons for German disquiet in the midst of this euphoria. Several thousand Soviet soldiers managed to escape the German net. And here and there a shocking Nemesis stalked and surprised the Germans.

On 23 June a KV had taken up position in a defile between marsh and forest blocking the center line of 6th Panzer Division. For two days it stayed there, its 76 mm gun first destroying 12 lorries and then at 600 m two of the latest 50 mm anti-tank guns sent to deal with it. It proceeded to knock out an 88 mm gun at 900 m before the German gun could fire a shot; to defeat the efforts of engineers to blow it up by stealth at night; and easily deflected shots from the PzKw III's 50 mm guns, before finally falling victim to an 88

T34/76

THE RUSSIAN T34/76, of which the Germans knew nothing up to the time their tanks first met it in 1941. It was a development of the Christie breed but incorporated much that was original. Its reliable diesel engine and wide tracks gave it a great advantage over its German opponents. The well-sloped armor was good (as the performance tables show) and the 76 mm gun could fire a useful HE round in addition to AP. The two-man turret, however, was badly designed, without a cupola and with hand traversing gear only.

Weight 26 tons
Speed 33 mph
Frontal armor 45 mm (sloped to great advantage)
Armament 1×76 mm, 3×mg

One of the last of the obsolete Russian T26 tanks, supporting infantry during the bitter winter war of 1941/42.

which got into position at 800 m while the Russian crew was distracted by some PzKw IIIs. It was then found that the 50 mm guns had barely dented the KV's armor and that only two out of seven 88 mm shots had penetrated, still without terminal results. Explosives dropped into the turret finished the job.

Even more impressive to Guderian were the T34/76 tanks he photographed on 10 July stuck in a bog beside the road. Already the Germans had met and overcome several of these tanks, but the sight of the sloped armor and the good 76 mm dual-purpose gun made the PzKw IIIs and IVs, with their lesser armament, seem all the more inadequate – despite the superiority of their three-man turret crew compared with the inefficient two-man Russian arrangement. This was a real technical revolution of tactical significance. Signals of alarm to Berlin from the front insisted that existing tanks must at once be powerfully up-gunned and up-armored and that, at once, the next generation of medium and heavy tanks, which had reached project model stage, should be further improved and put into production. Until those measures were implemented, the fighting men in the field had to improvise their anti-tank measures by, for example, deploying 88 mm dual purpose guns with advanced guards. In addition, the powerful medium weapon known as a 100 mm gun [it was actually 105 mm and called 10 cm gun], which was normally placed only in indirect support of formations, was integrated with leading units to enhance their chances against enemy KV types. For even that mighty AFV's 110 mm armor could not withstand a 31-pound shot fired at less than 1000 m when it struck at 835 m/sec (2740 ft/sec). Yet neither of these guns provided a satisfactory answer. Heavy and bulky, they were slow to deploy, difficult to conceal and deficient of crew protection against hostile fire.

For the time being, however, the Germans managed well, minimizing their losses and sustaining momentum despite logistic difficulties on poor roads against a shattered opponent. Carelessness, associated with over-confidence, was often their worst enemy. A typical example occured at Zhlobin on 6 July when the 3rd Panzer Division's I Panzer Battalion approached the town without previous reconnaissance. Moving at speed, without infantry, to capture a bridge over the River Dnieper, all 40 tanks

KV1

THIS RUSSIAN TANK WAS, AT THE TIME OF its appearance in large numbers in 1941, the most formidable tank in the world. Not only could it (as the performance tables show) defeat almost every weapon the Germans had, but its reliable 550 hp diesel engine also gave it a range of over 200 miles. As with all Russian tanks of rugged design, the under-trained crews of 1941 were unable to take full advantage of KV1's capability.

Out of over 1400 KVs and T34s available in the frontier zone in June 1941, only a few got into action and most were mopped up without firing a shot. Contemporary German combat accounts hardly mention it, so derisory was its impact.

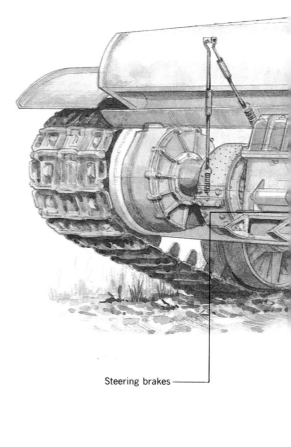

Steering brakes

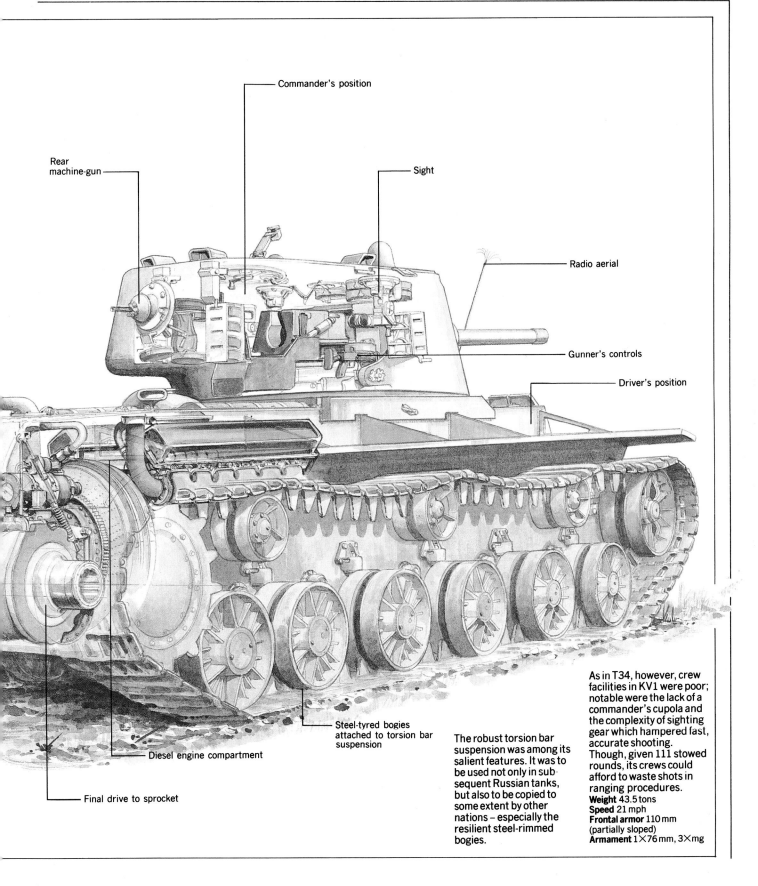

Commander's position

Sight

Rear
machine-gun

Radio aerial

Gunner's controls

Driver's position

Diesel engine compartment

Steel-tyred bogies
attached to torsion bar
suspension

Final drive to sprocket

The robust torsion bar
suspension was among its
salient features. It was to
be used not only in sub-
sequent Russian tanks,
but also to be copied to
some extent by other
nations – especially the
resilient steel-rimmed
bogies.

As in T34, however, crew
facilities in KV1 were poor;
notable were the lack of a
commander's cupola and
the complexity of sighting
gear which hampered fast,
accurate shooting.
Though, given 111 stowed
rounds, its crews could
afford to waste shots in
ranging procedures.
Weight 43.5 tons
Speed 21 mph
Frontal armor 110 mm
(partially sloped)
Armament 1×76 mm, 3×mg

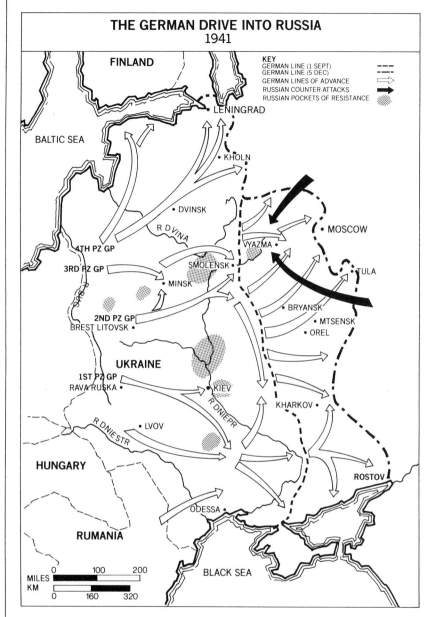

THE GERMAN DRIVE INTO RUSSIA
1941

KEY
GERMAN LINE (1 SEPT)
GERMAN LINE (5 DEC)
GERMAN LINES OF ADVANCE
RUSSIAN COUNTER-ATTACKS
RUSSIAN POCKETS OF RESISTANCE

FINLAND

BALTIC SEA

LENINGRAD

KHOLN

DVINSK

R DVINA

4TH PZ GP

3RD PZ GP

SMOLENSK

MINSK

VYAZMA

MOSCOW

TULA

2ND PZ GP
BREST LITOVSK

BRYANSK

MTSENSK

OREL

UKRAINE

1ST PZ GP
RAVA RUSKA

KIEV

R DNIEPR

KHARKOV

LVOV

R DNIESTR

HUNGARY

ROSTOV

ODESSA

RUMANIA

BLACK SEA

MILES   0   100   200
KM   0   160   320

The onrush of the German Army into Russia in 1941, spearheaded by the fast-moving panzer groups. The phase line in September marks the end of the easier victories. After that, up to the moment of the Russian counter-offensive in December, the Germans found life much more difficult as the weather worsened and their logistics began to falter.

unwittingly swept past a hidden Russian infantry and artillery position as they drew close to the outskirts. Suddenly they were caught in vicious fire from 30 Russian tanks hidden among the buildings, a blast which compelled the Germans to veer off and thereby expose their flanks to the bypassed Russian guns which now joined in. The tidy wedge formation was thrown into disorder, crews leaping from disabled and burning machines and in their turn being shot down in the open. No fewer than 22 German tanks were put out of action. This defeat might have had much more serious consequences had not the II Panzer Battalion, hearing cries for help over the radio and witnessing the

disaster from the flank, taken advantage of the Russians' absorption with the holocaust of their ambush. The Russians did not see the Germans swing right and enter the town in their rear. The tables were turned with a vengeance, and 25 Russian tanks were knocked out at pointblank range without further loss to the Germans.

Heavy losses the Germans could ill afford: their total tank production in 1941 was only about 1500 and they were to lose 2700 that year in Russia alone. Serious as this discrepancy was, it would have been bearable if only the Russian campaign had been completed with the alacrity of previous ventures. Then the panzer force could have been withdrawn to the central repair workshops in Germany and refurbished as efficiently as it had been after the campaigns in Poland and Western Europe. But by mid-August the Russians were still resisting strongly and among the Germans only the most supreme optimists thought that the struggle would be over before winter set in and Moscow had been taken. Meanwhile the Quartermasters Department, erring in its omission to provide for a longer campaign in freezing weather, also set back by the realization that the central maintenance and repair system collapsed when separated from the front by long and tenuous lines of communication. Because the Soviet rail gauge was different to the German, and relaying the track could not keep pace with the rate of the armies' advance, the back-loading of damaged vehicles was impossible, the forward transit of spares inadequate, and the existing field repair workshops proved quite unable and untrained to deal with the work-load thrust upon them. A steady decline in vehicle strength, above all tank strength, set in as summer dust, which damaged engines, gave way to autumn mud, which wore out running gear. All these defects placed still greater strain upon a creaking maintenance and repair organization.

Yet still the weakened panzer divisions rolled on, compelled to seek the total victory which had so far eluded them. The drive to Leningrad and the encirclement of the Russian armies in the Ukraine in August and September garnered fresh laurels and masses of captured men and equipment – yet without the capitulation expected. Far too late for comfort, on 26 September, Hitler instructed his commanders to strike at Moscow, the goal the generals cherished but the one Hitler seemed to feel was less important than the destruction of enemy armies. The main thrust was to start on 2 October when Central Army Group drove due east from Smolensk, with Hoth's and von Kleist's Panzer Groups (on the eve of being renamed, respectively, Third and Fourth Panzer Armies) leading. Farther south, having with breakneck speed completed the battle of encirclement for Kiev and then reorganized, Guderian's 2nd Panzer Group (soon to be named Second Panzer Army) set out for Orel on 30 September and, from the outset, made such astonishing progress that hopes rose that the enemy was in collapse – as the Russians so nearly were.

THE BATTLE FOR MTSENSK

The relative ease and low cost of Guderian's capture of Orel, by 4th Panzer Division, in conjunction with the capture of freshly defeated Russian armies, was sufficient to encourage the German High Command to ask Guderian to exploit the enemy's positions towards Tula and Moscow. Shortages of fuel and ammunition, apart from the inevitable decrease in tank strength due to wear and tear, were no discouragement. The weather was excellent, the ground firm, and the enemy in disarray. Moreover, the High Command expected that activity by Guderian's southern arm of the offensive should (as it did) distract opposition from the main effort, by von Bock's Army Group, from Smolensk to Moscow. Evidence that this was so came to hand on 4 October when air reconnaissance told of many Russian tanks detraining at Mtsensk railway yards.

Already alarmed on 1 October by Guderian's progress, which became shatteringly apparent to the Russians before von Bock opened his attack on the 2nd, Stalin sent Major-General D D Lelyushenko, along with a motor cycle regiment, to defend Mtsensk. To this force were added a few mobile Rocket Launcher (Katyusha) batteries and, most important of all, the 4th Tank Brigade, with its KV1 and T34 tanks, which arrived by rail from Leningrad. It was these tanks the German airmen had spotted on the 4th, generating a suspicion that KVs were among them. Lelyushenko aimed at confronting the Germans along the Lisiza stream where already a handful of light tanks, backed up by anti-tank guns and infantry, were dug in, holding a ridge between the railway and the village of Kamenewo, commanding the road bridge.

XXIV Panzer Corps resumed its advance on the 5th with 3rd Panzer Division directed on Bolchow and 4th Panzer on Mtsensk, the gap of 31 miles between them but thinly covered by air and ground reconnaissance. By nightfall 4th Panzer (Major-General W von Langerman) had driven in Russian covering forces and was poised to cross the Lisiza early next moring. At 0900 hrs a somewhat perfunctory artillery bombardment was loosed upon the known Russian positions, followed by the onrush of Colonel H Eberbach's 35th Panzer Brigade. Its five tank companies and a motor cycle battalion, supported by field artillery, a detachment of multiple rocket launchers (*Nebelwerfer*) and an 88 mm battery in the anti-tank role, drove hard for the bridge. Momentarily impeded by a few mines, they seized it intact and then drove to the crest beyond. At once a brisk exchange of fire erupted between the PzKw IIIs and IVs and the Russian T26s and anti-tank guns – leading at once to the latter's destruction. Russian infantry who bravely tried to destroy the German tanks with hand grenades were tackled by the motor cyclists and eliminated. A copybook all-arms assault had opened the way for the next wave of tanks, followed by a battery of six 105 mm gun howitzers and a single 100 mm gun plus two 88s (all these pieces with an anti-tank role as first priority) to pour across the ridge and occupy the crest line.

This was what the AFVs of General Katukov's 4th Tank Brigade had been waiting for. Moving forward on the night of the 5th/6th to concealed positions among the woods fronting Woin, they were content to allow the Germans to advance beyond the crest before opening heavy and accurate 76 mm fire. Having measured the range at leisure, they at once scored hits and kills, easily penetrating the German armor at ranges in excess of 800 m, but safe against shot from the short German 50 mm guns, which glanced off their thick and well-sloped armor. The unequal duel was of short duration. The German tanks retired first to hull-down positions and then back down the slope, abiding by doctrine and a technical superiority which prescribed that high-velocity field artillery could best kill tanks. But the two 88 mm guns by no means had it all their own way. No sooner had they opened fire from the crest, and each in turn claimed a victim, than they were put out of action by high-explosive from the tanks' guns, leaving the direct anti-tank defense of the river line to the battery of 105 mm howitzers of the 103rd Artillery Regiment and one 100 mm gun.

THE SHOCK AT KAMENEWO

The battle for Mtsensk developed into a fight between the German guns and the attacking Soviet tanks, sent by General Katukov of 4th Tank Brigade during the night of 5 October. Importantly, these tanks were used in concentration. Katukov launched his KV1 and T34/76 tanks to the assault as the German 4th Panzer Division

was in the process of attempting to advance across the Lisiza bridge at Kamenewo. Two 88 mm dual-purpose guns were deployed to hold the crest against the threat of just such an attack.

The T34s and KV1s advanced in two waves, the leading echelon supported by fire from those in the rear. One group moved straight down the road as another group of 25 machines emerged from the woods to turn the German flank.

The panorama shows how this charge by T34s developed, supported by 76 mm gunfire from the remaining KV1 and T34

(cont.)

GERMAN
ARTILLERY

100 MM GUN

RUSSIAN ATTACK

NORTH

TO OREL

TO MTSENSK

VIEWPOINT

R LISIZA

THE SHOCK AT KAMENEWO (continued)

tanks along the crest. Out of picture, the surviving German 105 mm howitzers are getting ready to limber up and move back across the bridge. There a PzKw III stands guard in trepidation, hoping the fast-moving enemy will come within effective range of its short 50 mm gun before it is knocked out. Linchpin of the local defense of the bridge is the solitary 100 mm gun, which has just disclosed itself at the last moment. Camouflaged and apparently unnoticed by the surprised enemy T34 commanders, this gun, firing a 32-pound shot at full charge with a muzzle velocity of 835 m/sec, plays havoc. Yet the T34s still reach the gun positions, knocking out a few 105s before being driven off by intense close-range fire and the action of German soldiers jumping upon them with gasoline to set them alight.

Even though they lacked artillery, the Russians still had an advantage, had they continued firing their 76 mm guns from the crest line at the longer range at which their armor was effective. By moving to close range, within 20 m, of the German guns they threw away that advantage. Such incaution cost them dear; five tanks being wrecked, three of them by Leutnant Krause from a concealed position.

Shaken, the Germans completed their withdrawal and the Russians reorganized for subsequent attacks better supported by artillery and infantry. But that night the first snows fell and a temporary stalemate, which spelled the beginning of the end for Guderian's advance upon Moscow, set in. Strategically, tactically and technically, therefore, the tank-versus-tank fight at Kamenewo represented a turning point of the war, let alone tank warfare. No longer could German armor prevail against an enemy fast learning to use his latest superior tanks concentrated instead of, as previously, dispersing them along the front, mixed in with obsolete AFVs.

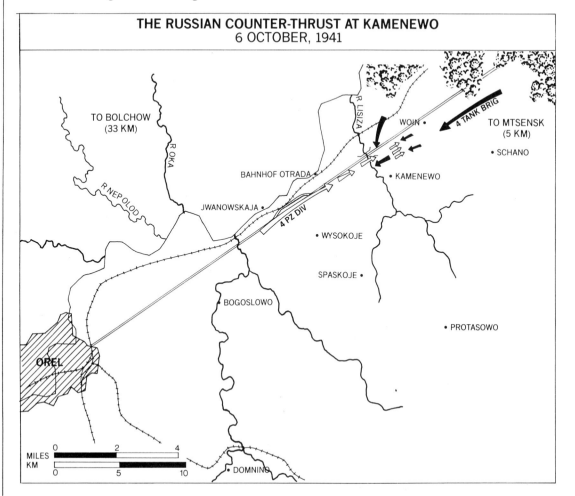

THE RUSSIAN COUNTER-THRUST AT KAMENEWO
6 OCTOBER, 1941

IMPLICATIONS FOR THE PANZERS

4th Panzer's losses of ten tanks, two 88 mm and one 105 mm howitzer, and one 100 mm gun were far from crippling, and had to be set against the destruction of 18 enemy tanks, including eight KV1s. But the effects of this, the first major encounter with a mass of the latest Russian machines, were far-reaching. To begin with, the check on this front, imposed by a coherent Russian defense, had repercussions elsewhere as German lines of communication began to collapse in alternating conditions of blizzard and frost, thaw and glutinous mud. Stop-go killed off the German momentum and presented the Russians with invaluable time and opportunities to assemble fresh forces to create new stop lines protecting the obvious enemy objective, Moscow. The Germans still frequently demonstrated that they were far ahead of the Russians in training, technique and execution of imaginative ideas. Yet in tank technology the Germans were far behind in firepower, protection and mobility. In a tank-versus-tank battle they were out-classed.

Within a matter of months, PzKws III and IV were to have their armor thickness doubled by the addition of face-hardened, spaced plates; and their guns improved, respectively by the L60 50 mm and a very good 'long', L43 75 mm piece with a muzzle velocity of 700 m/sec (2300 ft/sec). Simultaneously, pre-war design projects would be updated to put into production a 56-ton tank, armed with an 88 mm gun, the Tiger I, and a brand-new medium tank of 43 tons with sloped armor and an L 70, 75 mm gun, the Panther D. Power plants would be increased from the existing 300 hp of the PzKw IV to 650 hp in Panther and 700 hp in Tiger. Tracks would be made much wider to help match the superior cross-country performance of the wide-tracked KV1s and T34s.

None of these improvements, however, were ready in time to save the Germans from the bitter winter ahead. As a measure of what the combined resistance of snow, mud, KVs and T34s added up to in terms of resistance, it was another 18 days after the repulse at the Lisiza before Mtsensk fell. Progress on all fronts grew slower as the temperatures dropped 30 degrees below freezing, reducing the efficiency of men and machines to less than 20 per cent. Long before 5 December, when von Bock's troops arrived within sight of Moscow and a Russian counter-offensive opened against his Army Group, all German formations were reporting exhaustion. Tank strengths were at their lowest, due not only to the fierce and, by now, unyielding enemy resistance stiffened by the deadly KV1s and T34s [which assumed a dominance out of all proportion to their numbers], but also to the vulnerability to the cold of the German vehicles. Fuel and lubricants untreated for such low temperatures froze, as did engine coolants of insufficient density. Narrow tank tracks of too high a ground pressure sank in the mud and, frequently, were then frozen in solidly before the vehicles could be dragged out. For the first time in Russia, as the Germans began to withdraw, large numbers of their machines had to be abandoned.

Wholesale breakdowns and a widespread spares famine now broke the German maintenance and repair organization. In order to keep just a few tanks running, indiscriminate cannibalization was inflicted on tanks which might otherwise have been recovered and returned to action. Those which were backloaded by rail to Germany for overhaul usually arrived at their destination stripped of nearly everything movable and in need of a rebuild. Deleterious as these shortcomings were, the Soviet tank force was in only slighter better condition. The number and efficiency of its AFVs was seriously depleted and impaired by the inability of Soviet factories (overrun or uprooted by the invasion) to make good the losses plus the ineptitude of replacement commanders and crews who were pitched into battle with the most meagre training. With so few tanks operational on either side, they usually appeared only in 'penny packets'. Nevertheless, even a platoon of tanks, employed in these circumstances against a weakened opponent, could have the equivalent effect of a whole battalion by comparison with the early days of the campaign. When defenses were impoverished, just two or three tanks in working order were as terrifying to the defenders as had been, for example, the 16 German A7Vs which had advanced at Villers Bretonneux in 1918. And few tank-versus-tank battles during that terrible winter of deprivation were on a much larger scale than the first one of all.

SWINGS OF FATE IN THE DESERT

Logistic difficulties, plus maintenance and repair deficiencies, as afflicted the German Army deep in Russia, also hampered the German/Italian forces in North Africa. The slow accumulation of adequate stocks of fuel, ammunition, vehicles and spares across a

ARMOR-PIERCING (AP) SHOT
The shot with which all tanks went to war in 1939, but which soon proved inadequate as a penetrator of more sophisticated, face-hardened armor.

ARMOR-PIERCING CAPPED (APC)
The softer metal cap was added to prevent break-up of ordinary AP and thus assist penetration.

few hundred miles of Mediterranean sea meant that it was September 1941 before Rommel judged he had the capability to strike again, and late into November before he had recuperated from his incompetent and abortive raid on British supply depots near the Egyptian frontier. It cost 30 tanks (only five totally destroyed) from shelling, bombing, breakdown and fuel shortage. It postponed his crucial renewal of the assault upon Tobruk, enabling the British to attack before he was ready.

Despite being farther from their home supply bases, the British had built up their tank force to 756, (opposing the 400 in German/Italian possession) and suffered few supply embarrassments. Their principal weaknesses lay in gun power, the unreliability of the latest Crusader cruiser tank, and a fundamental flaw in their tactical doctrine. Their anti-tank guns were still the 40 mm, supplemented by the US 37 mm mounted in the US Stuart light tank, of which sufficient for a complete brigade had been supplied. British armor basis was the same as in France and over-matched by the German L60 50 mm anti-tank gun on its field ·mounting, and firing capped shot (APC), which added greatly to German killing power against all types of British and US tanks then in service.

Tactically there were similarities. Each side appreciated that tanks and guns were the dominant desert weapons, making infantry shift warily, escorted by tanks and guns, whenever they left fortified positions to join in the mobile contest. Both tended to adopt sea battle formations and maneuver like navies. Each sought to destroy the other's AFVs as a vital prerequisite of ultimate victory. But while the Germans persisted in employing their armored formations to lure the British onto concealed emplaced guns, the British hunted for outright confrontation, tank versus tank (as Fuller had decried in 1918). They thus fell victim to the enemy's ploys by chasing moving targets instead of adhering to the military principle of seizing and dominating the vital ground with their forces concentrated.

Repeatedly during the battle which began on 18 November to the east of Tobruk (and most devastatingly in its opening phase) the British allowed themselves to be cut to ribbons when charging emplaced guns and tanks. As one tank driver said, after seeing so many of his comrades slain: 'I was not so keen on this charging business'. Charging,

however, was almost unavoidable if the 40 mm gun with its ordinary AP shot was to have any chance of getting within killing distance of the German tanks, many of which were being fitted with additional 30 mm face-hardened plates upon which AP shot broke up except at the closest ranges. From the British point of view, the tragedy lay in the fact that, although they possessed specimens of every kind of German armor since April 1941, it was almost a year later before they rumbled that it was face-hardened. So, in November 1941, they fought under the false impression that it was failings in their own marksmanship rather than an enemy technical superiority which was causing them to come off second best in tank-versus-tank battles.

The clash of armored masses to the southeast of Tobruk erupted as a turmoil of formations and units seeking combat in dust clouds and battle smoke. Shooting might open from the 88s at 2000 m, but hits were rarely scored above 1000 m (where the L60 50 mm guns came into their own) and at 300 m, if their luck held, the British with their 40 mm guns might begin to take a toll. Notably on the vital ground of the Sidi Rezegh feature, with its airfield, the losses to the British, fanning out to seek their quarry, mounted alarmingly as they fell into ambush after ambush. They were overrun by adroitly concentrated enemy formations, skilfully apprised of the situation by reconnaissance units and deftly handled by commanders whose communication system was so much better served by radio sets superior to those of the British. The ground to the south and east of Tobruk was converted into a tank graveyard. At one point, two British armored brigades, which four days previously had set forth some 350 tanks strong, were reduced to 50, although far from all of these were total losses, many having merely broken down or suffered minor damage. But here again the Germans benefited because their recovery facilities were far better than those of the British.

Yet Rommel threw away the considerable advantage won in battle by departing from this vital zone and the tank battle in order to raid the British lines of communication with what remained of his own armor. Instead of concentrating upon collecting or destroying the helpless mass of disabled enemy tanks, he left the field clear for the British to repair their damaged tanks and reconstitute their armored force at Sidi Rezegh. As a result, when he returned to the vital ground, weakened himself by several damaging encounters with British artillery at the frontier, Rommel had to start all over again just as his logistics began to collapse. Come 4 December, despite a few more local victories over the out-classed British tanks, he had to concede defeat due to a shortage of machines and the loss of his supplies. By the end of the year he was back at El Agheila licking his wounds, while the British built up their strength for an invasion of Tripolitania.

Insecure British radio networks told Rommel that, in mid January, he would, for a fleeting moment, possess a numerical edge over the British at El Agheila. Even so the brusque spoiling attack he launched on 20 January should not have swept the British away if their gunpower had been stronger, if their command and control system had been better, and if the Germans had not been uplifted by an entirely justified confidence in their own superiority in the art of mobile warfare. With cool precision, the Germans combined their tanks and anti-tank guns to massacre fresh troops with limited desert experience. One German described how his twelve 50 mm anti-tank guns

*...L*EAP-
frogged from one vantage point to another, while our Panzers, stationary and hull-down if possible, provided protective fire. Then we would establish ourselves to give them protective fire while they swept on again'

...a marvellous encapsulation of the fundamental technique of fire and movement alloyed with all-arms cooperation. Once again charging to destruction, breaking down in retreat and scattering to the winds, the British armored formations were broken to the south of Benghazi, exposing the infantry formations, with their pathetic 40 mm anti-tank guns, to annihiliation. Only by cutting their losses and running fast to Gazala and Tobruk were they able to escape that fate.

THE NEW TANK GENERATION OF 1942
Exhaustion in the desert enforced a winter's pause for recuperation while on the steppe and among the forests the German struggle for survival continued against furious Russian attacks. However, the Russians over-reached and also exhausted themselves while everywhere behind the lines in training camps and factories the next generation of men and equipment prepared for still fiercer confrontations later in 1942. For the Russians

this build-up was an almost insuperable strain on their own current resources. New tank factories under construction in safety away to the east were nowhere near capable of producing the mass of machines demanded. Meanwhile, the tanks they were receiving from Britain were of types already out-classed by the Germans and, moreover, ill-suited for the most part to the harsh Russian environment. These tanks were employed for want of anything better, but not, it seems, with enthusiasm. Moreover, they would soon be faced by the latest PzKw IIIs and IVs. With its L60 50 mm gun and 60 mm spaced, face-hardened armor, the PzKw IIIJ was a useful fighting vehicle of proven reliability. Far better were the latest PzKw IVFs whose armor was the same as PzKw IIIJ but whose L43 75 mm gun was a match for T34/76 and might even take care of the KV1 if caught in flank. Likewise, developments of the self-propelled infantry assault gun class of AFV into a self-propelled tank-hunter (the Jagdpanzer) promoted a far more effective weapon system than the simple, towed anti-tank gun with its poor protection, slower time into action and limited mobility. In 1941 the first of the Jagdpanzers with the improved L48 75 mm gun (muzzle velocity 747 m/sec) on a PzKw III chassis made its debut, followed in 1942 by a 105 mm version.

AFVs thus armed, and especially if firing the latest tungsten carbide shot, could easily penetrate every existing British tank except the new Churchill III, whose armor only the 88 mm could overcome. But Churchill III would not enter battle until August 1942 during the amphibious raid upon Dieppe.

A Crusader I leaving a Tank Landing Craft during trials. Powered by a 340 hp Liberty ex-aircraft engine, this tank's high speed did not compensate, in 1941, for its thin armor, obsolete gun, and lack of a commander's cupola. Its combat life would be further extended in 1942 by fitting a 57 mm gun, but this meant reducing the turret crew to two men.
Weight 18 tons
Speed 27 mph
Frontal armor 40 mm
Armament 1×40 mm, 2×mg

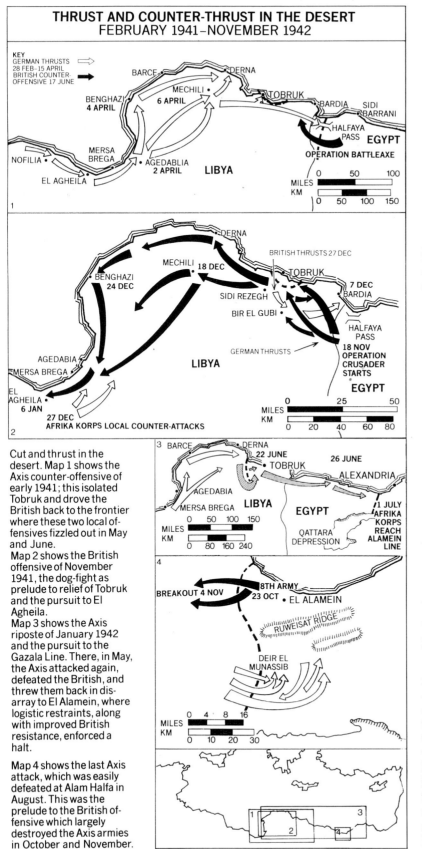

THRUST AND COUNTER-THRUST IN THE DESERT
FEBRUARY 1941–NOVEMBER 1942

KEY
GERMAN THRUSTS ⇨
28 FEB–15 APRIL
BRITISH COUNTER-
OFFENSIVE 17 JUNE ⬛➤

Map 1: BARCE, DERNA, MECHILI 6 APRIL, BENGHAZI 4 APRIL, TOBRUK, BARDIA, SIDI BARRANI, HALFAYA PASS, EGYPT, OPERATION BATTLEAXE, MERSA BREGA, NOFILIA, AGEDABLIA 2 APRIL, EL AGHEILA, LIBYA
MILES 0 50 100
KM 0 50 100 150

Map 2: DERNA, MECHILI 18 DEC, BRITISH THRUSTS 27 DEC, BENGHAZI 24 DEC, TOBRUK, SIDI REZEGH, BIR EL GUBI, 7 DEC BARDIA, HALFAYA PASS, 18 NOV OPERATION CRUSADER STARTS, EGYPT, GERMAN THRUSTS, AGEDABIA, MERSA BREGA, EL AGHEILA 6 JAN, 27 DEC AFRIKA KORPS LOCAL COUNTER-ATTACKS, LIBYA
MILES 0 25 50
KM 0 20 40 60 80

Cut and thrust in the desert. Map 1 shows the Axis counter-offensive of early 1941; this isolated Tobruk and drove the British back to the frontier where these two local offensives fizzled out in May and June.

Map 2 shows the British offensive of November 1941, the dog-fight as prelude to relief of Tobruk and the pursuit to El Agheila.

Map 3 shows the Axis riposte of January 1942 and the pursuit to the Gazala Line. There, in May, the Axis attacked again, defeated the British, and threw them back in disarray to El Alamein, where logistic restraints, along with improved British resistance, enforced a halt.

Map 4 shows the last Axis attack, which was easily defeated at Alam Halfa in August. This was the prelude to the British offensive which largely destroyed the Axis armies in October and November.

Map 3: BARCE, DERNA 22 JUNE, TOBRUK 26 JUNE, ALEXANDRIA, AGEDABIA, MERSA BREGA, LIBYA, EGYPT, 1 JULY AFRIKA KORPS REACH ALAMEIN LINE, QATTARA DEPRESSION
MILES 0 50 100 150
KM 0 80 160 240

Map 4: BREAKOUT 4 NOV, 8TH ARMY 23 OCT, EL ALAMEIN, RUWEISAT RIDGE, DEIR EL MUNASSIB
MILES 0 4 8 16
KM 0 10 20 30

And tungsten carbide shot would only rarely be available, because of shortage of tungsten. Nevertheless when the latest PzKw IIIJs began to arrive in North Africa in April, followed by the PzKw IVFs in July, the British had nothing of their own on tracks to compete, and only the newly delivered 57 mm (6 pounder) field anti-tank gun was capable of overcoming the latest German armor at 1000 meters. The one hope in the British stable, ready in time for the renewal of heavy fighting in May, was the M3 General Grant, put together quickly by the Americans in 1941 as a stop-gap AFV with a dual-purpose gun of 75 mm caliber. Based upon the experimental T5 tank of 1938, Grant evolved, under British guidance, from the initial M3, General Lee, into an AFV of tactical inconvenience. The sponson-mounted 75 mm gun, set low to one side of the hull and with limited traverse, could not be brought into line of sight without exposing the entire high-sided hull of an AFV whose 65 mm armor was good but whose rivets tended to fly about inside when struck. Nevertheless, even the 31 calibers 75 mm, first fitted before replacement with the better 40 calibers weapon, had the capability of defeating most German armor up to 1000 m; but more important, it at last gave British tank crews a weapon which could fire high explosive, desirably from turret-down positions, against enemy anti-tank guns. This spelt the eventual doom of the dual-purpose 88 mm gun and many another German gun besides.

1942 was indeed a turning point in the development of Anglo-American tank gun ballistic technology and techniques. Compelled, at last, to recognise the German superiority as a deadly threat to their own crews' effectiveness and morale, they at last began introducing into service improved optics, better firing gear, more powerful guns and much more sophisticated kinds of shot. The Americans, having settled upon the 75 mm gun, were already looking ahead to the need for a 76.2 mm gun. The British whose 57 mm gun was about to be fitted (with difficulty) into the too-small existing tank turrets, were dissatisfied with its lack of a useful high explosive round. They too were working upon a 76.2 mm gun which would be known as the 17-pounder. But the most immediate British improvements were to their shot with the introduction in May 1942 of capped shot (AFC) – the fitting of a soft nose to prevent break-up against face-hardened armor – and of a streamlined

ballistic cap to this (creating APCBC) which by reducing the drag helps to raise the muzzle velocity of a 40 mm gun, for example, from 689 m/sec (2260 ft/sec) to 792 m/sec (2600 ft/sec). They copied the Germans, who had used APC and APCBC ammunition almost from the beginning and were at an advanced stage in the production of longer 75 mm and 88 mm guns with muzzle velocities in excess of 914 m/sec (3000 ft/sec). Soon, too, the Russians would be introducing weapons of 85 mm and 100 mm as the gun/armor race accelerated.

WAR IN THE FAR EAST

Japan's attacks on the United States, British and Dutch in the Far East had rapidly spread the war across the Pacific basin and into Burma. The Japanese fought an amphibious-related war, with infantry and artillery predominant on land, supported in a subsidiary role by tanks of limited capability. Tank-versus-tank clashes were very few and far between because only a handful of light types had been deployed by the Allies in this war zone. In Burma, where the British sent two regiments of Stuarts, jungle and paddy fields generally confined the tanks to the roads and tracks. Here a couple of clashes between Stuarts and Japanese tanks took place at ranges of between 800 yards (when three Japanese tanks were hit by 37 mm shot and destroyed) and a few score yards (without result).

In the Far East as the course of war brought a decline in Japanese strength while that of the Allies rose to irresistible proportions, such armored warfare as occurred was very much one-sided. When the British and Indian armies turned to a major offensive in Burma in 1944, they vastly out-numbered the Japanese in tanks and were opposed by little more than bravely served anti-tank guns and

by men with charges attached to the ends of poles. When the Americans and Australians landed on Japanese-held territory during a series of amphibious operations to seize vital points and islands, there were but few Japanese tanks to resist the waves of swimming AFVs (invented in the 1920s by Christie) and the medium tanks which followed up. This was a very different kind of conflict to the vast wars of armored machines taking place in the wide open spaces of North Africa and Europe. It contributed virtually nothing to the history of tank-versus-tank fighting.

PLAN ORIENT

In June 1942 Hitler ordered a draft plan called 'Orient' to consider the possibilities of a link up in the Middle East between the German/Italian forces in North Africa with the German Army about to advance into the Caucasus, thus threatening the vital oilfields of that region and those of Persia and Iraq. Rommel had already struck at the British who held a fortified and mined system of infantry 'boxes' at Gazala. But in the face of an initially well-conducted defense, stiffened by

Above: Crusaders and Shermans advancing at El Alamein.
Left: An American Stuart Mk II light tank of the British Army passes a German PzKw III J, which has been demolished to prevent recapture. The reliable Stuart was used as a stop-gap tank when introduced to the North African desert in 1941, but was unfit for stand-up fighting in 1942 and soon relegated to reconnaissance work. Its high speed was of no great protection.
Weight 12 tons
Speed 35 mph
Frontal armor 43 mm
Armament 1×37 mm, 3×mg

the new Grant tanks and the 57 mm anti-tank guns, he had been checked and thrown back on the defensive. Forewarned of the attack (and, indeed, almost ready to attack themselves) the British met the Axis armor head on as it outflanked their positions from the desert and drove for the British rear, with tanks and guns maneuvering from prepared positions. The Grant's 75 mm gun made a considerable impression on the Germans; their losses mounted and their lines of communication could not be kept open. If the British could have swiftly mounted a fully coordinated tank, infantry and artillery counter-stroke against Rommel's mobile forces penned in with their backs to the minefields which littered the area, they could have won. In fact, so deprived was the Axis army of water that at one point Rommel was within a few hours of asking for terms of surrender.

Rommel wriggled out of trouble by reopening his lines of comunication and then, with superbly handled artillery backed up by tanks, defeating a British tank attack which came in several days too late and ill-supported by artillery fire which was directed against empty desert instead of its intended targets. The thrust by Rommel's tanks and guns capitalizing upon a massacre of British armor, as it once more charged, repeated what was by now an all-too-familiar pattern. It also showed that up-gunned PzKw IIIJs were a match for the Grant. No less than 138 British AFVs were lost by noon on 13 June and their tank strength, some 850 on 26 May at the start of the battle, fell to 70. This meant that facing about 150 Axis tanks and a strong core of anti-tank guns still in action, the British had no option but to quit the battlefield at Gazala and retire to the shelter of the Tobruk fortress and the Egyptian frontier.

Inefficient command and control apparatus, lax radio security and lack of a coherent doctrine lay at the root of the British troubles. Once more they had been defeated because not only had they dispersed their armor in attack but they had also utterly omitted to give support to their tanks and infantry with concentrated artillery fire. A pernicious practice of conducting operations with scattered groups rushing around in cavalier disunity had been exposed by an opponent who played all his weapons in concert and often had the knack of picking the right spot and the right time to do so. So devastating was their defeat, the morale of

ARMOR-PIERCING CAPPED BALLISTIC CAPPED (APCBC) SHOT A streamlined APC shot to increase muzzle velocity.

PZKW IVF

POST-1941, THIS GERMAN AFV BECAME the workhorse of German mobile anti-tank forces when the original short 75 mm gun was replaced by the 43 calibers 75 mm (and in due course by the even better 48 calibers weapon). At the same time, armor was increased to 50 mm (with some intermediate versions at 30 + 30 mm and subsequent models raised to 80 mm), making the PzKw IVF an extremely formidable weapon system, as was proved against the British at El Alamein, and against the Russians in the approaches to the Caucasus and Stalingrad.

Turret access periscope door

The Germans were introducing better sighting systems and improving their gunnery techniques in a desperate effort profitably to raise the hit and kill power of their AFVs against numerically superior foes. The basic PzKw IV, however, remained unchanged, except that far greater reliability was achieved in a machine which already enjoyed the confidence of its crews.

Weight 24 tons
Speed 25 mph
Frontal armor 50 mm
Armament 1×75 mm (43 cals), 2×mg

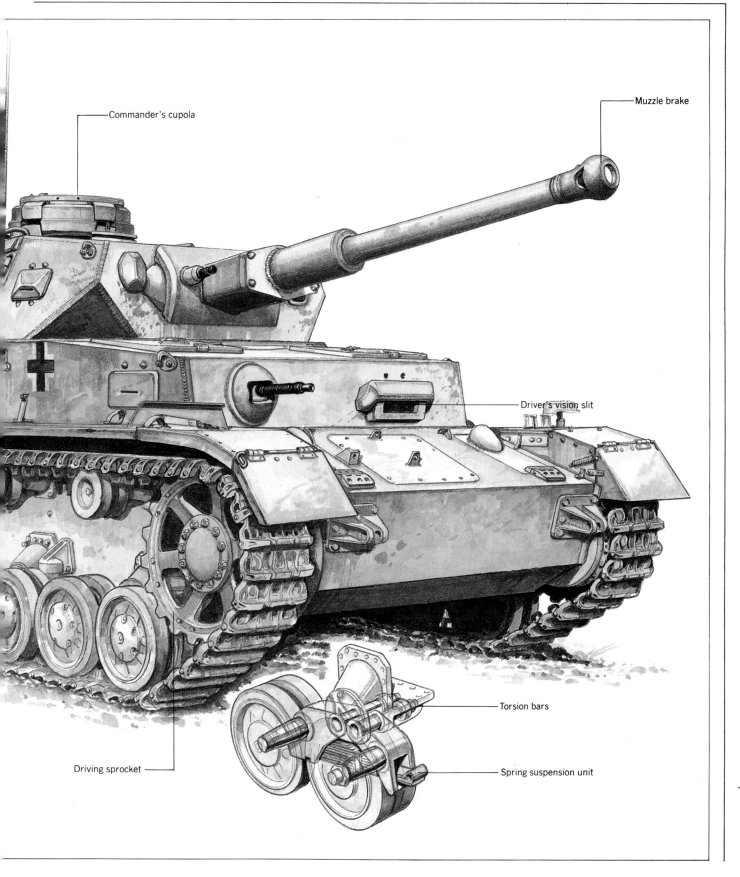

Commander's cupola

Muzzle brake

Driver's vision slit

Driving sprocket

Torsion bars

Spring suspension unit

the baffled British crews sank to an all-time low. As breakdowns of their cruisers and Matildas occured at far too high a rate, what became known as 'The Reliability Crisis' appeared along with a saying that 'A Grant will see you through – a Matilda will let you down'. This reflected a belief of the men who fought in them that a Grant was worth three British tanks even though it was inferior to the latest German machines. More damaging still, there emerged a school of British thought which declaimed that, because it was costly to stand up and shoot it out, vehicle against vehicle, it was preferable to revert to long-founded artillery methods by trying to engage enemy tanks with armor-piercing shot from turret-down positions. This not only abandoned the tank's role as an instrument of pin-point-accurate direct fire, but also further sapped each crew's offensive spirit when pitted against a supremely confident foe. Fortunately this retreat from fortitude was snuffed out before it became doctrine. But its gloomy adherents were listened to with attention during the desperate days of the fall of Tobruk and Rommel's bold but risky invasion of Egypt which overran Mersa Matruh and was stopped only by backs-to-the-wall resistance at El Alamein at the beginning of July when

the German logistic system proved unequal to operating too far from base.

Even so, it was air attack and the artillery, the latter at last directed to fight as a concentrated force to exert its full inherent flexibility when centrally controlled, which did the trick for the British. For in successive encounters, British tanks continued to be worsted almost every time they attempted offensive strokes. On 22 July, for example, the 23rd Armoured Brigade with Valentines, in their first action, lost some 116 tanks – nearly all of them were charging against 88 and 50 mm anti-tank guns at a moment when the German tank strength amounted to little more than 50 fit for action.

THE CAUCASUS AND STALINGRAD - THE OIL HUNT

On the Eastern Front the left pincer claw of the sketchy Plan 'Orient' thrust forward on 28 June on a 400-mile front between Voronezh and Rostov and, by its initial stupendous progress, indicated that the Panzer Armies, with restored strength and better machines, had recuperated well against a weary opponent whose tank strength was at its nadir. Although Soviet production was rising fast, it was not until later in the summer that a significant increase would be noticed at the

T34s carrying infantry into battle. This was far from being an exclusive Russian practice. Most other armies did it. Troops had to be careful to dismount swiftly once opposition was met, otherwise infantry casualties could be high and the tank deprived of its offensive capability.

front. In the meantime the Russians had to make do with captured German machines, with the inferior British types and a few US Grants, plus whatever they built themselves. T34s were being made in the largest numbers. Emphasis upon the less easily constructed KV1s fell off as efforts to introduce a greatly improved range of heavy tanks, the Josef Stalin breed, were put in hand. Of equal importance was the order issued by General Y N Fedorenko, Marshal of Tank Troops, at the end of June in which he laid down the principles for future employment of armored forces. The directive included little that was original. Largely it related what Fuller had called for in 1918 and the Germans had been practicing for years. But it was overdue for Russian commanders in the field, who were persisting with methods that had brought the French and British to disaster in 1940. Henceforward, insisted Fedorenko, armored corps would be concentrated upon strategic missions as directed by army group headquarters. They would not be allocated to armies and split up among the infantry nor would they be used for head-on attacks unless heavily supported by air and artillery. Instead they would seek weak spots and infiltrate gaps aiming at strategic targets, some 25 to 30 miles distant. Surprise would always be sought, favorable ground used, and logistics most carefully organized to ensure that men and machines could move and subsist for five days or more without replenishment.

For deep penetration operations of this nature only the T34 was suitable. Therefore the KVs and their successors would be regrouped into special assault units where they would no longer, as in the past, hamper the T34s. Although this doctrine would have no impact against the latest German offensive, the Germans nevertheless discovered in Russian tank-versus-tank tactics an improvement over 1941 – even though the number of radio sets issued to the Russians was still niggardly. In a battle for possession of crossings over the River Resseta in July, 11th and 19th Panzer Divisions found themselves under fire from well dug in anti-tank guns, harried in flank by groups of five to seven T34s emerging from forest hides and gullies to fire and then backing off before they could be tackled. With skill the T34s repeated these tactics, inflicting high casualties on the Germans. They avoided return fire, cowed the German infantry and held up the German advance – demonstrating, in effect, what a marvellous

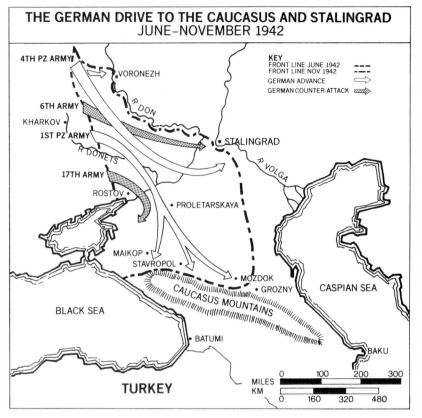

THE GERMAN DRIVE TO THE CAUCASUS AND STALINGRAD
JUNE–NOVEMBER 1942

defensive power even a small number of mobile tanks could exert.

It would be an exaggeration to suggest that Russian resistance to the German offensive totally collapsed, although there was no doubt in the Germans' minds that something had given way. A panzer sergeant remarked upon how different it was to 1941. '*IT'S MORE like Poland. The Russians are not nearly so thick on the ground. They fire their guns like madmen, but they don't hurt us.*'

With its old verve, Hoth's Fourth Panzer Army spearheaded the thrust towards Stalingrad which in company with Sixth Army, it reached at the beginning of August. Von Kleist's First Panzer Army which was rampaging through the Caucasus, seizing the Maikop oilfields on 9 August, entered the Caucasian foothills a few days later. Unhappily for the Germans, they also became fascinated by Hitler's ambition to capture Stalingrad, a miscalculation which offered the Soviet High Command an opportunity to transform the city into a fortress and a symbol of inflexible will to victory. Stalingrad was quite unsuitable for AFVs which are difficult to use in street fighting. If the

The German advance into the Caucasus and to Stalingrad. Their Russian opponents appeared to melt away, but then stiffened their resistance at key points.

Germans had persisted in the capture of the Caucasus and the oilfields at Baku, decisive strategic results might well have been achieved by von Kleist's armor, fully supported. Instead the vital resources were denied him and fed into an attritional mincing machine. Von Kleist's drive ground to a halt from lack of adequate logistic support as, steadily, pressure upon the Russians began to relax and they ceased to run before the Tank Terror. The position stabilised to the point at which, on 14 October, Hitler ordered a standstill except at Stalingrad where Sixth Army and Fourth Panzer Army lay concentrated in a salient with their northern and eastern flanks but thinly protected. Nine days later it came to his notice that the southern claw of 'Orient', already blunted at El Alamein, was in dire peril of being snapped off.

THE TURNING POINT AT ALAM HALFA AND EL ALAMEIN

A change of leadership, a rationalization of tactics, and the arrival in Egypt of a tank with a good dual-purpose gun in a turret were the decisive factors in the change of British fortunes. In August Lieut-General Bernard Montgomery imposed the discipline of military orthodoxy, adapted to modern conditions, upon the British Eighth Army. He insisted that possession of vital ground should be fundamental to operations, that artillery fire should be concentrated as a battle winning factor in support of infantry and tanks, and that the tanks should be integrated with the overall plan of battle and not permitted to rush off on their own, charging to destruction against unshaken enemy guns and tanks. His men were vastly assisted by the considerable improvement to British radio communications from the latest sets, and by the US Sherman tank. The Sherman, the first truly efficient combat tank produced by the United States, was a vastly superior AFV to the Grant. With its longer, more powerful 40 calibers 75 mm turret mounted gun, and its considerably thicker 85 mm armor, Sherman was as reliable as Grant, superior to T34/76 and a match for the first of the PzKw IVFs, which put in their appearance in larger numbers during August. It at once won the confidence of its crews when it entered action in October.

In the meantime Montgomery had to cope on 30 August with Rommel's last throw to reach the Suez Canal, a right hook through the desert aimed at the British rear, similar to the move he had made at Gazala in May. But this time there was no immediate tank clash. The British armor withdrew to the dominant Alam Halfa ridge, leaving their German adversaries to struggle in soft sand (thereby consuming more fuel than estimated) and in minefields where they were bombed and shelled without mercy. At once the German plan was thrown out of gear. Yet Rommel persevered, urging his tanks to within sight of the Alam Halfa ridge, the key to the British defenses and a most strongly held vital feature. Here the panzer divisions, deprived by concentrated artillery fire of infantry support, were hard-pressed to tackle the dug-in 57 mm anti-tank guns, whose gunners knew the range exactly. Mightily impressed though the British were by the appearance of the PzKw IVFs, they shot back with confidence, joined in the battle at the critical moment by Grants and Crusaders which moved into hull-down positions on the crest to counter each German maneuver. The PzKw IVs accomplished considerable execution by steady shooting, yet met some-

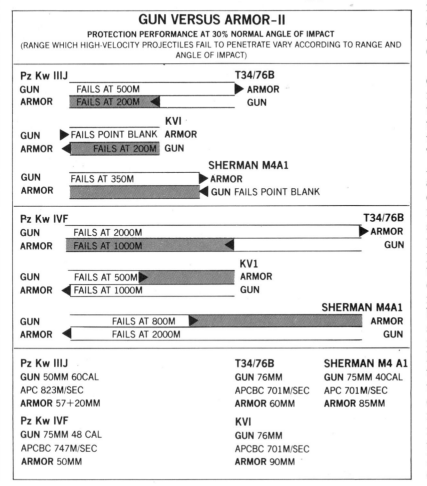

GUN VERSUS ARMOR-II

PROTECTION PERFORMANCE AT 30% NORMAL ANGLE OF IMPACT
(RANGE WHICH HIGH-VELOCITY PROJECTILES FAIL TO PENETRATE VARY ACCORDING TO RANGE AND ANGLE OF IMPACT)

Pz Kw IIIJ — T34/76B
GUN   FAILS AT 500M   ARMOR
ARMOR   FAILS AT 200M   GUN

KVI
GUN   FAILS POINT BLANK   ARMOR
ARMOR   FAILS AT 200M   GUN

SHERMAN M4A1
GUN   FAILS AT 350M   ARMOR
ARMOR   GUN FAILS POINT BLANK

Pz Kw IVF — T34/76B
GUN   FAILS AT 2000M   ARMOR
ARMOR   FAILS AT 1000M   GUN

KV1
GUN   FAILS AT 500M   ARMOR
ARMOR   FAILS AT 1000M   GUN

SHERMAN M4A1
GUN   FAILS AT 800M   ARMOR
ARMOR   FAILS AT 2000M   GUN

Pz Kw IIIJ	T34/76B	SHERMAN M4 A1
GUN 50MM 60CAL	GUN 76MM	GUN 75MM 40CAL
APC 823M/SEC	APCBC 701M/SEC	APC 701M/SEC
ARMOR 57+20MM	ARMOR 60MM	ARMOR 85MM
Pz Kw IVF	KVI	
GUN 75MM 48 CAL	GUN 76MM	
APCBC 747M/SEC	APCBC 701M/SEC	
ARMOR 50MM	ARMOR 90MM	

SHERMAN M4 A1

THE US SHERMAN, with the good dual-purpose 75 mm gun, at last gave the British a tank which could outmatch enemy 88 mm anti-tank guns, besides the improved PzKw IIIs and IVs. Produced in several different versions, some Shermans (like this model) had very reliable diesel engines; others had gasoline radial engines, some originally made for aircraft. Reliable and easy to operate, the main crew complaint about the Sherman concerned its propensity to burn – the Germans naming it the 'Tommy Cooker'.

Weight 31 tons
Speed 28 mph
Frontal armor 85 mm (partially sloped)
Armament 1×75 mm, 2×mg

thing unyielding. This time Rommel's men recoiled, tried again, wilted and began a retreat – in the vain hope that, as in the past, the British tanks would be sacrificed in yet another charge. However, this time (except in one isolated instance) nothing of the sort occured. The battle ended in stalemate with the British armor intact and the Germans sheltering behind minefields and seriously weakened at the end of long and vulnerable lines of communication which imposed a chronic fuel shortage.

Henceforward, as German offensive capacity declined and they fell back onto the defensive, the minefields they laid whenever tactically profitable were to have a cloying effect on tank movement. On the relatively narrow 40-mile frontage at El Alamein they imposed a decisive restriction on the British

offensive on 23 October, since they dictated the formulation of a combined assault by infantry, artillery and tanks at night in order to open up gaps to get at the enemy beyond. At El Alamein, too, mechanical 'flail tanks' (which beat the ground ahead to detonate the mines) were also used for the first time, thus reintroducing what had been conceived at Cambrai in 1917, specialized armored vehicles for the maintenance of mobility.

At the heart of Montgomery's plan was the aim of destroying the German/Italian tank force by taking a leaf out of the German book. This was, with all-arms attacks, to seize ground the enemy could not afford to yield and thus lure the German tanks (which Rommel had stationed all along the front) onto emplaced guns. In the initial phase, tanks mainly supported the infantry penetration of the forward defenses. In the next stage, the so-called dog fight, they combined with guns in the destruction of the enemy armor. Finally they broke out and enveloped most of what was left of their opponents. The British possessed not only more than 1100 tanks, but the great new advantage of among them 270 Shermans and 210 Grants – set against 200 German tanks (of which only 30 were PzKw IVFs) and 280 obsolete Italian tanks. The point had been reached at which General Sir Harold Alexander (C-in-C Middle East Land Forces) could insist. '**N**OW WE HAVE A LOT OF *armor we must be prepared to use it where it is wanted and to accept heavy losses.'*

This is precisely what happened against the enemy anti-tank guns at El Alamein during 11 days of attrition which witnessed losses of up to 90 per cent of tanks in some British formations, but led to almost 100 per cent of the Axis armor being eliminated. And once more it was anti-tank guns, rather than tanks, which accomplished the lion's share of tank destruction, leaving several hundred surviving British tanks to act the bully against a broken enemy. But this time even the anti-tank guns also had a miserable experience, the British artillery concentrations, supplemented by fire from the Shermans' and Grants' dual-purpose guns, wreaking havoc on their positions. Very few 88s escaped and not many more 50 mms and captured Russian 76.2 mms which had been put to German service. A combined attack won total victory at the turning point of the war as Germany lost the initiative.

COUNTER-STROKE AT STALINGRAD

As the southern claw of Plan Orient was broken at El Alamein and a large Anglo-American invasion force began landing in Morocco and Algeria on 8 November, the Russians were scheming the destruction of Orient's northern claw at Stalingrad and in the Caucasus. To each side it was obvious that both flanks of the salient were vulnerable. As early as September the Russians had started to explore possibilities, arriving at a positive commitment to counter-offensive at the end of October. Only slowly did the Germans come to convert their suspicions into a feeling of uncertainty about what was in train. Yet never did they credit their opponent with the strength or ability to carry out what was to be a double pincer movement in depth.

With masterly stealth, under General Zhukov, the Russians managed at a time of freeze and thaw, to move to their assembly areas the mass of men, the 13 500 guns and the 894 tanks which were to attack over a frontage of about 150 miles down four main axes of advance. This tank force, let it be noted, was smaller than the one employed by Montgomery at El Alamein over a frontage of 40 miles. Also at Stalingrad, Zhukov chose, as had Montgomery when he concentrated against the weaker Italian formations, to tackle initially the lower grade Romanian troops on the flanks of the German Fourth Panzer Army and Sixth Army in the vicinity of the city. The Germans were not themselves strong in AFVs. Their panzer divisions stood at about only 60 each: in all they had at their disposal somewhat less than 500 AFVs of all kinds, several of them obsolete Czech types, far too few of them the latest PzKw IVs.

Numbers and quality of AFVs, however, were to be of lesser importance than the merits of surprise achieved by the Russians as they obeyed the Fedorenko order. Maybe the Germans could have envisaged the effect of assault by KV1 tanks and massed artillery. What they did not allow for was the verve with which T34s, well supported by accompanying infantry and artillery, passed through the enormous holes rent among the Romanian formations; and how they would flow, with advances of 80 miles in four days by General Romannko's 5th Tank Army and of 60 miles by General Volsky's 4th Mechanized Corps.

The state of shock and unequalled panic assailing the German ranks as the Russian counter-offensive developed was mostly noticeable among administrative troops, but also detectable at the front where, caught unawares, units did not react with their customary fluency. When panzer divisions of Fourth Panzer Army were sent back from Stalingrad to block the approach of 5th Tank Army, their redeployment was reminiscent of French 1st DCR's move to Flavion in 1940. Leaving their infantry behind, they travelled piecemeal through the darkness across the snow-covered undulating plains without making adequate logistic arrangements. Fuel tanks had not been topped up at last light and the supply echelons were scattered. Spread across the steppe, they reached the vital crossings over the Don at Kalach, short of fuel and ammunition, and dispersed into small, improvised combat teams containing only a few reconnaissance, artillery and anti-tank

A T34/76 crew spying out the land.

elements, and no infantry. Before they could settle into properly coordinated defensive positions they beheld a sight never before seen by the German army – a solid phalanx of Russian T34s, motorized infantry and guns bearing down upon them in the early morning gloom of 21 November.

There was very little the German tank crews, still short of fuel and ammunition, could do to prevent a debacle. Caught in penny packets; unable, without infantry, to hold nodal points; and outflanked by the sheer dimensions of the broad Russian sweep, they managed to inflict quite severe casualties before themselves succumbing. Those who avoided an abortive head-on clash of armor scurried away either to the now-beleaguered Stalingrad or to the southwest to join the relief force hastily being assembled from under-strength units. The Fedorenko system had worked almost to perfection, leaving German soldiers to wonder at the systematic combination of Russian tanks, guns and infantry who often rode into action on the tanks' decks to leap off into the assault within a short distance from their objectives. Better trained though individual German leaders and crews remained, and superior their gunnery over T34 two-man turret crews (whose engagment of targets was less precise), there was nothing much the

Germans could do against odds of up to five to one in open terrain.

Locked up in Stalingrad when the Russian pincers met at Sovetsky on 23 November, General von Paulus reflected upon the planned attempts to organize a counter-stroke to break the enemy ring and enable the evacuation of the marching elements of his Sixth Army and the remnants of Fourth Panzer Army. 'But what if this attempt does not succeed?' he asked. 'If our Panzer formations are too weak, what then?' It was dawning upon the Germans that the undeniable individual skills of their magnificently trained and experienced mobile troops might no longer be a match for an enemy who shrugged off technical and training deficiencies and made do with mass and brute force. As 1942 drew to a close and the ring contracted around Stalingrad while the Germans tried desperately to break through from the south, the Russians built up their strength to a culminating moment on 23 December when, having smashed the relief attempts, they once more struck out irresistibly to roll away the Germans. Sixth Army in Stalingrad was doomed. Simultaneously the rear of the German army in the Caucasus was most dangerously threatened by Russian mechanized forces which, for the time being, were unstoppable.

CHAPTER SIX

THE GUNNERY REVOLUTION

IN OCTOBER 1942 RUSSIAN ANTI-TANK GUNNERS ON THE Leningrad front were confronted with a problem their German counterparts had long suffered against the KV1s – that of tackling a daunting AFV which looked impenetrable. In narrow forest rides they met the first of the new 56 ton German Tiger Is whose 100–110 mm frontal armor was proof against their 76.2 mm anti-tank gun and whose 80 mm side armor could only be defeated at the closest range. Fortunately for the Russians – and for the British and Americans, too, in December when four of these monsters turned up in Tunisia – the Tigers were few in number (having only entered production in August) and plagued by the sort of mechanical unreliability such as afflicts all untried machinery. But the writing was on the wall. 1943 was to witness a dramatic acceleration in the gun/armor race as the Germans took the lead against the Russian T34s and KV1s, the British Churchills, and the US Shermans.

Of greater tactical importance than the none too easily manufactured and somewhat immobile heavy Tigers were the latest generation of so-called 'medium tanks' (which, at weights between 30 and 45 tons, would have been categorized 'heavy' in 1940). These were the German Panther, the Russian T34/85, the British Mark VII cruiser (eventually called Cromwell), the American T20 project, and a host of self-propelled assault and anti-tank guns being made in profusion and ever-increasing size by each nation. These AFVs had power plants mostly significantly larger than those of their predecessors, and armor that was usually sloped and rarely less than 75mm thick, but their really momentous feature was their improved armament, gun-laying equipment and projectiles. For not only had the gage of the gun-versus-armor competition been taken up by each side, but also the vital necessity of hitting and killing hard targets with minimum waste of time and ammunition had assumed an overriding priority in the minds of commanders and technicians. As battlefields became saturated with massed armored formations, it no longer was permissible to take ten shots or more to score a single hit which might or might not kill. Moreover as gun caliber increased to between 75 mm and 88 mm, the quantity of much bulkier rounds which could be stowed within AFVs decreased, making it all the more important to make best use of what was available.

Germany's tank designers set the pace with the Panther and the Tiger whose gun controls, optical systems, firing gear and turret arrangements were well in advance of those of their antagonists. Serving the latest 70 calibers 75 mm piece in the Panther and the 71 calibers 88 mm, which was to be fitted to a monstrous 65-ton self-propelled gun called Elefant, remarkably accurate fire could be delivered with quite devastating results. For these two guns, respectively, had muzzle velocities of 836 m/sec (3070 ft/sec) and 1018 m/sec (3340 ft/sec), the former firing a 15-pound shot, the latter one of 22.25 pounds. They were slightly superior, in kinetic energy, to the latest 85 mm gun being produced by the Russians (at 899 m/sec (2950 ft/sec) with a 21.5-pound shot) and the British 76.2 mm (884 m/sec (2900 ft/sec) with a 17-pound shot), and a lot better than the latest American

76.2 mm (792 m/sec (2600 ft/sec), 15.4-pound shot).

Pieces of such high velocity brought with them, however, additional problems for commanders and gunners. No longer was it possible satisfactorily to base corrections of aim upon spotting the fall of shot, because the shot usually landed before the dust and smoke from the gun's discharge had cleared away. Field anti-tank gunners often overcame the spotting problem by employing a flank observer: tank commanders in a turret, jolted by the discharge, were in trouble. Moreover, although at the shorter (and more common) ranges of engagement, where line of sight virtually coincided with trajectory of projectile over the initial 800 meters and made it necessary only to lay at the center mass of target, the judging of distance at potentially effective ranges out to 2000 meters now became critical. In desert and steppes these difficulties faced the Germans as their Tigers, Panthers, Elefants and several more kinds of heavy Jagdpanzer came into service throughout 1943. The Russians, too, would have to consider it when the greatly improved T34/85 with its three-man turret, thicker armor and 85 mm gun appeared in August 1943 – although there is little evidence to suggest that they approached the subject with the same thoroughness and precision as did the Germans.

As for the British, the stage was not reached until mid-1943 when they took a universally firmer grip on tank gunnery development. For one thing they professed, at top level, in the belief that they could get by with the latest 50 calibers 57 mm gun with 7-pound shot at 802 m/sec (2630 ft/sec) – a contention thrust upon them, to some extent, by the impossibility of mounting the far superior 76.2 mm into their projected Mark VII cruiser. This cruiser, whose specifications had been settled in January 1941, was barely ready for action until the end of 1943, by which time it would be outclassed by most of its opponents – a matter to which we will return later. Meanwhile the Americans, to whom the possession of a powerful, turret-mounted large gun had always been essential, were pressing ahead with a new design of tank, the T20, which would easily accomodate the 76.2 mm piece, carry thicker armor, and possess a better automotive performance than the Sherman. But this project would suffer from policy vacillation. In fact, although the British in the summer of 1943 started a crusade aimed at developing indirect fire with

high explosive, accurate direct fire out to 2000 m and an all-embracing program to improve optics and gun control gear, there resided among them (and to some extent among the Americans) an illusion that the vast number of tanks coming out of the factories would compensate in quantity for any slight inferiority in performance compared with that of the German machines.

The size and sheer weight of the much larger caliber guns required to overcome the latest better-protected tanks was disturbing the balance between AFV and field anti-tank gun. For example, the German 37 mm piece of 1939 vintage which weighed about 970 pounds and was easily concealed and manhandled, was a lot different in tactical value from the bulky 71 calibers 88 mm which weighed 9660 pounds and had to be moved in and out of position by towing and winching. As a result of this clumsiness and inbuilt vulnerability, the big field anti-tank guns began to lose their edge over the far more tactically flexible self-propelled armored gun.

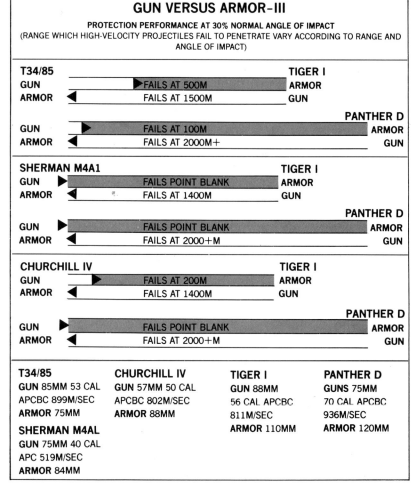

GUN VERSUS ARMOR–III

PROTECTION PERFORMANCE AT 30% NORMAL ANGLE OF IMPACT
(RANGE WHICH HIGH-VELOCITY PROJECTILES FAIL TO PENETRATE VARY ACCORDING TO RANGE AND ANGLE OF IMPACT)

T34/85		TIGER I
GUN	FAILS AT 500M	ARMOR
ARMOR	FAILS AT 1500M	GUN
		PANTHER D
GUN	FAILS AT 100M	ARMOR
ARMOR	FAILS AT 2000M+	GUN

SHERMAN M4A1		TIGER I
GUN	FAILS POINT BLANK	ARMOR
ARMOR	FAILS AT 1400M	GUN
		PANTHER D
GUN	FAILS POINT BLANK	ARMOR
ARMOR	FAILS AT 2000+M	GUN

CHURCHILL IV		TIGER I
GUN	FAILS AT 200M	ARMOR
ARMOR	FAILS AT 1400M	GUN
		PANTHER D
GUN	FAILS POINT BLANK	ARMOR
ARMOR	FAILS AT 2000+M	GUN

T34/85
GUN 85MM 53 CAL
APCBC 899M/SEC
ARMOR 75MM

SHERMAN M4AL
GUN 75MM 40 CAL
APC 519M/SEC
ARMOR 84MM

CHURCHILL IV
GUN 57MM 50 CAL
APCBC 802M/SEC
ARMOR 88MM

TIGER I
GUN 88MM
56 CAL APCBC
811M/SEC
ARMOR 110MM

PANTHER D
GUNS 75MM
70 CAL APCBC
936M/SEC
ARMOR 120MM

CHURCHILL IV

LAST OF THE BRITISH Infantry tanks, the Churchill was produced in 1940 in haste, and suffered from innumerable mechanical defects until the appearance of the much modified Mark IV in 1943. Although its 350 hp engine was quite reliable, trouble tended to occur with minor components while the transmission system (which incorporated an extremely ingenious regenerative system that, in principle, is used to the present day), had numerous teething troubles. Unfortunately the turret was not big enough to install guns larger than 75 mm. This defect made the Churchill obsolescent by 1943, even though it continued in service to the end of WW2, sustained by the thicker armor of the final Marks.

Weight 39 tons
Speed 16 mph
Frontal armor 88 mm
Armament 1×57 mm, 2×mg

To off-set the difficulties of penetrating very thick armor with kinetic energy projectiles, an alternative method now entered the lists – hollow charge ammunition, later known as High Explosive Anti Tank (HEAT). HEAT rounds penetrated by blasting a high-velocity jet of gas and molten debris through armor with a pressure of as much as 2000 tons/in². Optimum effect is downgraded by spin; but higher velocity and spin are required for range and accuracy, depth of penetration being conditioned by the diameter and profile of the cone which concentrates the explosive jet. Hence a lower-velocity 75 mm field gun could be every bit as lethal as a much larger high-velocity 88 mm piece – providing the jet was not deflected or dispersed, and providing a hit could be obtained by weapons whose lower velocity implied inaccuracy. Seen initially as a panacea solution to the anti-tank problem, HEAT ammunition, in practice, merely performed as a complement to existing weapons – as another club in the bag. However, as light-weight, hand-held, rocket-propelled weapons for infantrymen, unspun HEAT warheads offered considerable potential. From 1943 onwards the threat of the so-called bazooka type projector would considerably exercise AFV commanders and make it all the more important for them to cooperate closely with

escorting infantry who could eliminate or neutralize bazooka men.

Finally, along with the ever-growing number of anti-tank devices, had to be included the anti-tank mine which, as the war progressed and the Germans began their long retreat towards the homeland, were laid in vast numbers, significantly denying freedom of maneuver by immobilizing all kinds of vehicle. Costly in production and time to lay, mines nevertheless represented such a serious threat to AFVs that equally expensive measures to detect and destroy them had to be undertaken in order to sustain the tank's mobility and vital roles in battle. Mine-sweeping tanks of various kinds – fitted with flails, rollers, ploughs and so on – became essential elements in any armored force, demanding special skills in their operation and employment. Indeed all sorts of specialized armored vehicles were being devised in 1943, not only to help overcome natural and man-made obstacles but also to assume a leading role in the amphibious operations needed to land the British and Americans on the European mainland, and in the Pacific to regain the scores of islands held by the Japanese. Among these devices were swimming and wading vehicles, bridging equipment, flame-throwers and all kinds of projectiles to smash concrete fortifications.

SWING OF THE PENDULUM AFTER STALINGRAD

The latest tanks and technology had no part in the battles following the surrounding of German Sixth Army and elements of Fourth Panzer Army in Stalingrad. Once the ring had been sealed, the Germans had either to defeat the Russian army and restore the situation or break out from the ruined city and withdraw with what survived – at the same time pulling back from their by now directly threatened salient in the Caucasus. Uncharacteristically, they had been slow reacting to the initial threat. Thereupon Hitler made the wrong decision to stay put in Stalingrad. Now, with winter's grip upon the open steppe and a rapidly worsening logistic situation, the relief attempts by Field Marshal Eric von Manstein's newly formed Army Group Don were sentenced to attacks against an enemy firmly in place on vital ground straddling the obligatory approaches to the city. Compared with battles past the tables were turned. This time it was the German armored forces which were slow in concentrating and which had no other option than to butt their tanks against forewarned anti-tank guns. Meanwhile the Russian armor stood back in safety and reserve, emerging from its hides, heavily supported by artillery and rocket batteries, only when von Manstein's attacks, with a dwindling number of tanks, faltered.

Unlike most previous and later major tank encounters, numbers were low. 17th and 23rd Panzer Divisions, for example, possessed only 30 each and rarely did the Russians commit many more than 30 at any one time.

To begin with, Army Group Don managed on 12 December to achieve local numerical superiority and make progress. But at the crucial moment on 20 December, when a renewed Russian attack elsewhere threatened the German rear and 17th Panzer Division's tank strength fell to a mere eight, it became essential to call a halt and detach the stronger 6th Panzer Division to guard the vital bottleneck at Rostov. Russian tanks were beginning to enter the struggle in significantly larger numbers, confident that there was little fear of interference by a breakout from the encircled enemy at Stalingrad whose 100 or so AFVs contained less than 30 miles' worth of fuel. In the tank-versus-tank fights along the front of Army Group Don and on its flanks, the valedictory thrust by 60 German tanks towards Stalingrad on 22 December met solid, if improvised resistance from General R Malinovsky's 2nd Guards Army which, short of fuel, poorly trained, arrived piecemeal to the flight and several times used immobilized tanks as pill boxes. Yet it was enough. After the fight Malinovsky could justly explain: 'To-day we have finally halted the formidable enemy. Now we'll attack ourselves'. On Christmas Eve, he was as good as his word, plunging the Germans into a retreat of almost two months' duration.

Throughout January 1943, as a vast Russian offensive developed on a 1200-mile front from Orel to the Black Sea, the most critical sector remained the corridor funnelling back from Stalingrad in the east and from the Caucasus in the south to its neck at Rostov. Here von Manstein struggled first to keep

HIGH EXPLOSIVE ANTI-TANK (HEAT) ROUND
The cone directed a high-velocity narrow jet of molten gas and debris through armor with a pressure of as much as 200 tons/inch^2.

The German infantry 50 mm 42 cal anti-tank gun. Nearby is a self-propelled Assault Gun Stu III which, though conceived as an infantry support AFV, was rapidly developed along with other vehicles into a mobile anti-tank weapon system far superior to the field anti-tank gun.

T34/85

THE APPEARANCE IN THE SUMMER OF 1943 of the T34/85 restored to the Russians the superiority they had lost to the German PzKw IVFs in 1942. While retaining the same automotive system and armor basis as T34/76, this AFV amounted to a redesign of its predecessor. The frontal glacis plate was different, the front gunner was disposed of, and an entirely new up-armored three-man turret, with a commander's cupola, was introduced.

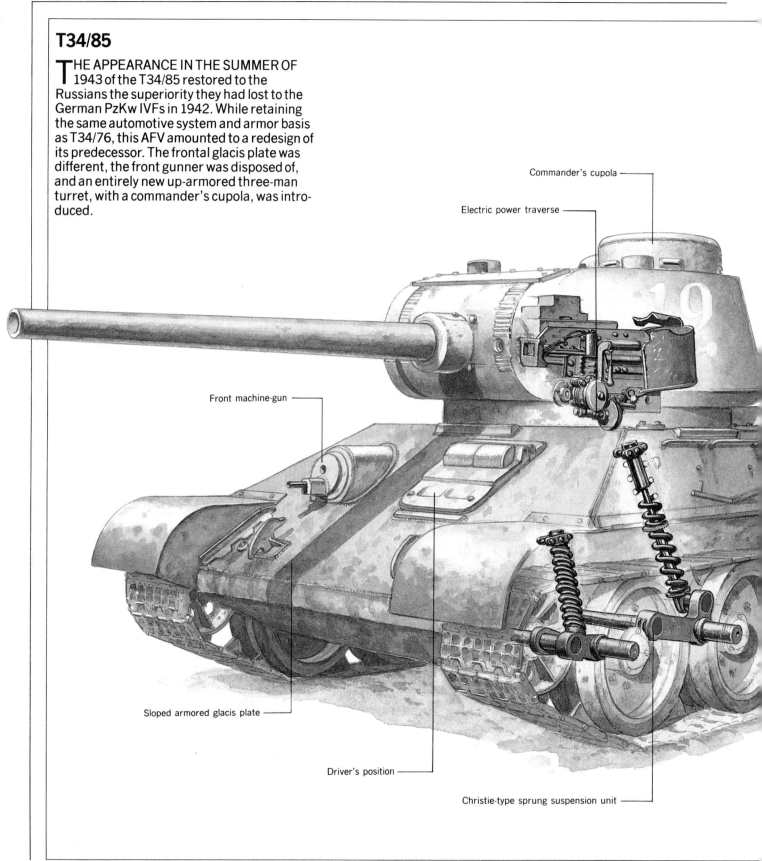

Commander's cupola

Electric power traverse

Front machine-gun

Sloped armored glacis plate

Driver's position

Christie-type sprung suspension unit

The electric traverse gave gunners a much better deal. However, this advantage was offset by the large 'shot-trap' between the bottom of the turret and the hull, which allowed many otherwise avoidable losses. Nevertheless, T34/85 remained combat-worthy to the end of WW2 and continues in service with some armies to this day.
Weight 32 tons
Speed 31 mph
Frontal armor 75 mm (sloped)
Armament 1×85 mm, 2×mg

Auxillary detachable fuel tank

Driving sprocket

Rubber tyres

General Hoth's Fourth Panzer Army intact against pressure from the Russian Southwest Front armies, while General E von Mackensen's First Panzer Army drove back to help resist the dangers from the South Front armies whose intention it was to seal off von Kleist's Army Group A in the Caucaus. Mobile armored warfare predominated as the Germans, losing AFVs at a faster rate than they could be replaced, gave way most unwillingly to mounting pressure. Frequently the thin German infantry lines broke and desperate measures were called for to restore cohesion. Far too slowly for von Manstein's peace of mind, reinforcements were being sent from the west, of which the II SS Panzer Corps under General Paul Hausser, with its especially well-equipped SS Panzer Grenadier Divisions, was the most potent in the German order of battle. Yet even as he survived crisis after crisis and the seemingly unstoppable enemy waves flowed onward, von Manstein's fertile mind, with its acute understanding of the logistical restraints controlling mechanized warfare and the overriding principles of surprise and concentration of effort which were keys to victory, was designing a tank counter-stroke unlike any attempted before.

Von Manstein realised that, as the Russian spearheads moved westward, the problems of keeping them up to strength and reasonably supplied must multiply to the point of breakdown and exhaustion. Always he was encouraged by the inveterate prowess of the élite panzer formations which, despite being outnumbered, continued to outfight an opponent whose inferior training, command and control arrangements became more apparent as combat reverted from positional to fluid format. The action at Manutchskaya on 23-25 January, when 11th Panzer Division in Fourth Panzer Army destroyed a strong Russian lodgement over the Manich River threatening the passage of First Panzer Army through the Rostov bottleneck, was a classic on this pattern. Here the Russian defense of their bridgehead collapsed because the German armor attacked in an unexpected quarter (subtly chosen by General H Balck because it had been the site of an earlier repulse) with intense concentrations of artillery fire and close cooperation with infantry. The German tanks quite easily broke into the key village enemy strongpoint from the rear, because the Russians had been distracted by a feint attack with light forces and artillery in another sector. Also the Russians had dug in

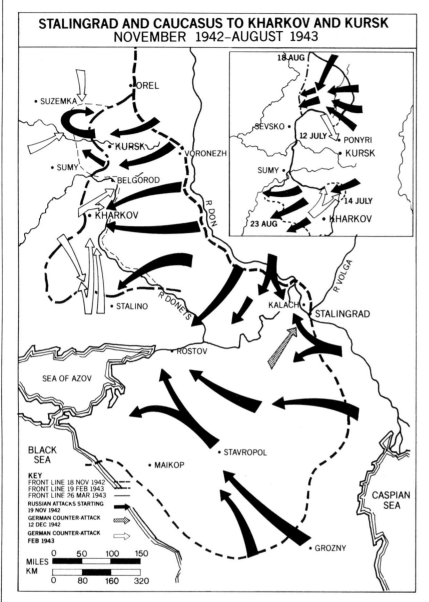

STALINGRAD AND CAUCASUS TO KHARKOV AND KURSK
NOVEMBER 1942–AUGUST 1943

KEY
FRONT LINE 18 NOV 1942
FRONT LINE 19 FEB 1943
FRONT LINE 26 MAR 1943
RUSSIAN ATTACKS STARTING
19 NOV 1942
GERMAN COUNTER-ATTACK
12 DEC 1942
GERMAN COUNTER-ATTACK
FEB 1943

0   50   100   150
MILES
KM
0   80   160   320

The Russian counter-offensive of mid-November 1942. It isolated the Germans besieging Stalingrad (leading to the destruction of Sixth Army in February 1943) and began rolling back the Germans toward Kursk and Kharkov in Ukraine. The adverse consequences to the Russians of their weakening lunge past Kharkov can be appreciated, the Manstein counter-stroke of February leading to a Russian retreat which ended at the Kursk salient.

their tanks, instead of employing them more effectively as a mobile striking force, with the result that they lost 20 tanks and 600 of their infantry, against just one killed and 14 wounded on the German side.

With First Panzer Army under his orders, and safe to the east of Rostov, along with Fourth Panzer Army and the arriving SS Panzer Corps, von Manstein could scheme the enemy's destruction. By trading time and space against the weakening of the enemy, he could attract them into a void until the right moment came to unleash his own revitalized armored troops. This the Russians feared as a possibility. Yet in mid-January, a fortnight before Stalingrad at last fell, they launched a renewed drive to the west with the intention of seizing the route center of Kursk and establishing strong bridgeheads across the River Dnieper before the spring thaw set in and clogged movement. Banking on a supposition that the Germans were so hurt and demoralized as to be incapable of protracted resistance, let alone any sort of major offensive action, Stalin insisted, against the doubts of some among his senior commanders, that the offensive be pushed to the limit. Generals Golikov and Vatutin, respectively commanding the Voronezh Front, which was aimed at Belgorod and Kursk, and the Southwest Front, aimed at Kharkov and the Dnieper river, were not only afflicted and worried by the devastated condition of their lengthening lines of communication but also concerned that the axes of their advances were divergent, opening up a gap between their Fronts. To offer the Russians as much rope as possible with which to hang themselves, von Manstein was only too happy to entice them onward, even surrendering such strategically and psychologically important centers as Belgorod and Kharkov to stimulate Russian convictions of their own immunity.

Yet as the Russians surged westward, with ever-decreasing and enfeebled tanks and artillery in columns whose supplies were, to a significant extent, transported by animals, von Manstein's principal concern, aside from assembling his main striking forces in the vital terrain to the east of the Dnieper bend, was to convince his superiors – Hitler and his entourage in the German High Command – that the plan would succeed. The debate between Hitler, the apostle of unrelenting struggle from position, and von Manstein, the high priest of mobile warfare, was perfectly highlighted by von Manstein's ability, on this occasion, to convince Hitler that his way was right. Just for once on 6 February, the Führer, shaken by the failure of his inflexible methods at Stalingrad, was prepared to give von Manstein a free hand. The gathering of three panzer corps menacing the flanks of Vatutin's over-extended spearheads to the south of Kharkov (which fell on 16 February) was permitted to go ahead – only to be threatened once more on the 17th when Hitler panicked and again met von Manstein with the intention of sacking the Field Marshal on the very eve of delivering his blow. But once more Hitler held his hand: convinced to some extent no doubt by the presentation of intelligence from radio intercept and other sources which showed how weakened the Russian columns were; and reinforced also in resolve by what amounted to a *fait accompli*. For von Manstein could announce that his arrangements were complete. II SS Panzer Corps was poised at Krasnograd to attack Vatutin's spearhead moving left to right across its front. Fourth Panzer Army's Panzer Corps stood concentrated near von Manstein's GHQ east of Zaporozhye, tasked to strike those same columns from the southward, while the neighboring First Panzer Army, with XL and LVII Panzer Corps, held the enemy at Krasnoarmeyskoye awaiting the order to strike northward in unison at Kharkov.

Ironically, as the German blow began to disclose itself (and there is little evidence to suggest that the Germans practiced anything other than routine security to conceal its preparation), the Russian Front commanders were enduring similar treatment from their high command to that borne by their opponents. Stalin uttered dire threats from Moscow at the slightest sign of hesitation or worry on the part of Golikov or Vatutin at the front. He convinced himself at the outset that the German counter-offensive merely foreshadowed a covering operation to permit the safe withdrawal of the German southern wing behind the Dnieper. In this state of blinkered self-delusion, the Russians fell headlong into the trap.

COUNTER-STROKE AT KRASNOGRAD, FEBRUARY 1943

The ranks of Waffen SS formations, as befitted the chosen élite of Nazi Germany, were composed of the best men available and a larger establishment of better equipment than their ordinary Army equivalents. For example, SS Leibstandarte Panzer Grenadier Division Adolf Hitler (LAH) commanded by Hitler's favorite Major General Sepp Dietrich, was with its Panzer Regiment mainly composed of the latest PzKw IV tanks and a heavy company of Tiger tanks. It was therefore much stronger than any of the panzer divisions then in service in the Eastern Front whose average number of PzKw III and IV tanks had fallen to 27 each. Therefore this single division, apart from its companions Das Reich and Totenkopf Panzer Grenadier Divisions, was a dreadful threat on 19 February when it moved against Major General VV Popov's Third Tank Army in the approaches to Krasnograd. The hotch-potch Russian columns streaming across the snow-covered undulating steppe were but thinly supported by T34 tanks, poorly served

by reconnaissance, and totally unready for what was thundering down upon them. Since crossing the Don their resupply had been hand-to-mouth. In the words of von Clausewitz more than a hundred years earlier, this was a 'culminating point of victory' for the Germans, when their enemy's attacking force stood on the verge of losing its impetus through exhaustion, although von Clausewitz can hardly have dreamt of mechanized forces so versatile as those under the hand of von Manstein that day.

Everywhere across the wide frontage of LAH, the Russian columns were made to pause, but nowhere was their discomfiture so dramatic as at Jeremejewska where Dietrich had concentrated his strongest mobile force to head off the enemy making for his own headquarters at Krasnograd. Here he had positioned Major Jochem Peiper's 3rd (Armd) Bn SS Pz Gren Regt 2; the 1st Pz Bn, SS Pz Regt 1 (commanded by Major Max Wünsche), and the SS Regt AA (the divisional reconnaissance unit under Major Kurt Meyer) – a battle group including some 30 PzKw IV and four PzKw VI Tiger tanks, accompanied by numerous armored cars and armored personnel carriers and supported by strong artillery. Their combined strength created immense firepower augmented by fluent mobility on the hard-frozen terrain.

Starting at 0400 hrs, Peiper's group, flanked by Meyer's AA, advanced from Ziglerowka to Jeremejewska. It met and put to flight an enemy covering force prior to seizing the village at 1500 hours and putting it into a state of defense against three hostile armored columns attacking from the direction of Paraskowejewakije. Joined by a panzer company and in concert with the AA, Peiper maneuvred against the enemy units, making best use of folds in the ground to find the flanks of the leading enemy tanks before engaging their anti-tank guns at long range, as well as bringing down counter-battery fire against artillery and mortars as they disclosed themselves. This fire fight had to be won before the PzKw IVs, backed by the Tigers, could get in among the fatally exposed Russian infantry. By nightfall the entire enemy spearhead had turned back, littering the steppe with T 34s, guns, burning equipment and scores of bodies. Yet this was but an overture in the realization of von Manstein's masterpiece. Now was the moment to capitalize on the local victory and convert it into a major collapse at a culminating point in enemy fortunes.

EASTERN FRONT, FEBRUARY 1943

COUNTER-STROKE AT JEREMEJEWSKA

This was the prospect before Major Kurt Meyer and his Panzer colleagues on 20 February, 1943. Moving southward from Jeremejewska was a long straggling Soviet column caught in the open. 'Is it an ambush?' Meyer asked himself. 'Probably not.' So the best method was to attack at once at top speed, hurling one company of tanks at the enemy center with a second company to provide fire support as the artillery opened up. The Germans, with the long 75 mm guns in the PzKw IVFs and the 88 mm guns of the Tigers, completely outmatched the mixed Russian groups of guns, tanks, trucks, bullock carts and marching men as they crossed the hard-frozen, snow-covered plain. It was no contest from the outset.   (cont.)

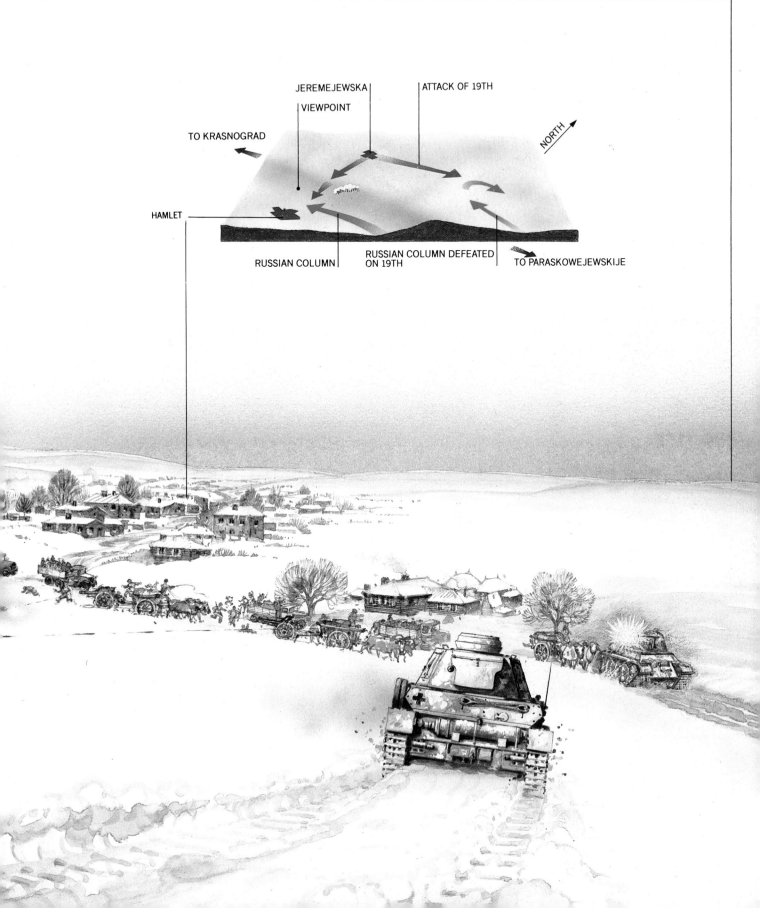

TO KRASNOGRAD

JEREMEJEWSKA

VIEWPOINT

ATTACK OF 19TH

NORTH

HAMLET

RUSSIAN COLUMN

RUSSIAN COLUMN DEFEATED
ON 19TH

TO PARASKOWEJEWSKIJE

COUNTER-STROKE AT JEREMEJEWSKA
(continued)

Major Peiper's Battle Group, moving from Ziglerowka to Jeremejewska, was intent upon establishing a strongly defended pivot of all arms from which to lash out with tanks and guns against an enemy whose straggling approach was meticulously reported by air and ground reconnaissance.

Although their rebuff at Jeremejewska (19 February) had blunted the Russian thrust, it did not deter the Soviet General V V Popov from urging his men on next day. Stalin and the Soviet High Command demanded it. Thus it was that when Peiper forayed southward on 20 February to ram home the proof of LAH's local dominance, it was to discover an unfortunate and vulnerable Russian battalion group doggedly plodding westward – marching infantry, towed anti-tank guns, trucks and bullock carts escorted by a mere handful of T34s. Peiper's leading PzKw IVs are shown here on the rampage, closing at high speed on the surprised Russian column whose T34s have already been picked off by PzKw IVs from hull-down positions. Russian anti-tank guns, caught on flank while on the move, have no time to unlimber and come into action. High explosive and machine-gun fire ravages the terrified enemy troops who fire back sporadically, but are unable to reach the shelter of Woroschilowa, and are wiped out.

The deed done [at minimal cost] Peiper, aware that fresh enemy attacks are in progress against Jeremejewska, turned about. A few minutes later he was back at base, reinforcing its defense against renewed enemy attacks while feverishly replenishing with ammunition from stocks dumped among the houses. German training and armored technique had again been justified, with a subsequent uplift in morale to the German forces fighting an enemy growing in strength and learning not to make the same mistake twice.

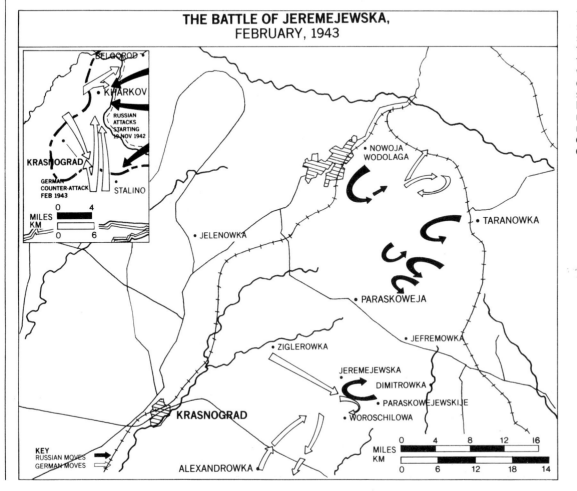

THE BATTLE OF JEREMEJEWSKA, FEBRUARY, 1943

BELGOROD

KHARKOV

RUSSIAN ATTACKS STARTING 19 NOV 1942

KRASNOGRAD

GERMAN COUNTER-ATTACK FEB 1943

STALINO

MILES
KM
0   4
0   6

NOWOJA WODOLAGA

TARANOWKA

JELENOWKA

PARASKOWEJA

JEFREMOWKA

ZIGLEROWKA

JEREMEJEWSKA

DIMITROWKA

PARASKOWEJEWSKIJE

WOROSCHILOWA

KRASNOGRAD

KEY
RUSSIAN MOVES
GERMAN MOVES

ALEXANDROWKA

MILES
KM
0   4   8   12   16
0   6   12   18   14

The Manstein counter-stroke in February 1943, showing how both horns of the Russian advance were tackled. The northern one was blunted by the stolid defense, while the southern one was stopped by a more mobile method rapidly converted to a ruthless pursuit of an enemy already logistically crippled.

THE PANZER TRIUMPH

German losses at Jeremejewska, in exchange for a complete battalion group wiped out, were a mere two killed and a handful wounded. Their task completed, the triumphant mobile troops returned to replenish at Jeremejewska where Peiper already had beaten off the first of many attacks to come by enemy troops whose commanders, for the next three days, remained ignorant of the overwhelming forces poised to crush their southern flank.   Doggedly Popov's Third Tank Army persisted in its attempts to break through at Jeremejewska and in the neighboring northward sector. Always they were rebuffed by Peiper's mobile defense pivoting on the village, from whence tanks forayed whenever the attack began to fail. Timing was all in attaining the best results; the Russian attackers yielded most readily when distracted by chaos within their own ranks. With his eyes still fixed on the goal at Krasnograd, Popov seemed to ignore (or was unaware of) how Hausser was inserting the mass of his II SS Panzer Corps into the 25-mile gap which had opened up on Popov's southerly flank. There Das Reich and Totenkopf were wheeling in from the west to hit, in conjunction with Fourth Panzer Army, the flank of General Kharitonov's Sixth Army, prior to surging northward to encompass Vatutin's entire Southwest Front. Yet Vatutin, pressed by Stalin, nevertheless called for a continuation of the advance and for an attack upon First Panzer Army as it too began to advance against the base of the Russian salient!

Such folly could not for long withstand four panzer corps in full flood, and there was to be no help from Golikov's Voronezh Front, which itself was about to be engulfed by II SS Panzer Corps and Fourth Panzer Army as they approached Kharkov. Total disaster loomed for the Russians. As usual, Stalin called upon Zhukov to put matters right and gave the best of his commanders a fresh tank army plus two infantry armies to restore the situation. Even so, for a whole month the Germans stormed northward, recapturing Kharkov and Belgorod, claiming 40 000 Russian soldiers as casualties, along with 600 tanks and 500 guns captured, before the thaw set in and further ambitious maneuvers were prevented by the mud.

Von Manstein's counter-stroke had done practically everything hoped of it. The German southern flank had been saved and the Russians had been hurt, though by no means fatally. German training, technique and equipment had once more been demonstrated as vastly superior to that of their opponents. Confidence had been restored. The only niggling disappointment lay in the failure to recapture the ultimate objective of Kursk, and with it the elimination of the salient at whose center it stood; for that the thaw and the arrival of Zhukov with reinforcements could be blamed. But von Manstein had this to the forefront of his intention as the next target, just as soon as the state of the ground permitted.

RAPIER AGAINST BLUDGEON IN TUNISIA

The pursuit of Rommel by Montgomery from El Alamein to the Mareth line at the Tunisian frontier was marked by small tank-versus-tank encounters, small since the Germans had but few tanks to offer in battle. Priority of deliveries of all resources was given to the build-up of a strong Axis force in Tunisia where Fifth Panzer Army under General Jurgen von Arnim came formally into being in December, after the initial Allied thrust against Tunis had been stopped by the hastily assembled German/Italian XC Corps under Lieut-General Walther Nehring. Very correctly, Field Marshal Albert Kesselring appreciated that a prolonged defense of Tunisia was unlikely in face of the logistic difficulties posed by Allied control of air space over the sea passages. He hoped for permission to withdraw at an appropriate moment. In the meantime, he was encouraged by the performance of the German armored forces, notably the PzKw IIIs, PzKw IVs and the handful of Tigers belonging to 10th Panzer Division, whose tanks were among the first to meet the American 1st Armored Division in battle, as well as similarly inexperienced units of the British 6th Armoured Division.

From the outset, and with some justification, the Germans tended strongly to denigrate the Americans whose Lee tanks were hardly a match for the PzKw IVs and whose Shermans were not always handled to best advantage. On the other hand, they treated the British with more respect, despite the obvious inferiority of their out-moded, Crusader and Valentine tanks. But the Americans, on occasion, enjoyed success, notably when several of their light Stuart tanks charged across the airfield at Djedeida on 27 November to shoot up 20 German bombers on the ground and arouse such panic in the mind of that experienced tank

The Allied advance into Tunisia after the defeat of the Axis spoiling offensives at the beginning of 1943. With their lines of communication to Europe constantly threatened and eventually cut, the Axis forces were doomed from the start.

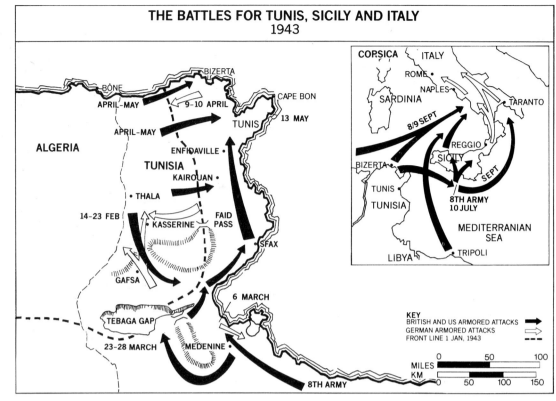

THE BATTLES FOR TUNIS, SICILY AND ITALY
1943

officer Nehring that, with Allied tanks within nine miles of Tunis, he concluded all was lost. 'Nehring rang me up in a state of understandable excitement and drew the blackest conclusions', remarked Kesselring, who shortly afterwards used this as a pretext to remove the shaken Nehring from command of XC Corps. But when the Germans went on the offensive themselves a few days later on 1 December, the frailty of the opposition was revealed. Forty German tanks thrown against a mixed force of 1st Bn 1st US Armored Regt backed up by Crusaders of the 17th/21st Lancers at the Chouigi Pass taught an object lesson in mobility. Compelled by the direction of the German thrust to move to fresh positions, the Lancers were caught on the move in the open and lost five tanks without reply.

Far worse was to follow on 10 December when, on ground made heavy by rain, the Allied offensive petered out. Preparing to withdraw at night under slight German pressure, Combat Command B (CCB) of 1st US Armored Division panicked at the sound of distant firing, tried to move along an unreconnoitered track, sank to the tops of their tracks in mire and eventually, to the delight of the Germans, abandoned 18 tanks, 41 guns and 130 other vehicles. Further setbacks were

to follow in January as the Germans began deep raiding to disrupt the Allied build-up, spoiling attacks which repeatedly exposed the inexperience of their opponents and most serious of all, the amateurishness of the Americans' command and control system. An order by Brigadier-General Robinett, commanding CCB (Combat Command B) on 19 January which went: '*Move your command, ie the walking boys, Baker's outfit and the big fellows to M which is due north of where you are now, as soon as possible...*'

tells much. Linked to direction-finding, such insecure chatter in clear on the air was manna from heaven for information-hungry professional Germans. But there was worse yet to come.

On 14 February von Arnim launched 10th and 21st Panzer Divisions against the Faid Pass. They bypassed or mopped up US infantry holding the commanding high ground and rapidly occupied concealed fire positions when air reconnaissance reported the approach of CCA in its attempt to restore the position. Hit by fire from the front, CCA recoiled and was then tackled in flank by another skilfully maneuverd German battle group. Some American tank crews stuck gallantly to their guns to the last, but far too many drove off the road into soft sand, abandoned their vehicles and were taken prisoner. 'I know panic when I see it' remarked one American infantry onlooker. Forty tanks and 15 SP guns fell into German hands, a score which rose steadily next day in the German favor when CCC, deficient of reconnaissance, charged to the rescue. Seeing them coming, 21st Panzer shifted adroitly to the flanks, let their assailants enter broken ground – and then struck with a torrent of well-aimed fire. At 1630 hrs some 50 American tanks were fighting fit; by 1800 hrs only four survived. The remainder were burning or being salvaged by the Germans.

What followed goes down in history as the Battle of Kasserine Pass, the poorly coordinated link by von Arnim and Rommel (the latter shifting northward from the Mareth Line to join hands with von Arnim) in an attempt to envelop the Allies by an imaginative sweep northward across their opponents' lines of communication. This was a classic gambler's throw by German mechanized troops of dwindling number and insufficient logistic support, one that relied on pace and shock to unhinge a beaten foe. The Allies gave ground with alacrity to fall back on prepared positions with secure flanks at Sbiba and Thala. Where maneuver became difficult tanks clashed but artillery held the ring. For example, at Thala, where Rommel's spearheads arrived in full cry (but without reconnaissance) on 21 February to be faced by obsolete Valentine tanks with their 40 mm pieces, it was a deluge of British and American artillery fire, concentrated by slick radio control and the latest simplified techniques, which undermined Rommel's thrust and made him retreat. Of tank-versus-tank fighting in the final stages of this Rommel offensive there was but little; and no call for an Allied counter-stroke in the von Manstein manner. The Allies had only to follow up a disgruntled enemy, and did so with caution.

German spoiling attacks in Tunisia were not yet finished. In the mountainous terrain, von Arnim's thrusts were curbed on ground that was better suited to the defense than to panzer drives. Tanks attempting to advance through defiles between picketted hill tops depend on infantry to see them through, but here the Germans lacked enough of the latter. And across desert on 6 March when Rommel tried for the last time to win a spoiling victory with a phalanx of three panzer divisions with 142 tanks and 200 guns, he too paid the price

for a faulty concept and plan. Amply forewarned by reconnaissance, radio intercept and decryption of what was impending, Montgomery dug in 467 anti-tank guns, backed up by 350 medium and field guns and 400 tanks, barring the approaches to Medenine. Forming up in full array prior to their assault – some of the tank crews reportedly kicking a football around in sight of the British before mounting – the Germans took the line of greatest expectation and rolled into fearsome fire. It was far worse than anything Rommel had met before and made all the more deadly by the debut of the latest 76.2 mm (17-pounder) anti-tank gun with its muzzle velocity of 884 m/sec (2900 ft/sec) which could penetrate even the frontal armor of the Tiger at 1000 m. Holding their fire to the last moment, the British gunners twice massacred advancing German formations, allowing them no significant gains at all and at low cost to themselves. Almost from the outset Rommel did little to impose control over his disconsolate divisions. The familiar German dash fizzled out in an ignominious disaster in which British tanks were hardly called upon and suffered no losses. The Germans, however, left more than 50 tanks behind with 635 casualties.

The rest of the Tunisian campaign was a foregone conclusion. Denied Hitler's approval to withdraw to Europe, the Axis armies were condemned to extinction, outnumbered in every department and progressively starved of supplies. Transient triumphs – such as the initial repulse by panzers on 22 March of the British tanks and infantry

A Churchill III in action at Longstop Hill in Tunisia in 1943. Note the 57 mm gun and the slab-sided turret which was dispensed with in later Marks of this tank.

which crossed the anti-tank ditch of the Mareth Line, and the massacre of British tanks on mines and against anti-tank guns at the Fondouk Gap on 8 April – could not forestall an inevitably rapid withdrawal into a bridgehead defending Tunis and Bizerta. Likewise, despite sterling work in defense against massed (and often expensively abortive) Allied tank and artillery attacks, supported by overwhelming air superiority, the German armor and anti-tank guns wilted. Even so, in this period there emerged two most significant developments. One was a variation of the Tank Terror theme, the 'Tiger Terror' – as for example when two British armored divisions were flooding through the Medjerda valley in the culminating drive to Tunis only to be stopped dead by the report of a single Tiger commanding the axis of advance. Such over-reaction to the threat of this admittedly formidable tank would be commonplace in the future. From this moment until the end of the war, at the slightest hint of a lurking Tiger, Allied tank crews grew exceedingly cautious, with the resultant loss of momentum and opportunity often leading to still greater cost in life. Moreover, it was by no means uncommon for any old enemy AFV to be misreported as a Tiger, such was the obsessive fear of Allied crews for a clumsy machine which, in fact, was both vulnerable and by no means well-favored by German Panzer leaders imbued with the spirit of mobility.

The second development was an up-surge of support for the anti-tank gun in German circles by those who believed that, in defense, a mass of cheaper anti-tank guns and panzerjägers were better value than the more expensive but tactically more flexible tank. Even Rommel, whose victories had been won by the tank and mobility, lent his voice to a tune he had heard Hitler sing. During conversation in July 1943 he stated: '*THE main defense against the tank is the anti-tank gun . . . If we can give the German infantry divisions first fifty, then a hundred, then two hundred 75 mm anti-tank guns each and install them in carefully prepared positions, covered by large minefields, we shall be able to halt the Russians . . . There is not the slightest hope of our keeping pace with the enemy in the production of tanks, but we certainly can in anti-tank guns . . .'*

Clearly this reflected his own upsets in the final phases of North Africa. As practice had shown, and would show again, static defense against massed artillery, tanks and infantry was no guarantee of success. Mobility, allied to firepower, was the most economic counter to mobility when AFVs exploited gaps in the front which were certain to exist or be made by the enemy. Moreover, Rommel overlooked the sheer magnitude and cost in material and labor needed to create such complex, endless defensive systems. But he was by no means alone in this contention. The same cry would be heard again and again in the years to come.

It might, indeed, re-echo as the outcome of the next German experience of static defense in Russia, when they once more went on the attack against an emplaced opponent at Kursk in July 1943.

THE PENT-UP TORRENT AT KURSK

From the moment his thrust was stopped by the March thaw, von Manstein had in mind a mere pause before continuing his proposed advance to capture Kursk, somewhere about the end of April when the ground had dried out and before the Russians could construct strong defenses. Events and Hitler thwarted him. Time was wasted in conferences at the highest level about what best to do to delay the next major Russian offensive. General Kurt Zeitzler, the Chief of General Staff, believed that ten to a dozen panzer divisions, adequately supported, would do the job by pinching out the Kursk salient at once. Hitler procrastinated; he was beset by worries about collapse in North Africa and the expected Allied invasions of southern Europe and in the West. In any case, he had recently appointed General Heinz Guderian as Inspector General of Armored Troops in realization that the decline of the panzer force was too serious to be allowed to continue. Furthermore, Hitler convinced himself that success in any future offensive must depend upon use of as many Tigers as possible, plus the commitment of the brand new Elefant SP gun and the PzKw V Panther, even though their trials were incomplete. To do so meant delaying the offensive until June, which in turn raised the number of formations required to overcome the inevitably strengthened Russian defenses. All at once the demand for panzer divisions alone increased from 10 to 20.

At the same time the Russians became convinced, by a wealth of intelligence from many sources, that the Kursk salient was not only the most obvious but also the selected

ELEFANT

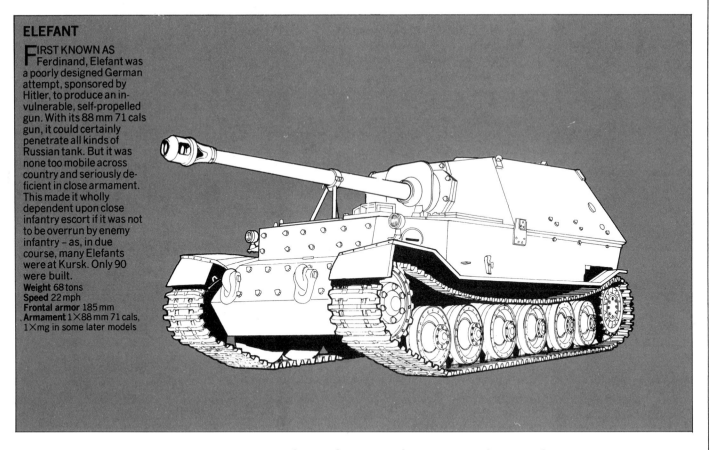

FIRST KNOWN AS Ferdinand, Elefant was a poorly designed German attempt, sponsored by Hitler, to produce an invulnerable, self-propelled gun. With its 88 mm 71 cals gun, it could certainly penetrate all kinds of Russian tank. But it was none too mobile across country and seriously deficient in close armament. This made it wholly dependent upon close infantry escort if it was not to be overrun by enemy infantry – as, in due course, many Elefants were at Kursk. Only 90 were built.

Weight 68 tons
Speed 22 mph
Frontal armor 185 mm
Armament 1×88 mm 71 cals, 1×mg in some later models

German target. On 8 April, taking Zhukov's view that it would be preferable to allow the Germans to exhaust themselves in attack before launching their own offensive, the Russians opted for defense. Throughout April, May and June with a 300 000-strong labor force, they constructed field defenses of a scale and density the equal of anything seen on the Western Front in 1917 and 1918. Immense concentrations of infantry, artillery and self-propelled guns were established in strong points defending six separate belts of earthworks, barricades and minefields. No less than 2400 anti-tank and 2700 anti-personnel mines were laid to each mile of front. 6000 anti-tank guns covered them. Lying in wait behind and to the flanks of these static positions accumulated a mass of KV and T34 tanks (mostly the latter) ready to counter serious penetrations when they occurred but also poised to execute the major Russian offensive the moment the German effort seemed to be lagging. Meanwhile air fighting of increasing intensity took place as both sides attempted to interfere with the other's logistic preparations and to make the gathering of information more difficult.

A further three-week delay was introduced by Hitler in mid June in order to take advantage of additional tank production to help overcome the Russian defenses whose enormity could not be concealed and which caused immense worry to a majority of German commanders who wished to be rid of this Operation 'Citadel'. Prior to the assault when at last it was launched at dawn on 5 July, the German AFV strength stood at 2500, significantly less than the 3300-odd on the Russian side, of whose number the Germans were unaware. And whereas the Russian machines were proven (if less powerful than the latest German types) there was serious weakness on the German side. The Elefant was virtually defenseless on its own due to lack of a close-in weapon system. The Panther, straight from the production line and underdeveloped, was a mass of technical faults requiring urgent modification, of which shortcomings in the optical and gunnery system were fundamentally disabling: in effect, it was uncombatworthy and prone to breakdown.

The German plan, predictably, undertook attacks against the north and south shoulders of the salient aimed at the closing of pincers at its base. The northern attack by Ninth

TIGER I

IN 1941 THE GERMANS PRODUCED TIGER in haste to combat KV1 and it first saw action in the autumn of 1942. A brilliant robust design, with a 700 hp engine, a gearbox with eight forward and four reverse gears, yet a range of only 70 miles, Tiger I had serious defects in combat. For one thing it was incompatible with fast operating panzer divisions, despite the ingenious interleaving of bogies in the torsion bar suspension to enhance mobility.

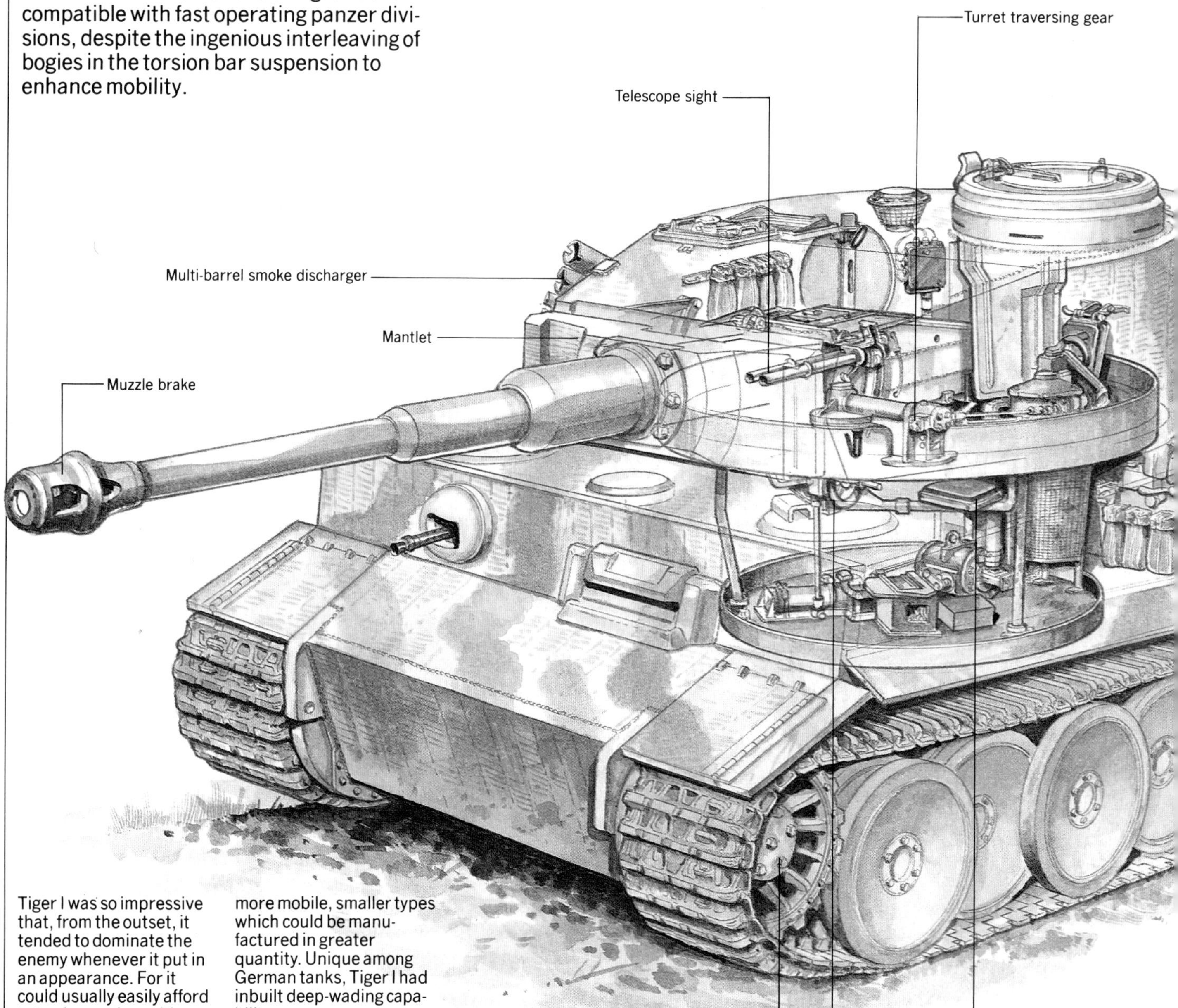

Turret traversing gear

Telescope sight

Multi-barrel smoke discharger

Mantlet

Muzzle brake

Gunner's position

Gun elevation wheel

Driving sprocket

Tiger I was so impressive that, from the outset, it tended to dominate the enemy whenever it put in an appearance. For it could usually easily afford to trade punches with most enemy tanks at long range (as the performance tables show). Yet for the most part the German tank leaders denigrated this AFV, preferring the more mobile, smaller types which could be manufactured in greater quantity. Unique among German tanks, Tiger I had inbuilt deep-wading capability.

Weight 55 tons
Speed 23 mph
Frontal armor 100 mm
Armament 1×88 mm 56 cals, 2×mg

Section of turret

Commander's seat

Racks

88 mm round

Suspension torsion bar

Racks

Army (with three panzer corps) was pre-empted by a hurricane Russian bombardment which disrupted the crossing of the start line. At once it was in trouble and largely held up in the first belt of defenses. Only the Tigers and Elefants working in groups of 10 or 15 were much help in face of a storm of fire. The infantry suffered dreadful losses. Moreover, once deprived of close infantry escort, the Elefants became helpless victims of any Russian tank-hunting party which cared to cripple them with explosive charges draped around the gun or fastened to the side armor: they were a total failure from the outset, particularly since at this stage the Russians provided few of their own tanks to be shot at by the Elefant's long 88 mm gun. So slow was the progress of Ninth Army's assault in the north that the Russians had ample time to lay still more mines across its all too discernable axis of advance. Gradually the Germans became enmeshed in minefields and ravaged by artillery. On 6 July, no sooner had they seemed to be making headway with the panzer divisions at last committed to the lead, than they ran into more Russian defenses backed by substantial armored reserves. In a last convulsive heave by three panzer divisions to break through on the 8th, the attack broke down before a hail of fire and repeated counter-attacks by Russian tanks. This repulse with the loss of about 200 AFVs and 25 000 men did more than point to the bankruptcy of the concept; it indicated a malaise inherent in the fundamental deterioration of the German army which had now spread to its élite formations. Infantry units in particular were reduced, for the most part to 50 per cent fighting strength. Their heavy losses were reflected in a collapse of morale, the commander of 18th Panzer Division, one of those involved, noting in an order: '*IT HAS happened that companies, on hearing the cry "enemy tanks", spring on their vehicles ... and drive away to the rear in wild confusion'*.

Any hope remaining for 'Citadel' had now to be pinned on Army Group South on the other side of the salient.

Hoth's Fourth Panzer Army, which included XLVIII Panzer Corps and II SS Panzer Corps, constituted the central punch of von Manstein's effort, while III Panzer Corps in Operation Group Kempf propped up the right flank. If Grossdeutschland Panzer Grenadier Division and the three SS Panzer Grenadier Divisions are counted as full

Above: A German tank graveyard in Russia. These are mostly PzKw IIIs, probably collected by the Germans for repair and then captured by the Russians.

panzer divisions (which in establishment they certainly were), von Manstein had at his disposal ten panzer divisions, four of them equipped with the latest PzKw IVH (with 80 mm spaced armor) and four with Tigers. In all he had 94 Tigers and 200 Panthers included in a total of 1150 medium and heavy AFVs. But although better progress was made on his front than that of Ninth Army, it was by no means fast enough to push the Russians on the run. Throughout the first 36 hours it was mainly a question of Hoth overcoming the successive rows of enemy trenches and mine-fields in the teeth of unremitting fire with hardly an enemy tank in sight. Remorselessly the German schedule was set back. After each step forward some new but predictable manifestation of defensive technique was un-veiled.

The symbols marked on maps of each panzer corps tell the tale. On the 5th the blue arrows of II SS Panzer Corps chop through no less than seven lines of defense; on the 6th and 7th, with the enemy hanging onto their flanks and beginning to mount local tank counter-attacks (which are brushed off by the flank guards), they depict a gap. They plunge ahead, exposing their flanks still further. On this day, too, XLVIII Panzer Corps, on their left, is stopped dead when Grossdeutschland

is checked by a very strong Russian tank at-tack. On the 8th and 9th the number of enemy red tank symbols multiply as the Germans try, without immense success, to widen and deepen their penetrations. The war diaries record local successes which momentarily suggest that the vital breakthrough has been achieved. But, as quickly, hopes are snuffed out. To quote, as example. FW von Mel-lenthin, Chief of Staff in XLVIII Panzer Corps (which was still 55 miles from Kursk):

'H*EIGHT 243...WAS HELD BY Russian tanks, which had a magnificent field of fire. The attack of the panzers and grenadiers broke down in front of this hill; the Russian tanks seemed to be everywhere and singled out the spearhead of Grossdeutsch-land, allowing it no rest. That afternoon the battle group on right of Grossdeutschland repulsed seven attacks by Russian armor and knocked out 21 T34s'.*

On 10 July Allied forces landed in Sicily and this event, creating a Second Front in Europe, was used by Hitler as a pretext for calling off an offensive which was doomed before it started because it had upturned every principle of German tank doctrine. Abandoning the match-winning formula of

to put the Germans at a technical disadvantage. For with the Panthers breaking down by the dozen and still not ready to put their excellent 70 calibers 75 mm guns to proper use, the PzKw IVs, which remained the work horses of the panzer divisions, found themselves dangerously outclassed because their 75 mm gun could not with certainty penetrate the new T34. This meant that only the handful of Tigers and the latest jagdpanzers could cope with the deadly enemy tank threat.

Yet cope the Germans still did to a remarkable extent against almost everything the Russians could throw at them. Though they gave ground at Orel, they never permitted the Russians an outright breakthrough. Indeed the Russians indicated the great difficulties under which they strove when their major offensive against Kharkov was delayed until 3 August by all manner of problems and ineptitudes, with benefit to the Germans. And in the last fight for Kharkov itself the attrition rate was well in the German favor. Russian tanks rolled in, wave after wave, against six infantry and three panzer divisions – all of them understrength – but paid a stiff penalty. In one of several ferocious encounters 32 Tigers, 96 Panthers and 25 heavy jagdpanzers, at relatively low cost, knocked out 184 T34s in a struggle which, unusually for the Russians, continued into the night by the light of burning buildings when commanders and gunners could barely pick out their targets at ranges of less than 100 m. Sometimes, states one German account,

'*THE ANTI-TANK COULD NO longer fire properly since they could hardly distinguish friend from foe. German tanks entered the fray, ramming Russian tanks in a counter-thrust or piercing them … at gun barrel range in order to block the breakthrough*'.

Inevitably under such pressure Kharkov fell. Remorselessly, yet rarely at the pace of the German mechanized columns in 1941 and 1942, the Russians moved westward, engulfing the Ukraine and extending their offensive along the entire Eastern Front from Leningrad to the Black Sea. And in unison with these setbacks, the Germans had also to deal with disaster in the Mediterranean where, in August, Sicily fell and early in September Italy abandoned her Axis partners as Allied landings took place on the Italian mainland.

rapier-like thrusts through chinks in the enemy defenses, the Germans had allowed their crucial offensive Panzer divisions to be employed like bludgeons without benefit of surprise or subtlety. They had utterly failed to upset the enemy's cohesion or his long-term plans. Two days later the deliberately witheld Russian summer offensive opened against Ninth Army and Second Panzer Army, directed against Orel, to be followed shortly by a blow of equally great dimensions (with at least 1000 AFVs involved) against Fourth Panzer Army and Group Kempf, directed against Kharkov. Undeniably the greatest tank battles seen so far, these engagements were crucial not simply because they put an end to prospects for future major German offensives in the East, but also because they compelled the German High Command to dedicate their armored forces to essential offensive/defensive tasks. Henceforward the cut and thrust of the armored battle groups would be dictated, for the most part, by an opponent with the strategic initiative. Only locally could the outnumbered Germans call the tune with their tactical prowess.

In August, as the Russian offensive raged ever more furiously, the appearance of the first few T34/85s with their 85 mm, 53 calibers gun and 75 mm sloped armor began

SICILY AND ITALY – THE INHOSPITALITY OF TERRAIN

For only a few months short of two years, from July 1943, the Allied and Axis armies grappled in Sicily and mainland Italy on ground that was far from conducive to mechanized warfare. Therefore, the incidence of tank-versus-tank fighting was low. For one thing, although the Allies committed considerable numbers of the AFVs they by now possessed in super-abundance, the Germans, pinched by the demands of Russia and later by the opening of a new front in France, begrudged allocation of tanks to Italy. Adopting a wholly defensive posture amid mountain and river topography ideal for their purpose, the Germans correctly calculated that few tanks were necessary to deal with whatever usually short-lived spells of high mobility occured. They chose to rely upon jagdpanzers, towed anti-tank guns, and a profusion of minefields to keep the Allied tank masses in check – and achieved their aim to a remarkable extent throughout an extremely prolonged and skilfully delayed withdrawal.

What distinguishes these tank actions, and sets them apart from others, was the pioneering use of armor in amphibious operations. They include the first examples of major tank landings from the sea against a hostile coastline – and the nature of the fighting in country that was mostly either enclosed or predominantly mountainous.

It had been apparent since the summer of 1940 that the day must dawn when an amphibious invasion of the European mainland must be launched. With this in mind the development of suitable assault craft and of swimming and wading equipment and techniques for vehicles had gone ahead, mainly in Britain but also in the United States. Nevertheless, by the time of the Allied landings in Sicily in July 1943, at Salerno in September, and at Anzio in January 1944, the equipment and the techniques to land tanks *ahead* of infantry had not been sufficiently developed to encourage this tactical method. Tanks came ashore from tank-landing craft of shallow draft in the second or third waves of assault. The Allies got away with it because each of these three operations achieved strategic surprise, preventing Axis mobile forces from concentrating against the beachheads before a coherent anti-tank defense, based on armor, could be formed.

As a result of piecemeal commitment of tanks and the closeness of the terrain, there was rarely much opportunity or room for the deployment of tank formations much above company strength. Indeed, narrrowness of a sector as the result of natural or man-made restrictions, often dictated frontages of little more than a platoon or even a single tank. Hardly ever could tanks operate without close infantry escort; quite apart from their need for anti-bazooka support, almost invariably they were held up by minefields and demolitions blocking the defiles which featured in every feasible axis of advance. Feats as marvellous as that performed by Sgt A McMeeking of the Scots Greys in his Sherman tank during the initial phase of the Salerno landing were rare indeed. Extracted from the chaos caused by boggy ground in the beach exits and sent forward as one of a few individuals to help the hard-pressed infantry, McMeeking's arrival at the front coincided with a fierce German tank and infantry counter-attack. Solo, he saved the situation by knocking out four PzKw IIIs and IVs in the space of a few minutes. But for the most part on this day, and on nearly all those to follow, the AFVs of both sides were condemned to suffer fire from frowning peaks, at close range amid orange groves or from the walls of fortified villages, all of which controlled essential routes or approaches. Occasionally it was found possible by dint of skilful driving and determination to site tanks on hill tops where they acted as pill boxes or in direct artillery support. Sometimes the Germans mounted tank turrets on concrete bases to cover crucial approaches, thus saving on machines.

Try hard as the Allies did, it was only in the closing weeks of the war in 1945 that they achieved a major breakthrough in depth in Italy and they did so only because the enemy was everywhere at the end of his tether. The greater tank encounters were thus fought elsewhere and in increasing fury.

HARD SLOGGING IN RUSSIA

When the Germans speak of the traumas of winter fighting in Russia and when both sides record their triumphs and tragedies as the liberation of conquered territory gradually took place, it is often forgotten how very gradual that liberation actually was in relation to the sheer size of the attacking Russian armies. In the so-called autumn battles of 1943 which included the crossing of the mighty River Dnieper, it took some $2\frac{1}{2}$ million Russians with 51 000 guns and 2400 tanks to advance about 150 miles in about four

ACTION IN THE DIFFICULT TERRAIN OF ITALY

Left: An American M3 tank destroyer with 76 mm gun and vulnerable open turret engaging targets at long range in typically hilly country.
Below left: Shermans in a badly damaged town which, like so many of its kind, had been converted into a tank-proof bastion by the Germans.
Below: Churchill IVs and Bren gun carriers, well dispersed while forming up for an assault on the fortified enemy.

months' combat against half that number of Germans armed with only 12 000 guns and 2100 tanks – slow going by comparison with past German performance on the same ground. As usual, mechanical attrition as well as logistic debilities played conclusive roles. Frequently, too, German interception of their enemy's radio traffic provided the vital intelligence which enabled them to judge the timing, scale and placing of their counterstrokes to perfection. The aftermath of the recapture of Kiev by the Russian Voronezh Front under Vatutin on 6 November, followed by exploitation towards Korosten, is a classic example of this kind of situation as the Russians began to falter and the Germans bided their time.

The counter-attack by XLVIII Panzer Corps under General Hermann Balck in Fourth Panzer Army between mid-November and Christmas rates as among the most sustained and competent of its kind, taking advantage of alternating conditions of freeze and thaw. With six panzer divisions (only three of which were anything near 75 per cent of full establishment) and a single infantry division, they endeavored to chop off at its base the salient which bulged beyond Kiev. They might have done so had not General E Rauss, the exhausted Hoth's replacement as commander of Fourth Panzer Army, diluted the main blow through a subsidiary attack at Zhitomir. As it was, the Panzer Corps' successive thrusts, chopping at the horns of Vatutin's charge, inflicted a toll of losses which the Russians could ill afford – even though annual production of T34s was by now running at about 10 000.

Von Mellenthin describes the encirclement of three Russian armored corps at Brussilov on 21 November and the netting of 153 tanks, 70 guns and 250 anti-tank guns along with 3000 dead. Reproduction of the operational maps of the day draw a very different picture to the scene as it had been at Kursk in July. Now the blue German arrows record fast-moving deep penetrations overrunning red enemy blobs; criss-crossing his rear areas, meeting and parting in concentric moves which bewilder and scatter the enemy. Yet the arrows rarely encounter elaborate supply convoys, such as the Germans depended upon, since to a considerable extent each Russian battle group tended to carry what it could. They stopped only when they ran out of fuel (as too did the Germans), and collapsed only when they ran out of ammunition. Von Mellenthin also describes the saga of the Meleni pocket between 16 and 23 December when XLVIII Panzer Corps, with three panzer divisions, essayed the encirclement of an enemy force which, quite unexpectedly, was discovered to consist of three strong armored and four rifle corps poised to attack. He tells of how the Germans hoped for 'a miniature Tannenberg' but instead met resistance that compelled them to revert to the mobile defensive and ride with the blows the Russians began to throw in efforts to prevent their own encirclement. The Kiev salient would not be eliminated. XLVIII Panzer Corps would simply function as Army Group South's 'fire brigade', rushing from one enemy outbreak to another to check, but never entirely extinguish, the blaze. Though they might capture 700 Russian tanks and 600 guns in this period of high mobility, they merely postponed ultimate defeat.

The remarkable feats of the German tank force during this period should not be attributed only to superior handling. A slight but vital change in the technical balance also helped. As the worst of the Panther's faults were eradicated, this basically fine AFV mastered the T34/85s as they appeared in increasing numbers. The heavy tank balance also, at the year's end, stood in the German favor; indeed, by Russian standards, Panther was a heavy and Tiger a super-heavy, and both out-classed the by-now-obsolescent KV1 and also were more than a match for the KV1's successor. For KV85, which Z A Kotin has already made in small numbers by autumn 1943, mounted only the 85 mm gun, while its armor was little better than KV1's. Nor was his next offering, Josef Stalin I/85, much better even though its armor was thicker and its automotive and running gear improved; quite simply, its gun was not powerful enough. In fact, not until Josef Stalin 1/122 (JS 1/122), with its 122 mm gun mounted in a far better designed cast turret, was ready early in 1944 was a viable competitor to the Panthers and Tigers available. It was only when this tank began to make its presence felt in larger numbers that year that the battle of giants was fully joined and the German qualitative superiority at the beginning of 1944 seriously challenged. Even so, the clumsier heavies and super-heavies still had their detractors. Useful though they might be in powering through against the heaviest anti-tank defensive position, they were difficult and slower to move from place to place and tended to be much more unreliable than the older, proven, lighter machines. Moreover, they placed an immense strain on logistics. The Germans often left the heavies behind when projecting one of their swift counter-strokes, preferring to use them to lead a break-in and then do duty as the core of a position or as stand-bys in case the enemy made a serious counter-attack. In any case, once a Tiger had been committed far ahead of the support and repair echelons, the chances of recovery if it broke down or was damaged were less than reasonable. By 1944, the Russians on the other hand, assured of a constant general advance, could guarantee the recovery of lost tanks within normal operational circumstances.

And normal circumstances in 1944 meant, in the tank-versus-tank context, that in the majority of engagements a chronically outnumbered German tank force would be trying to cope with an opponent whose current technical capability was forever improving. For at last, Soviet, US and British tank designers began to overcome the ravages of the 'locust years' that had set them back so far at the beginning of the war.

CHAPTER SEVEN

DUELLING MONSTERS

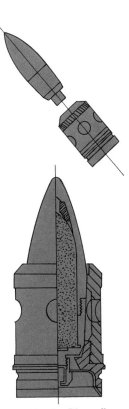

I N PARALLEL WITH THE NOTABLE INCREASES IN CALIBER and barrel length which had taken place since 1941 in order to achieve higher muzzle velocities with large shot for great penetrative power, there had also been more subtle attempts by technologists to raise muzzle velocities without modification of barrel characteristics. As earlier mentioned, the Germans had experimented with tapering barrels to squeeze special shot to achieve higher terminal velocity, but they had abandoned this method because of shortage of tungsten to make the shot. The British had developed a muzzle adaptor for the 40mm gun, but introduced only a few into service: a weapon of that kind could not be dual-purpose [by also firing high explosive shells] and, in any case, in 1943 a better method was on the way.

This new method worked on the principle of firing a shot of smaller caliber and dense material encased in a lightweight carrier through a standard gun barrel: increasing velocity was obtained because the full-caliber projectile had a greater base area for the charge to act upon than the normal AP, APC or APCBC round. The new projectile was also lighter in weight. With a German round of this kind, known as Armor Piercing Composite Rigid (APCR), both shot and carrier travelled to the target, but generated higher air resistance and a rapid falling-off in accuracy beyond 600 m. However, with the more sophisticated British Armor Piercing Discarding Sabot (APDS), the sub-caliber shot was carried in an aluminum shoe (or sabot) which detached itself after leaving the gun muzzle. Increases in muzzle velocity were highly significant, as is shown below by a comparison of the penetrative powers of the British 76.2mm and the German 88mm against homogenous armor at 30° to normal.

Armor Piercing Discarding Sabot (APDS)

76.2mm	APCBC	884m/sec penetrated 118mm at 1000 m.
	APDS	1204m/sec penetrated 170mm at 1000 m.
88 mm	APCBC	811m/sec penetrated 101mm at 1000 m.
	APCR	936m/sec penetrated 103mm at 1000 m [but with a lower chance of a hit]

This shows not only the superiority of APDS but also the importance of the British 76.2 mm gun, commonly known as the

17-pounder. For this was the only gun in Allied service which had a reasonable chance of penetrating the latest German AFVs at normal battlefield ranges – that is, up to 1000 meters. Hence the priority attached by many British soldiers to equipping a percentage of their tanks with this gun before they invaded Western Europe in 1944, and their horror at being thwarted at every step to fit this gun to the Sherman. For in autumn 1943 the Americans shelved development of T20, the tank intended as Sherman's successor but armed with a 76.2 mm gun that was inferior to the British version. The US 76.2 mm, which was being fitted to the latest mark of Sherman, was also inferior as an armor penetrator to the British 57 mm gun with APDS, then currently arming Cromwell, the latest (and already obsolete) British cruiser tank. It was, indeed, fortunate for the British, and indirectly the Americans, that a handful of determined British officers managed, towards the end of 1943, to demonstrate the feasibility of mounting the 17 pdr in Sherman. They were just in time to force through enough conversions to build what became known as Firefly Sherman which in Normandy, that summer, would just hold the balance against the Tigers, Panthers and such powerful SP guns as the 46 ton Jagdpanther with its 71 calibers 88 mm gun. Yet, in cancelling T20 development and opting to concentrate instead on vast production of the obsolescent Shermans and an up-gunned and

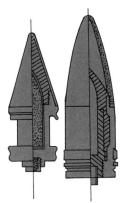

Armor Piercing Composite Rigid (APCR)
These, respectively, were British and German attempts to raise the muzzle velocity of shot by applying the principle of firing a projectile of smaller, dense material through a standard gun barrel. The performance tables show how effective this method was – and remains.

up-armored so-called Easy Eight Sherman, the Americans deliberately chose a policy of quantity versus quality – which was tantamount to gambling on the lives and morale of Allied crews pitted against superior enemy AFVs.

PAY-OFF IN WESTERN EUROPE

Throughout the winter of 1944 the Soviet armies prolonged their autumn offensive to push the Germans back from Leningrad in the north and almost to complete the reconquest of the Ukraine in the south. Encounters of thrust and counter-thrust raged, involving several grand encirclements in which large German formations fought their way westward, virtually surrounded by the enemy. By the time of the thaw, the German tank force had been seriously whittled down with no chance before year's end of complete refurbishment in the operational pause. For despite rising production in German factories, it was now essential for them to concentrate a large mobile force in Western Europe where an Allied invasion was expected at any moment.

When the Allied armies came ashore in Normandy on 6 June 1944, one revolutionary tactic comprised the landing of swimming tanks ahead of the infantry and, on the British beaches, the employment on a large scale of specialized tanks to clear and to cross obstacles, and to sweep mines. The success of these measures enabled the British to advance several miles inland before dark, thus establishing defenses in depth against the expected German armored counterattacks. In the American sector, on the other hand, failure in rough seas of the swimming tanks and the absence of the other special devices (because the American generals thought they could do without them) exposed

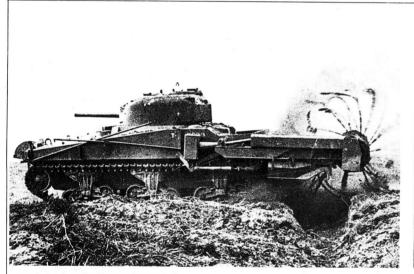

SPECIALIZED WW2 AFVs

A NUMBER OF SPECIAL vehicles were employed in amphibious warfare and in assaults on heavily fortified defenses.
Above: The Sherman minesweeping tank (called Crab) flailing for mines. This special AFV had the advantage of being usable as an ordinary gun tank, as was often required of it.
Above right: The Buffalo tracked carrier which was propelled through the water by its special scooped tracks. First used in the invasion of North Africa in 1942, it was later used extensively in the Pacific campaigns and in Europe, although not in the invasion of Normandy.
Far right: A Churchill IV converted into an Armoured Vehicle Royal Engineer (AVRE) for close-range assault with its Spigot Mortar, on steel and concrete structures. It could also lay fascines and bridges, in addition to carrying out other tasks.
Right: A mass of British amphibious tanks and other specialized AFVs clutter a Normandy beach on 6 June 1944.

unsupported infantry to heavy fire and serious casualties. Deep inland penetration was prevented and for a few vital hours the landing was in jeopardy, had the German tanks been able to strike at once. Allied immunity to a serious counter-thrust that day was principally thanks to a delayed and attenuated German reaction which had its roots in disagreements over the appropriate use of mobile reserves; unawareness of the sophisticated Allied landing techniques and surprise at tanks being in the van; and vacillation over where and when to strike back, associated with a conviction that the real invasion was aimed for the Pas de Calais.

The Germans did not expect a main Allied effort in Normandy. In any case, old-school mobility addicts such as von Rundstedt and Guderian considered that the right strategy was to hit the enemy with massed mobile forces once the main lodgements had been identified. Opposed to this was the Commander of Army Group B, Field Marshal Rommel, who believed that overwhelming enemy air attacks would prevent the assembly of a tank mass; he held that the invasion must be defeated at the coast by fixed defenses, minefields and large numbers of anti-tank guns. He wanted to spread the mobile forces thinly, close behind the beaches, for immediate intervention. Eventually Hitler settled the dispute by a bad compromise with the results described. Nevertheless, the Allies were contained within a bridgehead because, to begin with, the presence and arrival of German forces managed to keep pace with the Allied build-up from the sea. Subsequently the Allies were held up because the extremely dense *bocage* terrain of Normandy was ideal for defense. Within its confines, the outnumbered but superior German AFVs could, with minimum effort, check each successive,

armor-preponderant Allied offensive.

Bocage posed peculiar problems in tank-versus-tank combat. Not only did the thick, double hedges and narrow lanes severely restrict mobility and visibility, but also the smallness of the enclosed fields to all intents and purposes reduced most ranges of engagement to about 400 meters with a great many at 150 m or less. In bocage, therefore, even the best-armored Allied tank (the British Churchill VII with its 152 mm frontal armor) was likely to be vulnerable to the least well-armed German Pz Kw IV (Pz Kw III was virtually wasted out of service by this time); while for the Germans, only the Panther's sloped frontal plate was reasonably proof against the British 57 mm gun with APDS (1219m/4000ft/sec) and the 76.2 mm APCBC. Likewise at the closest of ranges, the American 76.2 mm stood a good chance against Tiger, although by now the 75 mm gun, which had been adequate in Tunisia and Sicily, was outclassed; this meant that both the early Shermans and the latest Cromwells were in trouble, their crews' morale suffering accordingly. Indeed, throughout Normandy – in the bocage of the center and the west flank as well as in the more open country to the south of Caen on the east flank – a dread of German tanks was oppressive, above all of the Tiger of which, in fact, only 1353 were ever built and only a few score were in Normandy. Quite as important was German prowess, the skill of crews whose selection and training was as good as ever.

Nevertheless, on 29 June when Rommel did at last manage to assemble a sufficient number of six panzer divisions (each of about 100 tanks) to make a unified counter-attack against British attackers in the bocage, the blow was absorbed by anti-tank guns and finally stopped dead by rows of tanks blocking his thrust line and backed up by a storm of artillery fire which eliminated the vital infantry support element during the move into close country. Barely a dozen German tanks broke in and half of these were instantly despatched.

Tank losses in Normandy were extremely high, as was to be expected when so many were being thrust into action against well emplaced anti-tank guns, and where skilfully deployed AFVs had only to cover the relatively few predictable avenues of approach without prematurely disclosing their fire positions. A supreme example of losses related to density of deployment was Operation 'Goodwood', the aim of which,

PANTHER D

DEVISED IN 1941 AND FIRST INTO ACTION at Kursk in 1943, Panther eventually became the best tank of WW2. It was built primarily to beat T34/76, but its designers thought ahead to match the next generation of Russian tanks – T34/85 and KV1's successors – which, on the whole, Panther managed to do.

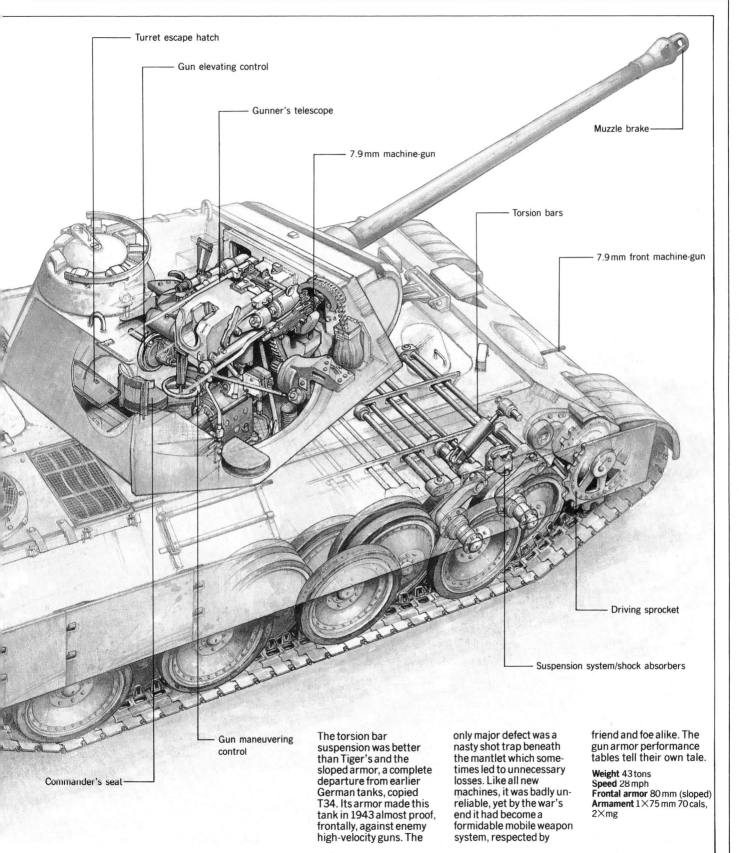

Turret escape hatch

Gun elevating control

Gunner's telescope

7.9 mm machine-gun

Muzzle brake

Torsion bars

7.9 mm front machine-gun

Driving sprocket

Suspension system/shock absorbers

Gun maneuvering control

Commander's seat

The torsion bar suspension was better than Tiger's and the sloped armor, a complete departure from earlier German tanks, copied T34. Its armor made this tank in 1943 almost proof, frontally, against enemy high-velocity guns. The only major defect was a nasty shot trap beneath the mantlet which sometimes led to unnecessary losses. Like all new machines, it was badly unreliable, yet by the war's end it had become a formidable mobile weapon system, respected by friend and foe alike. The gun armor performance tables tell their own tale.

Weight 43 tons
Speed 28 mph
Frontal armor 80 mm (sloped)
Armament 1×75 mm 70 cals, 2×mg

ENTANGLEMENT IN NORMANDY

Above: Panther on its way to the front to counter the Allied advance.
Above right: Sherman with locally manufactured Culins hedgerow-cutting device. This was used to drive gaps through the thick Normandy hedgerows that threatened to impede tank movement.
Far right: Shermans in action in France shortly after the D-Day landings.
Right: The Allied landing in Normandy in June 1944. Shown here is the subsequent expansion of the bridgehead, along with the attrition of German AFVs. The map shows the US breakout at St Lo, leading

to the closing of the Falaise pocket, and the subsequent pursuit of a routed foe to the fixed defenses along the German frontier and the River Maas. At this point the overstretched Allied logistics failed, easing the pressure on the enemy.

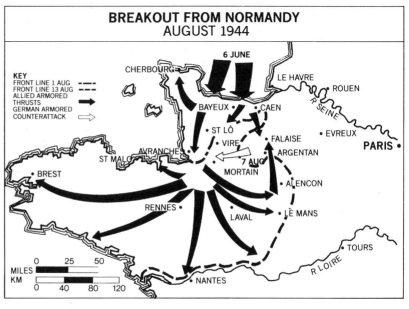

BREAKOUT FROM NORMANDY AUGUST 1944

KEY
FRONT LINE 1 AUG
FRONT LINE 13 AUG
ALLIED ARMORED THRUSTS
GERMAN ARMORED COUNTERATTACK

6 JUNE

CHERBOURG · LE HAVRE · ROUEN · R SEINE · BAYEUX · CAEN · ST LÔ · VIRE · FALAISE · EVREUX · PARIS · AVRANCHES · ST MALO · ARGENTAN · 7 AUG · MORTAIN · BREST · ALENCON · RENNES · LAVAL · LE MANS · TOURS · R LOIRE · NANTES

MILES 0 25 50
KM 0 40 80 120

according to General Montgomery, was 'to engage the German armor in battle...' It resembled 'Crusader' indeed, parallelling the unrealistic desert hunt for German tanks in November 1941; but here Montgomery was attacking vital ground the enemy had to defend. Across open country south of Caen on 18 July nearly 2000 assorted AFVs of both sides clashed in an area 8000 m square. Three days of fighting, every bit as intense as that at Kursk in 1943, concluded with the loss of 300 British and about 60 German AFVs, the majority the victims of SP guns and tanks. On the first morning it was panzerjägers, in conjunction with anti-tank guns, which absorbed the shock of the first of three armored divisions which were being forced through a bottleneck to the arena beyond. Only later did German tanks move to the vital crest over-

looking the scene and contribute their gun power to the carnage, but they suffered losses themselves when attempting to move down the slope to close the range to less than 1000 m. Yet it is worth noting certain, typical proportions of losses: out of 126 tanks lost by British 11th Armoured Division, only 40 were total write-offs, the rest being recoverable; in one tank battalion which lost 41 tanks there were only 17 dead and 39 wounded, several of whom were hit outside their machines.

The blunting of 'Goodwood' took place at the entrance to so-called 'good tank country', similar to that of Salisbury Plain in England or the steppes of the Soviet Union. Yet paradoxically, most decisive tank battles in Normandy were in bocage where the attrition rate also was extremely high, but where the issue was decided by the sheer availability of

Allied tanks and the devastating effects of artillery and air power. In this terrain, where the short-range bazooka and panzerfaust played their part in infantry ambushes of AFVs, the Germans declined to commit tanks, leaving limited mobile defense to panzerjägers. This policy worked quite well while the bridgehead was compact but began to fail as each successive expansion stretched the German defenders more thinly. Gradually the number of uncovered gaps increased and became wider. Infiltration by quite large numbers of Allied tanks became feasible, with exploitation much more promising so long as the Germans persisted in withholding their mobile armored formations from the 'poor tank country'. It is noteworthy that the Inspector General of Panzer Troops, General Guderian, who had exploited the close country of the Ardennes in 1940, disagreed with the strategy adopted. Massed counter-attacks in the bocage by two or three panzer divisions, he said '...*WERE POSSIBLE, but only outside the range of naval gunfire, and the panzer divisions would have had to be broken down into small groups of tanks and infantry, because of the terrain. We had prepared for this eventuality.*'

But the Germans did not make use of that preparation. The big break came on 25 July, when General Hodge's First Army (followed a few days later by General Patton's Third Army) pushed well-balanced tank, infantry and artillery task forces, adequately supported by engineers, deep into the bocage south of St Lo. What little chance the

SHERMAN M4 A3 E8

THIS MARK OF THE SHERMAN represented an attempt to prolong this versatile tank's life by up-gunning and up-armoring . The suspension was an improvement on earlier Marks, with wider tracks fitted. The engine was larger, at 450 hp, (earlier models were only 350 hp) while the armor was thickened by 15 mm. Though reliable as ever, this tank nevertheless was inadequate against Panthers and Tigers due to its gun's shortcomings (as the performance tables show). It mattered not that large numbers were available. Crew morale suffered because of a sense of technical inferiority.

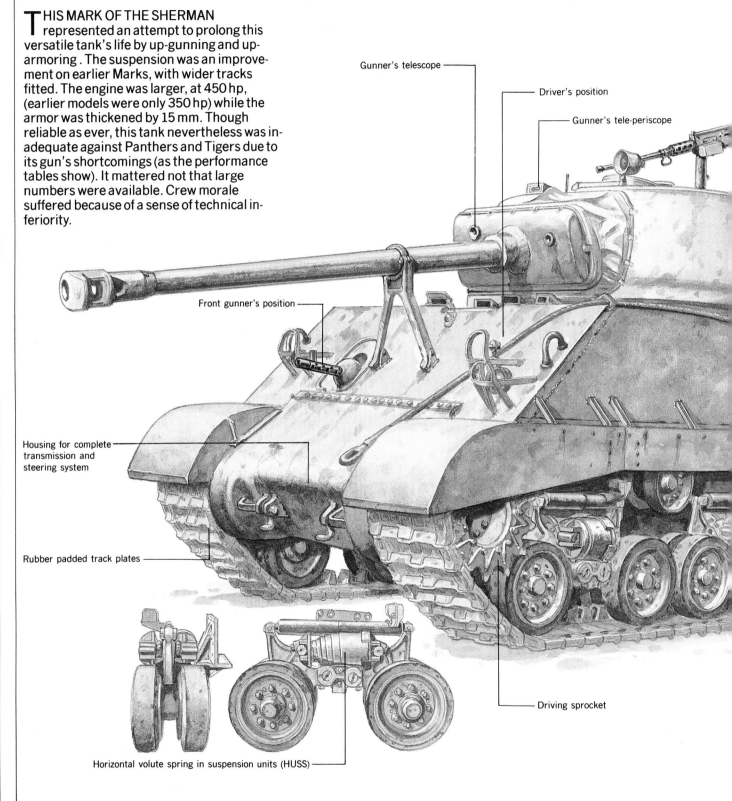

Gunner's telescope

Driver's position

Gunner's tele-periscope

Front gunner's position

Housing for complete transmission and steering system

Rubber padded track plates

Driving sprocket

Horizontal volute spring in suspension units (HUSS)

5-inch machine-gun

Engine compartment

Track adjusting roller

Weight 33 tons
Speed 26 mph
Frontal armor 100 mm
Armament 76.2 mm 53 cals,
2×mg

Germans ever had of blocking this strong drive behind crushing air attack was fatally diminished by the continuing absence of panzer divisions. These were concentrated to the east, guarding the obvious line of expectation from Caen.

Far too late, Hitler insisted upon sending four understrength panzer divisions to counter the breakthrough. Their losses mounting as they moved westward, their intent well-advertised to Allied intelligence, by radio intercept and code-breaking, their defeat in bocage at Mortain was inevitable and crushing. Deprived of their supplies by interdiction from the air, and held up in traffic-congested lanes, the panzer divisions came into action piecemeal and were torn to shreds. Frequently enough, it is true, a single Tiger or a few Panthers might triumph locally to the extent of knocking out four or five opponents to one of their own. But an already frail crust was sure to crack and allow a hostile surge through.

When German containment of the bridgehead collapsed, pockets of resistance only, and a few fleeing columns of mobile troops, barred the way of a torrent of Allied mobile troops hurtling into the heart of France toward Belgium, Holland and Germany. The last major tank battle in France erupted around the perimeter of the largest pocket of all, in the vicinity of Falaise. British and Canadian troops pressed in from west and north, Americans from the south – compressing the Germans into a tightening ring which was pounded day and night by bomb and shell. The overriding aim of German tanks at this stage was to escape, but only a few won clear. On the face of it there was nothing to stop the Allies overrunning France and engulfing Germany in a towering wave. Nothing, that is, except a logistic brake – which is precisely what did begin to act within a few days of the pursuit's commencement. Yet throughout the Allied surge towards the German frontier not a single counter-offensive, so typical in Russia, was mounted – not even when indications that the tank spearheads were embarrassed by fuel shortage – a shortage, incidentally, which was caused as much by a scarcity of trucks as it was by distance or the shattered state of the lines of communication. It was not unwillingness to try, but sheer inability which restrained the Germans. German reserves were run down and almost irreplaceable. Moreover, as will be described, on 22 June the Russians had launched another large-scale offensive from one end of the Eastern front to the other and the German armies there were also being consumed in a quite disastrous manner.

Yet the Allied advance ground to a halt at Germany's western frontier, partly from lack of supplies, but also in face of a defense based on natural and man-made obstacles (the Siegfried Line) reinforced by AFVs which were rushed from one trouble spot to another. Sometimes, as happened at Arnhem, AFVs happened to be standing just where they were wanted, on this occasion to hit the First Allied Airborne Army when it landed, without tanks. A mere handful of German tanks and jagdpanzers contributed to the fatal delay inflicted upon a British armored division as it advanced to link up with the airborne divisions which had seized river crossings along a route into the North German Plain and the Reich's industrial heartland. Loss of momentum by the British division gave the two SS Panzer Divisions at Arnhem just sufficient opportunity to grind unsupported parachute infantry into the ground – by practicing in the long-standing manner the tank's underlying role as a 'battlefield bully' when left free to pick its punches.

The failure at Arnhem put paid to the expectation of an Allied rampage through Germany even as the Soviet drive into Poland was running out of impetus. Until mid-December the main Allied effort in the West had to be concentrated upon improving their logistics and assembling the men and material needed for the final effort. Numerous subsidiary operations to gain control of the approaches to the port of Antwerp and of jumping-off places along the German frontier were essential, and most of them incited tank-versus-tank skirmishes in which the Germans, in retreat, tended to deploy a high proportion of jagdpanzers. Meanwhile, the Germans concentrated upon delaying tactics to keep the Siegfried Line intact as a start line for one last counter-offensive in the grand manner. Tank clashes broke out when the conflicting longer term preparations met opposition – to the south of Saarbrücken, for example, where Patton's Third Army struggled ahead in the winter mud of Lorraine and the German First Army fought to retain the Ardennes along with this important industrial and communication center. On 5 December CCA of US 4th Armored Division (Maj Gen Hugh Gafney) was advancing along the main road to the village of Bining, but had been diverted left to a minor road in order to avoid fire from a forest along its right flank. In the path of its leading tanks lay the village of Singling overlooked from the north by high ground.

THE FIGHT FOR SINGLING – SHERMANS VERSUS PANTHERS

Towards evening on 5 December, Company C of 37th Tank Battalion (Lt Col Creighton Abrams) approached Singling and at 800 m was struck by a fusillade of shot from Panthers, Jagdpanzer IVs (with L48 75 mm guns) and 75 mm anti-tank guns hidden among the houses. Within a few minutes five were knocked out by shot and nine more, stuck in the soft ground as they tried to escape, crippled by artillery fire. Along with its two artillery observation tanks, (FOO) Company C was annihilated without striking a blow in its own defense against I/111th Panzer Grenadier Regiment of 11th Panzer Division.

Next morning Abrams tried again with a carefully coordinated plan. Capt Leach's Tank Company B and Lt Belden's Company B from 51st Armored Infantry Battalion, well supported by artillery, approached across the same sodden ground as had the ill-fated Company C the previous afternoon. Most of Leach's tanks were Shermans with the 75 mm gun, but five were M4A3 E2 models with the 76.2 mm gun firing the latest HVAP shot (Hyper Velocity AP, which was similar to the German APCR) at 1036m/sec (3400 ft/sec). The infantry rode in open-topped armored half-tracks until these bogged down in the fields when the men transferred to ride the tanks. Two batteries of artillery and a platoon of open-topped M18 Hellcat tank destroyers with 76.2 mm guns supported the advance.

Knowing that enemy AFVs and guns in the village and along the crest beyond dominated the surrounding ground, Leach and Belden had agreed to make a run for the houses under cover of a dense artillery White Phosphorus (WP) smoke screen laid across the village and Welschoff Farm. The Hellcats were to lie back and pick off any enemy tank which disclosed itself – really only those in the village since there was little chance of the 76.2 mm gun doing much harm to tanks on the ridge at 1600 m or more. This plan worked even though the smoke screen failed to cover the entire ridge and German artillery, directed by FOOs on the ridge, managed to drive off the poorly protected Hellcats. As the leading platoons of Shermans reached the

The later Tiger family, sponsored by Hitler who thought bigger things must be better.

Left: Jagdtiger was a monstrosity of a tank destroyer. Its utility was as suspect as that of the equally monstrous Elefant.
Weight 70.5 tons
Speed 22 mph
Frontal armor 250 mm
Armament 1×128 mm, 1×mg

Below: Tiger II (known as Royal) appeared in two versions but not in large numbers. The most formidable tank of WW2, it was limited by its immense size and relative immobility.
Weight 70 tons
Speed 24 mph
Frontal armor 185 mm (sloped)
Armament 1×88 mm 71 cals, 3×mg

outskirts of Singling, the enemy infantry dived into cellars leaving the defense at ground level to the guns and AFVs.

A game of hide and seek between vehicles began. First blood went to the three Panthers, the Jagdpanzer and the anti-tank gun tucked in at the west end – three of their shots at 150 m knocking out the Sherman of the leading platoon leader on Leach's left flank. Yet this acted sufficiently as a distraction to allow the two tank platoons carrying the infantry to reach the outskirts of Singling and deposit the men in the center and east end of the village. Almost at once, however, the infantry were sprayed by bullets from the Jagdpanzer IV and by infantry, compelling them to seek cover in houses and cellars, where they became mixed up with the Germans already there. Largely hidden from view, they now fought a private battle while the tanks duelled outside. For at this moment the five Panthers and two Jagdpanzers on the ridge eased into pre-reconnoitered hull-down positions and opened up from 1200 m.

A two-tiered battle ensued. At one level, the American infantry in the village tried to round up Germans (with little help from the Shermans which had only to stick a gun round a corner to draw Jagdpanzer fire down the main street) and also went tank-hunting until they crippled the village Jagdpanzer and made its crew bail out. At the other level, deadly fire from the ridge made two Shermans erupt in flames, pinning the surviving tanks to the shelter of the houses. Moreover the Germans refused to be budged from the west end, their Panthers ripping the houses

apart with shot and shell, to the great encouragement of their own infantry.

With most eyes fixed on the street brawl, Leach's right flank tank platoon nevertheless spotted in time two counter-attacking Panthers rumbling down the slope from the northeast, supported by four comrades back on the crest. At the same time concentrations of artillery fire fell on the east end. At 150 m Sgt Fitzgerald with his 76.2 mm gun hit an obligingly halted Panther, its turret still traversing to engage at the thinnest part of its side armor, and set it alight. But the second one he fired at a moment later at 400 m was luckier and backed off under cover of its own local smoke screen. At 500 m, however, a third Panther, missed by Fitzgerald's initial sighting shot, took two hits in quick succession and brewed up. But when Fitzgerald tried for a hat trick on a fourth Panther at 800 m (and hit it) the shot simply bounced off the glacis plate.

GUN POWER AT SINGLING

In the difficult approaches to Bining the US 4th Armored Division was attempting to outflank anticipated enemy resistance by a move through Singling. The strong enemy armored presence at Singling was to counter the very sort of indirect approach the Germans anticipated – the kind of thing they too would have tried, had they been on the offensive.

Here the German counter-attack is developing, following the attempts by US Hellcats and Shermans to take control of Singling. While infantry fights and tank duels take place in and around the village, a crucial moment comes when Fitzgerald's Sherman jockeys for a shooting position.

(cont.)

SINGLING WELSCHOFF FARM PANTHERS

SP GUNS ON RIDGE

NORTH

AMERICAN ADVANCE FITZGERALD VIEWPOINT

GUN POWER AT SINGLING (continued)

Fitzgerald's Sherman M4A3 E2 is engaging a Panther at 400 m with his 76.2 mm gun. He has already disposed of the Panther to his front at 150 m. He misses the one at 400 m, which backs off under cover of smoke, but a third Panther at 500 m is about to be engaged, and penetrated at 500 m by HVAP. A hit on a fourth Panther's glacis plate at 800 mm fails, however. The shot bounces off.

However, the German counter-attack has been soundly defeated by the action, largely because Fitzgerald has skilfully fired from positions defiladed by houses from enemy direct supporting anti-tank fire. Indeed the tank of Fitzgerald's platoon leader can be seen attracting most of the supporting fire from Jagdpanzers up on the ridge and it is about to be hit and crippled. Its driver, Pte Nelson, was cleaning his periscope when

'...*W*HAM! IT SOUNDED AND FELT *like our own gun firing, but it wasn't. A shell had hit our turret. I looked back and saw smoke behind me. I was thinking of getting out when – blam again. And I'll be damned if I didn't have a German armor-piercing shell in my lap'.*

He and the rest of the crew bailed out, while the rest of the platoon, now under Fitzgerald, drew back into hull-down positions.

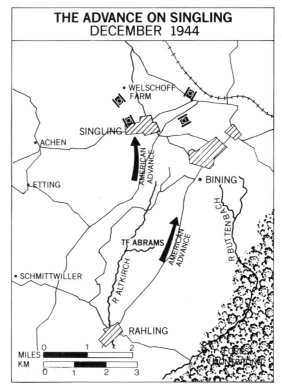

THE ADVANCE ON SINGLING
DECEMBER 1944

Tank gunfire from covered positions generated a stalemate. Neither side could make further progress. With nightfall the Americans withdrew, leaving 20 tanks knocked out by the Germans – who themselves had soon to withdraw as pressure built up to their flanks.

Infantry/tank co-operation. A Sherman supports infantry entering a burning village.

AN INCONCLUSIVE RESULT

The German counter-attack had failed in its intention of wiping out Leach and Belden but had contained the American thrust and enabled their comrades in Singling, intensively supported by artillery, to hold firm. They did so to such effect that when Abrams attempted that afternoon to send in fresh tanks and infantry, they were raked by Panthers and compelled to withdraw. That put an end to capturing Singling that day. Under cover of darkness the remains of Leach's and Belden's command were pulled back, encouraged to depart by flashing tracer from German high-velocity guns, spurred on by the tank-hunting parties who tried, unavailingly, to start up and drive off two of the disabled Shermans.

In 24 hours no fewer than 20 American tanks had been lost or disabled in exchange for three German AFVs. Abrams could perhaps claim that the diversion of German attention was worthwhile, even at so high a price. The Germans could rest content with yet another demonstration of how their tanks outclassed the Americans – just so long as they managed to sit a little beyond 800 m range. Had they not counter-attacked, unnecessarily as it turned out, they might have held the village without the loss of a single Panther. For that matter, however, Singling itself was hardly worth the loss of so many tanks, with the usual proportion of killed and wounded. For the main objective, Bining, was evacuated a few hours later. Furthermore, far greater events were on the eve of disclosure as to the northward the Germans began the concentration of armor destined soon to be hurled into the Ardennes in the panzer divisions' valedictory charge.

DEBUT OF THE SUPER-HEAVIES

The anti-tank gun contest, so apparent as early as 1941, moved a stage forward in 1943 when the Germans introduced a 70 calibers 88 mm piece, and began work on a 128 mm model, and the Russians began introducing new 100 mm and 122 mm guns. Since towed mountings for these guns were excessively heavy and clumsy, suitable AFVs were essential. The result, in terms of vehicle weight and size, therefore also called for overall increases, particularly from Germany. Yet power plants remained much the same as in earlier models, thus inducing a progressive decline in power/weight ratio and, therefore, a further decline in mobility of the giants. Germany's 68-ton Tiger II (Royal Tiger), for

example, had the same 700 hp engine as the 56-ton Tiger I, while Russia's 46-ton JS2 managed, like the earliest KV1 from which it was derived, with 550 hp. Similarly the 70-ton Jagdtiger with its 128 mm gun and the Russian JSU 122 retained the earlier, standard engines – although there any similarity ended since the Germans fitted 150 mm armor while the Russians settled for only 45 mm. Thus the Russians produced more battleworthy AFVs built largely of proven components – a policy to which they were to adhere for many vehicle generations to come. Of the Russian self-propelled guns, perhaps the most important was the SU 100, based on the T34 chassis and armed with the latest 100 mm gun. SU 100 was a match for the Jagdpanther, although hardly for the clumsy Jagdtiger if the latter managed to get in a shot. In one vital area, however, the Russians were well behind their Allies and therefore in difficulty against the more thickly armored German tanks; they did not adopt APDS and had to make do with APCBC shot at velocities below 914 m/sec (3000 ft/sec) – little better than the American 76.2 mm gun with APCBC.

As for the Allies, both the British and Americans dabbled in super-heavies, – the former with the 50-ton Black Prince (76.2 mm gun and based on Churchill) and the 76-ton limited traverse Tortoise (94 mm gun); the latter with the 54-ton M6A2 (76.2 mm gun) and 200 mm armored M6A2 E1 (120 mm gun). But each for several reasons stopped short of production, among which the problems of shipping such bulky equipment to the war zones was prominent. Instead, the British concentrated upon what in 1945 turned out to be their best cruiser of the war, the Comet, with the 50 calibers so-called 77 mm gun (actually 76.2 mm). The Americans produced the 42-ton M26 General Pershing with its 90 mm gun that made it, in US and Soviet terminology, a heavy tank but which by German rating was a medium, as well as an effective opponent for Panther and Tiger I.

Throughout 1944, therefore, the main battle of the giants was confined to the Eastern Front. There, at the start of the great Soviet offensive on 22 June, Tiger crews began to experience something disturbingly new, as JS2 entered action for the first time.

CONVULSIONS IN THE EAST

If the ordeals of the autumn and winter offensives of 1943/44, with the revelation that the Russians had so many good tanks in inexhaustible supply seemed bad enough to the Germans, the experiences of summer 1944 were totally unnerving. It was not that Russian training and techniques had improved all that much over the standard of 1943. They simply kept on coming in large numbers, no matter how fast they were knocked out by German tanks whose crews were still amazingly effective. Deprived of adequate reinforcements by the demands of the Southern and Western theaters, they inevitably faced terrible odds. The artillery barrage preceding the Russian attacks on 22 June along the Baltic and Central Fronts, called on something in the order of 14 000 guns, against 600 German; and for the assault and exploitation, 5200 AFVs were available against only 900.

The fighting in the forests which dominated the ground between Smolensk and the old Polish frontier, where Guderian and Hoth had triumphed in 1941, was intricate and without the incisions of the earlier campaign. On a frontage of 450 miles, six converging assaults were aimed at steamrollering Army Group Center into submission. Yet the density of combat was thinner than that of Normandy, even if similar in certain interesting aspects. As was happening at that same moment in the Normandy bocage, the enemy's sheer numerical preponderance over the Germans was overcoming the difficulties of operating in close country. Compared to steppe operations, the Germans here found it difficult to pick out a plethora of attacks before out-maneuvering or blocking them. They might have done better if Hitler had not stuck so rigidly to his obsession with clinging to bastions, and thus condemning whole armies to encirclement and the subsequent inevitable costly breakout operations or annihilation. Eventually, of course, the result would have been the same; but the retreat (which halted at Warsaw when the Russian momentum expired at the end of August) could have been delayed and might have been more economical if the German generals had been granted a greater degree of flexibility and mobility. For one thing, they would not have lost so may AFVs in head-on duels. Repeated flank attacks would have prolonged the agony and perhaps saved Army Group Center from the total defeat it suffered. The panzerfaust hollow charge weapon, used in increasing numbers, would have been a much cheaper substitute at the closer ranges for expensive AFVs.

It was farther south, in the more open

northern Ukraine (where the Russians struck on 13 July using 14 000 guns and 1600 AFVs) that the latest heavy tanks with their big guns came into their own. Here the 76.2 mm Russian anti-tank guns, which were viable at the closer, forest ranges in the north, were outclassed in highly mobile encounters which were often fought at ranges beyond 1000 m. Well forewarned and badly outnumbered, the Germans planned to withdraw a thin screen of troops into lay-back positions in order to escape the opening blast of artillery fire. But so fast did the Russians advance that these plans were overtaken. Tank task forces appeared in depth sooner than expected. German control began to slip, permitting a hopeless situation to arise out of an inherently perilous one. As infantry assaults, well-supported by the JS2 tanks and SUs, opened up wide gaps, infiltrations of vast dimensions (similar to those on the eve of being created in Normandy) took place. There was no need for Hitler's connivance this time to permit encirclements. The Russians did it for themselves and often with fatal consequences for their enemy. Moreover, the Tiger and Panther crews, who previously had enjoyed a monopoly of domination through gun and armor, now met their match.

General Hasso von Manteuffel had already fought JS1 tanks at Iassy on the Romanian frontier in the final stages of the Russian winter offensive. '*IT WAS A SHOCK TO FIND that, although my Tigers began to hit them at 2200 m, our shells (sic) did not penetrate them until we had closed to half that distance. But I was able to counter their technical superiority*

RUSSIAN SELF-PROPELLED GUNS
Although the Russians did not embrace the self-propelled gun to the same extent as the Germans, they nevertheless, with their SU 76 (**left**) on a light tank chassis, engineered a useful, fast AFV to keep pace with and give fire support to their mobile formations. In SU 100, (**below**) based on T34, they built an extremely useful anti-tank system, the equal of such German Jagdpanzers as Stu IV and Jagdpanther.

by maneuver and mobility in making best use of ground cover'.

He implied that the Russians were failing to hit pin-point targets at that distance, which no doubt was due to the usual difficulties of spotting and ranging at anything above 1200 m. But it was certainly another kind of shock for a Tiger crew (even those of the handful of Tiger IIs now coming into service) when it received a JS2's 56-pound 122 mm shot. At 2000 m the 122 mm could just penetrate Tiger I's frontal armor, a feat which could also be performed by the SU 100 at 1500 m with a 34-pound shot. No longer could the German heavies in their arrogance, afford to stand up and shoot it out. The discipline of enemy firepower reimposed the tactical discipline of old.

Firepower discipline varied tactics and, to some extent, strategy. A single tank's ability to kill its opponent at twice the range of what had been possible in 1940 generated a measure of economy; a modern tank could now dominate wider and deeper stretches of country. Theoretically, fewer tanks were needed – although the reverse effect applied since tanks of higher combat value were in greater demand, with a correspondingly increased load on manufacturing facilities and on maintenance. In other words, each improvement stimulated requests for further improvements in tank technology which, in a manner of speaking, fed on itself. By comparison with the Russians, the Germans were in no state to benefit fully from improved technology or increased numbers. Panzer divisions in the east possessed a mere 40 or 50 tanks each, at this time, because they were de-

prived of full establishment by the diversion of a far higher proportion (about 100 per division) to the West.

The picture which emerges of fighting in the Ukraine, in Poland and in Romania is one of ever-smaller German battle groups and combat teams scurrying to and fro in desperate endeavors to stem the mighty Soviet onrush. Out-maneuver the enemy they frequently did and, as in the West, they frequently out-shot less well-trained or managed opponents, but they could only inflict enough delay until the Russians ran out of fuel – as they did on the frontiers of Bulgaria and Yugoslavia towards the end of September.

ARDENNES COUNTER-OFFENSIVE
When the battle lines closed in on Germany's pre-war frontiers, Hitler had the options of surrender (rejected) or fighting to the bitter end. Abandoning any immediate hope of delivering a knockout blow against the Russians, he chose to tackle what he rated the

SU 76
Weight 11.5 tons
Speed 35 mph
Frontal armor 55 mm
Armament 1×76.2 mm 42 cals, 1×mg

SU 100
Weight 30 tons
Speed 35 mph
Frontal armor 45 mm (sloped)
Armament 1×100 mm, 1×mg

THE END-OF-WAR GENERATION OF ALLIED BATTLE TANKS

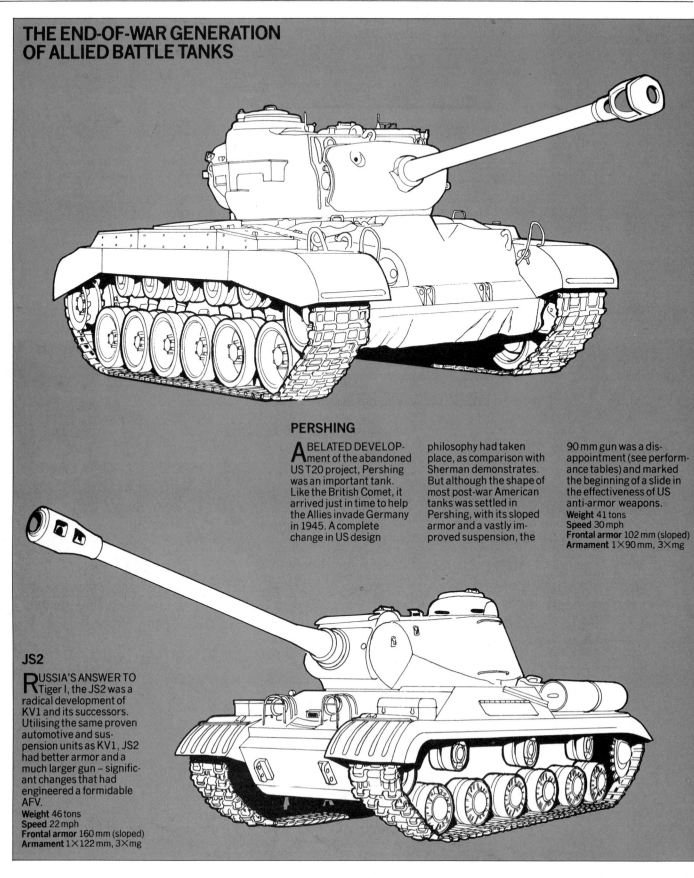

PERSHING

A BELATED DEVELOP-ment of the abandoned US T20 project, Pershing was an important tank. Like the British Comet, it arrived just in time to help the Allies invade Germany in 1945. A complete change in US design philosophy had taken place, as comparison with Sherman demonstrates. But although the shape of most post-war American tanks was settled in Pershing, with its sloped armor and a vastly improved suspension, the 90 mm gun was a disappointment (see performance tables) and marked the beginning of a slide in the effectiveness of US anti-armor weapons.

Weight 41 tons
Speed 30 mph
Frontal armor 102 mm (sloped)
Armament 1×90 mm, 3×mg

JS2

R USSIA'S ANSWER TO Tiger I, the JS2 was a radical development of KV1 and its successors. Utilising the same proven automotive and suspension units as KV1, JS2 had better armor and a much larger gun – significant changes that had engineered a formidable AFV.

Weight 46 tons
Speed 22 mph
Frontal armor 160 mm (sloped)
Armament 1×122 mm, 3×mg

GUN VERSUS ARMOR–IV
PROTECTION PERFORMANCE AT 30% NORMAL ANGLE OF IMPACT
(RANGE WHICH HIGH-VELOCITY PROJECTILES FAIL TO PENETRATE VARY ACCORDING TO RANGE AND ANGLE OF IMPACT)

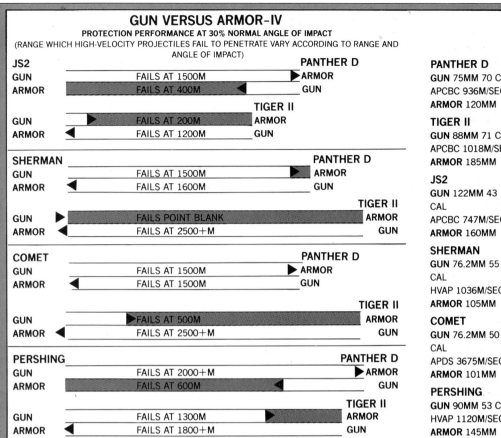

JS2
			PANTHER D
GUN	FAILS AT 1500M		ARMOR
ARMOR	FAILS AT 400M		GUN

			TIGER II
GUN	FAILS AT 200M		ARMOR
ARMOR	FAILS AT 1200M		GUN

SHERMAN
			PANTHER D
GUN	FAILS AT 1500M		ARMOR
ARMOR	FAILS AT 1600M		GUN

			TIGER II
GUN	FAILS POINT BLANK		ARMOR
ARMOR	FAILS AT 2500+M		GUN

COMET
			PANTHER D
GUN	FAILS AT 1500M		ARMOR
ARMOR	FAILS AT 1500M		GUN

			TIGER II
GUN	FAILS AT 500M		ARMOR
ARMOR	FAILS AT 2500+M		GUN

PERSHING
			PANTHER D
GUN	FAILS AT 2000+M		ARMOR
ARMOR	FAILS AT 600M		GUN

			TIGER II
GUN	FAILS AT 1300M		ARMOR
ARMOR	FAILS AT 1800+M		GUN

PANTHER D
GUN 75MM 70 CAL
APCBC 936M/SEC
ARMOR 120MM

TIGER II
GUN 88MM 71 CAL
APCBC 1018M/SEC
ARMOR 185MM

JS2
GUN 122MM 43 CAL
APCBC 747M/SEC
ARMOR 160MM

SHERMAN
GUN 76.2MM 55 CAL
HVAP 1036M/SEC
ARMOR 105MM

COMET
GUN 76.2MM 50 CAL
APDS 3675M/SEC
ARMOR 101MM

PERSHING
GUN 90MM 53 CAL
HVAP 1120M/SEC
ARMOR 145MM

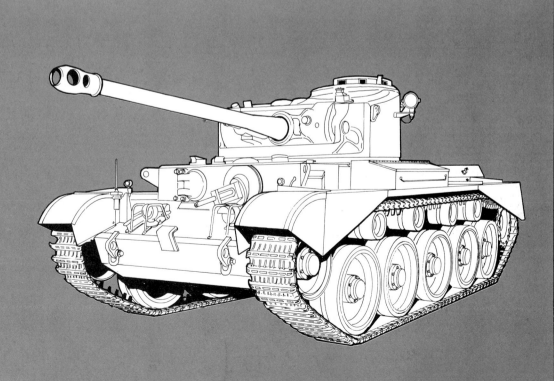

COMET

THIS WAS THE FIRST British cruiser design to dispense with the Christie suspension. The so-called 77 mm gun was about the equal of the 17-pdr (76.2 mm) fitted in the Firefly Sherman. Still there was no pronounced attempt to install sloped armor. Comet was a reliable tank and a considerable improvement on Cromwell, but its shortcomings indicated how far British design still lagged behind.

Weight 33 tons
Speed 29 mph
Frontal armor 101 mm
Armament 1✕77 mm, 2✕mg

Sherman in the Ardennes snow.

greater danger presented by the Allied forces in the West. Planning began early in October for an attack in mid-November through the Ardennes where, under the cloak of closer country, the suffocating effects of Allied air power might be mitigated. If all went well, the victorious panzer divisions could be transferred to the East in time to meet the next Russian offensive expected in January. A host of difficulties, among which the catastrophic effect of bombing was by no means the least, postponed the starting date to 16 December. Tank strengths remained below establishment, also as the result of air attacks on factories. Total production of Tigers, Panthers and PzKw IVs which had been 2438 from June – August, slumped to 1764 from September – November, although the figure for new panzerjägers had risen from 766 in August to 1199 in November. So the quantity of AFVs available was little more than 1500, spread between seven battle-hardened (and weary) Panzer divisions and 14 infantry divisions in the first wave of the assault – a meagre total by comparison with the numbers that had attacked so brilliantly against superior numbers in 1940.

The pattern of fighting in the Ardennes repeated that of most such combat carried out by determined troops when pitted against each other in close country. As in the bocage and in the Russian forest, issues were often decided at the level of tank or infantry platoon – frequently hinging upon the initiative (or lack of it) of one man or one tank. Frequent encounters took place between single

tanks or, at most, groups of two or three. Mines took their toll. Germans who had depended upon rapid and deep penetrations of the thinly held American lines within the first few hours were disappointed, even though to begin with, the surprised Americans in many places gave way under shock. Although there had been enough information to indicate what was brewing, the American intelligence staffs declined to accord this indication the credit it deserved. Their commanders were caught out strategically and tactically; they lost much equipment. Whenever they could, the Germans crewed captured US Shermans into action so that there were instances of Sherman fighting Sherman in the winter's cold and snow among the dense trees, hedges and narrow lanes and rides of the Ardennes forest.

A key to the German failure to reach Antwerp within the first few days was to be found in the inability of their crack Sixth SS Panzer Army to capture the Elsenborn ridge on the first day. This would have opened the way to much-needed American fuel dumps near Stavelot on the way to crossings of the River Meuse at Liège, which it was hoped to seize within 48 hours. As elsewhere, Hitler's dream of a repeat performance of 1940 was turned into a nightmare because the enemy and the conditions were totally different. Unlike the French in 1940, the Americans were committed to hold their ground and not withdraw to the Meuse. Also unlike the French, the Allies possessed armored forces which were well versed in the latest techniques of command and control and adept at switching mobile forces quickly from one front to another, without creating appalling traffic jams. Unlike the German forces of 1940, those of 1944 lacked complete air superiority, a serious defect which was mitigated at first by thick weather which largely prevented flying, but which reverberated to their discomfort when the clouds cleared away at Christmas. Above all, because the Germans were unable to expand their bridgehead, as they had in 1940, they were channelled into one single lancelike thrust. The check at Elsenborn meant that only von Manteuffel's Fifth Panzer Army, directed on Bastogne and on the Meuse bridges at Dinant, made significant progress; it thus became the principal instrument of decision, thereby attracting the heaviest weight of enemy counter-measures.

Fifth Panzer Army's success, based on surprise and a dubious American decision to hold unimportant ground which should have been yielded, was nevertheless too slow for victory. Infiltrate the torn enemy front its combat teams did, but the sheer complexity of the country and an accumulation of American local ambushes denied it essential objectives. Above all, the American determination to cling to route centers, such as Bastogne, automatically throttled the German supply system besides diverting troops to unwanted siege operation. It thwarted von Manteuffel's bypassing strategy and won time for the Allied high command to overcome its shock, to plug the gaps, and then to mount counter-strokes against both enemy flanks that invitingly extended in a westerly direction. The American forces built up their anti-tank content at the front with AFVs hastily repaired in field workshops and any unit available being sent forward from rest areas. The British also committed a corps, strong in tanks, to block the approaches to Dinant. Patton began executing a 90-degree left wheel to send his Third Army to relieve Bastogne as the overture to a powerful counterstroke against Fifth Panzer Army. Meanwhile, a gradually stabilized northern front, along a line from Elsenborn to Malmedy to Stavelot, formed the springboard for another counterstroke, also against Fifth Panzer Army.

Within two days of the offensive's beginning, senior German officers realised that they had fallen short of their first objectives, and Antwerp was beyond reach. It would be wise, they said, to conserve Germany's remaining armored mobile reserve for more pressing purposes. But Hitler resisted and drew encouragement from every breath of success at the front. When a spearhead of 1st SS LAH Panzer Division under Jochem Peiper made a local breakthrough near Elsenborn, he crowed – without knowing that the bulk of the division, held back by possession of only two out of the four routes it needed, was being pounded by artillery fire. In the days to come the loss by Peiper of 39 tanks, all his transport and over 1000 of his 2000 men, merged with a tale of encroaching ruin. Traffic jams stifled mobility. Von Manteuffel, helping personally with traffic control as he hustled his armored columns towards Dinant, was another inspiration of Hitler's insistence upon going on. But on 25 December his Fifth Panzer Army's leading elements, its weakened 2nd Panzer Division, were still short of the Meuse. Out of fuel, deprived of ammunition, awaiting support and already aware of British tanks strongly posted ahead, the Germans were quite unaware of 2nd US Armored Division poised to hit their northern flank with devastating power. That day Hitler rejected the plea of Guderian (who had taken over as Army Chief of Staff in July and, therefore, was responsible for defense in the East) that the offensive should be called off and the reserves sent to him. In mid-January, it was calculated, the Russians would launch an offensive against Berlin.

The delay in cancellation proved fatal to the German tank force. In addition to the losses already suffered by the SS Panzer Corps in its abortive attacks, the stranded leading elements of Fifth Panzer Army – 2nd, 9th and Lehr Panzer Divisions – were enveloped by 2nd US Armored Division and the British. Now it was the turn of German tanks, like those of the French 1st DCR at Flavion (only a few miles off) in May 1940, to be caught fuelless and virtually annihilated: 82 tanks, 16 panzerjägers, 83 guns and 280 motor vehicles were left on the battlefield. The handful who escaped represented the survivors of the last full-scale panzer offensive of the war – doomed to a fighting retreat until the enemy, converging from west, south and east, squeezed the life out of Germany.

THE CRUSHING OF THE PANZER FORCE

When Hitler belatedly called off the Ardennes offensive on New Year's Day 1945 and began transferring divisions to the Eastern Front, far too much damage had been done for any hope of recuperation. German arms production was falling catastrophically, due to the disruption of industry, and the transport system was under constant air attack. Moving troops from one place to another became a desperate and deadly slow process. The SS Panzer Corps that Guderian urgently wanted to guard Berlin was diverted to prop up Hungary where the Russians stormed the entire front on 12 January. German armored troops were now to be shuttled from one insoluble crisis to another – always outnumbered, ever-deprived of supplies and spares, falling to pieces and compelled to abandon irreplaceable AFVs, yet never quite surrendering that combat skill, pride, and resourcefulness under pressure which had kept them fighting for almost six years.

Thousands of Allied tanks, the majority of them technically inferior to their opponents, rampaged among the German defenses. Growing numbers of Russian JS2s and

The crushing of Germany by the converging Allied armies in 1944 and 1945. Each arrow represented masses of AFVs supported by artillery, infantry, and aircraft. These masses bore down on German armies whose tank forces retained their prowess to the end but which had no hope against such armored might and fire-power.

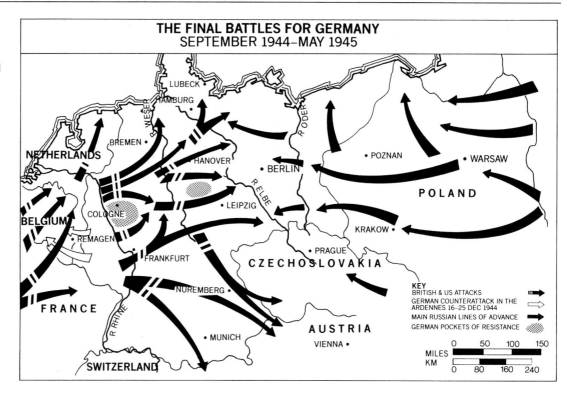

THE FINAL BATTLES FOR GERMANY
SEPTEMBER 1944–MAY 1945

KEY
BRITISH & US ATTACKS
GERMAN COUNTERATTACK IN THE ARDENNES 16–25 DEC 1944
MAIN RUSSIAN LINES OF ADVANCE
GERMAN POCKETS OF RESISTANCE

American M26 Pershings could hold their own with the best Germany could still field. The latest M4A3 E8, the so-called Super-Sherman, and British Comet (better-armed than their predecessors) promoted higher crew confidence thanks to their improved protective qualities. Of major importance, ammunition protection was upgraded and the fire hazard reduced, the Americans having installed protective jackets filled with ethylene glycol (later water) to flood ammunition in the event of penetration.

A mere 700 German tanks faced up to some 4000 Russian AFVs on 12 January 1945, and inevitably were driven back until the Russians again ran out of supplies and the disparity of numbers, in effect, was compensated by logistic breakdown. Tank-versus-tank contests often ended locally in the German favor, but it was interdiction of chaotic supply routes which mainly applied a final brake to the Russians – as it usually had everywhere else throughout the war. Indeed, the Russian supply system would have been even further impaired had not the Americans provided them with 400 000 wheeled load carriers to fill a gap that was beyond Soviet manufacturing capacity. Still fewer German AFVs stood guard in the West and in Italy as the Allies rebounded from their setback in the Ardennes and began remorselessly to grind down the defenders of the Rhine. When the

Russians came in sight of the River Oder in mid January, the last Germans were being ejected from the west bank of the Rhine, leaving behind scores of AFVs which would fight no more. The mobile forces which could be assembled to counter the Allied assaults over the Rhine, when they took place later in March, were more symbolic than real, possessing a pronounced majority of panzerjägers over tanks and a distinct preponderance of AFVs which had been patched up to carry out hopeless tasks.

Tank-versus-tank engagements were fragmentary. In Italy the single understrength panzer corps which, on good defensive terrain, had held back five times its strength for nearly two years, was overwhelmed by a deluge of enemy armored forces and swept headlong into Austria until the day of surrender in April. Allied forces which first crossed the Rhine by a seized bridge at Remagen on 7 March got across on a much wider frontage, starting on 22 March, to advance much as they chose. Here and there lay an ambush by a few tanks or panzerjägers, but rarely anything like a local counter-attack to disturb the Allied plans. It is appropriate to compare the German AFV situation of 1945, in relation to their enemies, with that of 1918. Tank-versus-tank fights were only occasionally on a bigger scale than at Villers Breton-neux, even if the vehicles engaged were immensely more powerful. A resolved issue would be finally decided by Allied forces of all arms, backed by stupendous air power rolling ahead irresistibly. As defenders of Germany, AFVs merely injected a hindrance. Two examples demonstrate this.

The fight near Kustrin on 22 March occurred when a scratch panzer division of 27 Panthers and 28 Tigers (the last considerable tank force left to Germany) barred the Berlin Highway against a typical massed Russian tank and infantry attack. By excellent shooting from prepared positions, the Germans picked off their approaching opponents. The Russian infantry went to ground; their tank attack withered away, only to be renewed when a flanking column, well supported by artillery, seized a village which sheltered the German command post and reserve Tiger company. In confusion, the Germans withdrew under a smoke screen to reassemble just in time to face the Russians emerging from the village. Silhouetted by the smoke at close range, the Russians were massacred, leaving the field strewn with 60 disabled or burning T34s against a mere handful of lost German AFVs.

The fight for the last bridge at Vienna took place on 12 April when a Panther and five PzKw IVs of 2nd SS Panzer Division held a bridgehead on the south bank with the intention of gaining sufficient time for a defense of the north bank to be prepared. In command of a Panther tank was Leutnant Arno Giesen who had to his credit 97 tank kills – at Kursk, in Normandy, the Ardennes, and Hungary. Giesen's Panther was sent across the bridge at night to reinforce the garrison and also to carry in badly needed ammunition. The tank fight into which he plunged among burning buildings and rubble, had at the heart of its inspiration the commander of the Panther in place, Sergeant Barkman – who was seriously wounded a few minutes after Giesen arrived. Over the ensuing hours the fight was dominated by tanks as Russian JS2s and T34s charged the bridge along the wide river front park. But Russian infantry too played a deadly role in stealth; no fewer than four of the PzKw IVs were killed by infantry tank-hunting parties that night. Many T34s were knocked out next day at point-blank range whenever they tried to rush the bridge. They blocked all approaches with their scarred carcasses. At one point Giesen dismounted and, with panzerfausts, stalked Russian tanks which his Panther could not get at; by the end of the day he had added 14 kills to his score

and still was able, that night, to cover the retreat across the bridge before it was demolished. He was last to arrive in safety.

COUP DE GRÂCE IN THE FAR EAST

When the Russians attacked the Japanese on 8 August 1945, the army of $1\frac{1}{2}$ million men and 5500 tanks they unleashed into Manchuria was hardly likely to be held up for long by 1 million men with only 1155 obsolete tanks. Japanese tank development had been uninspired throughout the war and her production in 1944 was only 295. Furthermore, Japanese tactical handling of armored units was hopelessly out-of-date, largely from lack of practice against a sophisticated enemy on open ground. Tanks were deployed in penny packets against the strong British tank forces in Burma and against American landings on Pacific islands. The 2nd Tank Division used against the Americans on Luzon in 1944 was split up and never used concentrated – a fate reserved also for the so-called Tank Army in Manchuria with its three tank divisions. Even so, against Japanese tanks armed mainly with small 47 mm and 57 mm guns, and protected by nothing thicker than 50 mm armor, there was little competition for T34/85s or obsolete T34/76s.

The Russian invasion of Manchuria was executed with all the practice acquired in four terrible years against the Germans and was regarded as a model of mobility by Russian commentators: '*T*HE AVERAGE daily rate of advance (of Sixth Tank Army) was 80 km, and on some days of the operation it reached 160 km. This was in spite of the difficulty of operating in mountain-desert terrain on the Bolshoi Khingan. The Soviet troops skilfully created high densities of men and weapons on axes of main attacks, especially when breaking through fortified regions.'

In these circumstances, Japanese tanks were destroyed fighting or were simply by-passed and left to rot. By 23 it was virtually all over, the Japanese government having put out peace feelers on the 10th in the wake of an event that left the Russian invasion of Manchuria in the shade. For on 6 and 9 August the Americans had exploded atomic bombs over the Japanese cities of Hiroshima and Nagasaki and introduced to the world a weapon that would revolutionize not only politics and warfare, but also, almost as an incidental, significantly change the nature of AFVs in future settings.

CHAPTER EIGHT

NEW TANK POWERS AND TECHNOLOGY

IN THE AFTERMATH OF WORLD WAR II A VAST TANK-scrapping program was begun by all the victorious belligerents, with the exception of the Soviet Union which continued to build tanks in large numbers as well as retaining the thousands it already possessed. Quite apart from the political significance of these trends, with their underlying atmosphere of suspicion between previous allies and the fear of renewed warfare, a new strategic and tactical threat was created. While there were those who thought the tank was outmoded by the latest infantry chemical energy, hollow-charge weapons, there was visible evidence of a mighty tank host pointing not only at Western Europe but also at other parts of the world. For the Soviets were exporting obsolete but still useful T34/85s and heavy tanks to so-called non-committed nations as well as to their allies. Inevitably the military balance was disturbed. Within a few years of the war's end, the Western non-Communist nations sensed the need to rearm and rebuild tank fleets capable of resisting a massed tank attack from the east. In this period were born many new tank forces of considerable power – throughout the communist countries China, North Korea, Eastern Europe and in newly created nations such as Israel, Egypt, Syria, India and Pakistan.

The Communist army of Mao Tse-tung, which completed the overrunning of China in 1949, was mainly an infantry force with a few AFVs captured from the Japanese, and American tanks supplied to their Nationalist enemies. Not until North Korea, with Chinese and Russian support, invaded South Korea in June 1950 did serious tank-versus-tank combat erupt in the Far East. North Korea had about 240 T34/76s and T34/85s, and the South was soon reinforced by US AFVs, of which the M24 Chaffee light tank with its 75 mm gun was first into action. The North Koreans used tanks mainly in the infantry-support role, the T34s having it much their own way (except in pointblank engagements against the Chaffee) until they began to come up against M26 Pershing and the latest M46 and M47 Patton tanks.

The North Korean invasion followed a classic pattern of gradual debilitation and deceleration once it advanced beyond its logistic base and ran headlong into stiffening resistance. In the tank-versus-tank encounters, which occurred principally on roadsides running between paddy and steep hills and mountains, the advantage eventually lay with the better armed and armored American tanks. But air attack with napalm on North Korean AFVs and their supply vehicles weakened the invaders far more, and eventually brought them to a standstill facing a bridgehead covering the vital port of Pusan. After that it was a matter of time as the Americans built up their assault forces to the point at which they could land from the sea in their enemy's rear and overrun the force which stood immobilized before Pusan. Within a matter of a few days the North Korean tank force was wiped out. Although the war would continue for nearly three more years, the North Koreans, joined by the Chinese Army, would never again commit tanks to direct combat.

Pershing in the assault with infantry across difficult Korean hills and paddy fields.

THE NEW GUN/ARMOR RACE

When the Western allies assessed what they took to be the Societ tank threat in Europe, they were conditioned, among other factors, by concern that the latest extremely well protected JS3 tank would be impenetrable by the 90 mm and 83.4 mm guns then entering service. Also, they feared they would be seriously outnumbered by a host of T34s and their successors. In response to the JS3 threat, both the Americans and the British designed heavy tanks – respectively the 55-ton M103 and the 65-ton Conqueror – armed with a 120 mm gun and protected by sloped armor of between 178 and 200 mm. At the same time they initiated a series of research projects aimed at further raising the penetrative power of anti-armor weapons and radically improving rates of fire as well as accuracy.

The introduction of very large, high-velocity guns posed tank designers with many problems, principally those of how to keep vehicle cost, size and weight within practical bounds. Similar problems also affected the design of simple anti-tank guns, of course: they too became far too big and unwieldy. Determined efforts were made to invent weapons which could achieve the same effect as the high-velocity gun without paying the same penalties. Various types of recoilless guns, firing chemical energy warheads, were tried but these had disadvantages of their own, notably in terms of range and accuracy. Most revolutionary of all was the guided rocket missile which could be launched from a light vehicle or from the ground and flown to its target by a controller (thus eliminating the ranging problem) and which, because its chemical energy warhead did not rely on high velocity for its effect, could be effective at any range. Originating from a 1944 German project for an air-to-air missile called X7, a number of Anti-tank Guided Weapon (ATGW) designs featured control by electrical signals through a very thin wire paid out in flight from inside the missile. Versions of anti-tank weapons developed in the 1950s and 1960s were to pose a serious threat at up to 4000 m range to AFVs, not only from ground launchers but also from helicopters.

The balance of arguments in favor of the high-velocity gun remained, nevertheless, overwhelming. It was upon this weapon that the Western allies, with the British to the fore, chiefly concentrated their attention. Longer gun barrels, increased velocity of improved shot, (the most promising of which was the fin-stabilized kind with discarding sabot APFSDS) all contributed to retention of a situation in which the gun, at acceptable battle ranges, could penetrate any practical protection an enemy could adopt. But that effort was wasted if crews were unable to hit the target with a high degree of certainty – and a figure of 90 per cent coupled with a rate of fire of 10 shots a minute was deemed necessary to offset the peril posed by enemy massed tank attacks at high closing speed, supported by additional tanks at a distance.

The problem of ranging through the obscuration generated by the gun's discharge had to be solved by a simple drill. Optical

ARMOR PENETRATING PROJECTILES AND THEIR EFFECTS

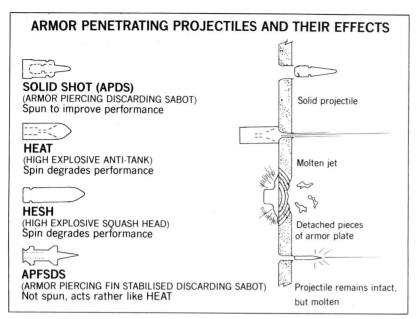

SOLID SHOT (APDS)
(ARMOR PIERCING DISCARDING SABOT)
Spun to improve performance

HEAT
(HIGH EXPLOSIVE ANTI-TANK)
Spin degrades performance

HESH
(HIGH EXPLOSIVE SQUASH HEAD)
Spin degrades performance

APFSDS
(ARMOR PIERCING FIN STABILISED DISCARDING SABOT)
Not spun, acts rather like HEAT

Solid projectile

Molten jet

Detached pieces
of armor plate

Projectile remains intact,
but molten

range-finders tended to be difficult to use, unreliable, and insufficiently accurate to provide hits on small targets. To begin with, the British devised a method in which the gunner fired three successive shots at targets within 1000 m range – the first with his telescope aiming mark at 800 m, the second at 1000 m and the third at 600 m. Thus a hit was virtually assured providing the ammunition was reliable and the gun accurately zeroed to the sight. Beyond 1000 m a high-explosive round was fired, to establish the range, followed by the standard three-round engagement. This was expensive in ammunition, of which few tanks carried more than 60 rounds. It was also fallible since ammunition was usually of variable performance, sighting gear often defective, and zeroing disturbed by any one of several factors, of which the prime culprit was 'barrel bend' The effects of rain or a cold cross-wind on a hot barrel could cause it to drift off zero by 5' of arc within two hours – quite sufficient to cause a miss at 1000 m.

Throughout the 1950s and the 1960s the struggle to enhance shooting standards by the improvement of ammunition quality; by the improvement of sighting and ranging equipment allied to easily practiced drills; and by the careful preparation of armament became central to the solution of the anti-tank problem. To reduce ammunition wastage and to improve ranging, the British introduced in the mid-1950s the idea of a sub-caliber 'ranging' gun which fired tracer ammunition at the target to establish the range before firing the main armament. This was done by mounting the US .5 inch machine-gun coaxially with the 105 mm main armament of the later Centurion tanks. This system, in which the ranging gun fired bursts of three special tracer rounds at the target, produced the 90 per cent first-round-hit chance required and far outclassed any other hand-cranked or automatic optical system yet devised. The Americans, nevertheless, did not adopt it. For the problem of barrel bend remained unsolved and in the early 1960s the introduction of the laser, with its potential as a range-finder, gave promise of a far better method of ranging which could be allied to still more sophisticated methods of fire control.

Also associated with gunnery was the problem of moving and shooting by night. During World War II, when tank fighting by night was rare but movement by the light of searchlights and moonlight common, attempts had been made to fit night vision equipment to AFVs. The British had experimented extensively with (but hardly used) a 13-million-candle-power arc lamp fitted to Matilda and Grant tanks to illuminate the battlefield, to assist in the acquisition and engagement of targets, and to blind the enemy by use of a flicker device: this was called for security cover, Canal Defense Light (CDL). The Germans, well advanced with research into invisible infrared light beams, had exploited their knowledge to build tank searchlights which enabled the crew to see in the dark without disclosure to the naked eye. But infrared light, being 'actively' projected, is detectable; so the advantage of being invisible was good only so long as the enemy lacked suitable viewing instruments. After the war it was the Russians who seized most eagerly on the infrared equipment which fell into their hands. By the mid 1950s the West suddenly became aware that the latest Russian T54 and T55 tanks were fitted with infrared equipment which enabled the crew to drive and shoot in the dark. It was naturally only a matter of time before the United States, France and Britain also began fitting infrared lights and detectors to their own tanks to counter this latest threat.

THE TANK IN THE ATOMIC ENVIRONMENT

In the immediate post-war era it was the Soviet Union, the United States and Britain, closely followed by France, who put the most effort into producing a new generation of

POST-WAR RUSSIAN REVOLUTIONS

JS3

JS3 INDICATED AN-
other step forward by
the Russians in developing
the KV and JS breed of
heavy tank. When first it
came to notice in 1945 it
created a great stir with its
dome-shaped turret and
divided glacis plate.
Setting aside that, there
had to be a high degree of

crew discomfort in such a
cramped AFV, although it
was reasoned that it must
be largely proof against
existing anti-tank guns. In
fact, JS3 turned out to
have certain fundamental
weaknesses of which a
piece of sheet armor fixed
on the top front of the
turret was the most
obvious.

Weight 46 tons
Speed 25 mph
Frontal armor 200 mm (sloped)
Armament 1×122 mm, 2×mg

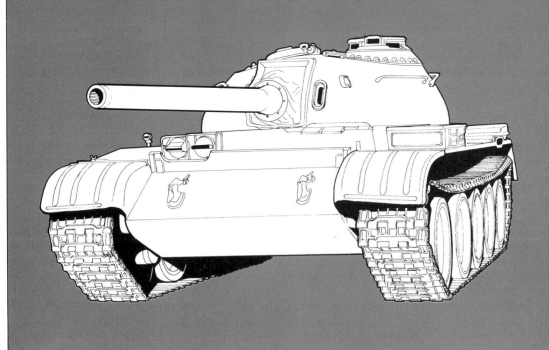

T54

THE DESIGN OF THE
T54 illustrated once
more the pragmatic
Russian policy of founding
each new tank on pre-
viously successful Marks.
The Christie suspension
was retained in this suc-
cessor to T34; a more
powerful engine (520 hp)
installed; and a dome-
shaped turret with the
good 100 mm gun adopted
as the Russians pursued
their intention of raising
gun power and protection
while reducing silhouette.
Of note was the fitting to
later Marks of a gun stabil-
izer, to match earlier US
and British models. In due
course, there would
appear the even more
sophisticated T55 which
incorporated a 35 cm
searchlight, with infra-red
capability to enable it to
fire by night in clear conditions at 1000 m range.

Weight 36 tons
Speed 31 mph
Frontal armor 75 mm (sloped)
Armament 1×100 mm, 2×mg

tanks. The Russians followed a policy of phased development of existing models, putting into service the heavy JS3 and, in due course, its even heavier successor, the T10 – both armed with the 122 mm gun – and the latest derivations from the Christie-based T34/85, the T54 and T55, with much-improved turret, 170 mm armor and 100 mm gun. In similar vein, the Americans continued to develop the M26 Pershing with successive marks of Patton tanks – the M47, M48 and M60 all armed with the 90 mm gun. Unfortunately for them the experimental T95 project (with a gas turbine engine, variable level suspension and smooth-bore 90 mm gun) was a complete failure, forcing them later to adopt the British 105 mm gun as an essential replacement to the outmoded 90 mm gun. The British also failed with a radical project. The FV 200 series, upon whose hull various kinds of AFV were to be based, proved unsuitable in all sorts of ways. This left the way open to develop the Centurion which, in the years to come, would be fitted with thicker armor, night-fighting devices, and ranging gun, and would be successively up-gunned from 76.2 mm to 83.4 mm to 105 mm. Centurion, despite a certain early automotive unreliability, was to prove a fine battle tank as we shall see. But it was the 105 mm gun, fitted to the same breech ring as the 83.4 mm, which proved a superb dual-purpose weapon of immense accuracy and was adopted by the vast majority of the world's tank forces, outside the Soviet bloc.

The advent of these new tanks, along with many other kinds, restated a belief in the future of AFVs, and not only as a means of offensive and/or anti-tank action. For AFVs offered one way of achieving protection against the fire, blast and radiation effects of nuclear weapons which, in the 1950s, were sufficiently miniaturized for tactical use on the battlefield. Armor would resist to a significant extent the nuclear physical effects; mobility would help land forces to avoid nuclear strikes or pass rapidly through irradiated or devastated areas. The tank's future was assured.

THE ARAB-ISRAELI CONFLICT

From very small beginnings – a solitary Sherman, two Cromwells and 12 Hotchkiss H35 light tanks, plus several locally armored lorries and cars – emerged the most significant tank force of the post-1945 era. When the newborn state of Israel found itself at once in conflict with neighboring Arab

M48 A2

M48 A2 WAS THE FOURTH US TANK DEsign in line of succession to the Pershing, which had seen the US Army through to the end of WW2, and played a part in the Korean War. Pershing had been followed by M46, M47, and M48 (known as Patton I, II and III). None of these were really satisfactory, even though they successively introduced into service such improvements as better semi-automatic transmission systems, joy stick steering controls, stronger hulls, better designed turrets, and stereoscopic range finders of dubious accuracy.

Designed in 1951, M48 A2 was a considerable advance on its predecessors with its 850 hp fuel injection engine with slightly modified hull and turret. Yet it retained the inadequate 90 mm gun, due to American fascination with a projected smooth bore weapon which unfortunately failed (expensively) to come up to specification.

Weight 46 tons
Speed 32 mph
Frontal armor 178 mm (sloped)
Armament 1×90 mm, 2×mg

Engine/transmission

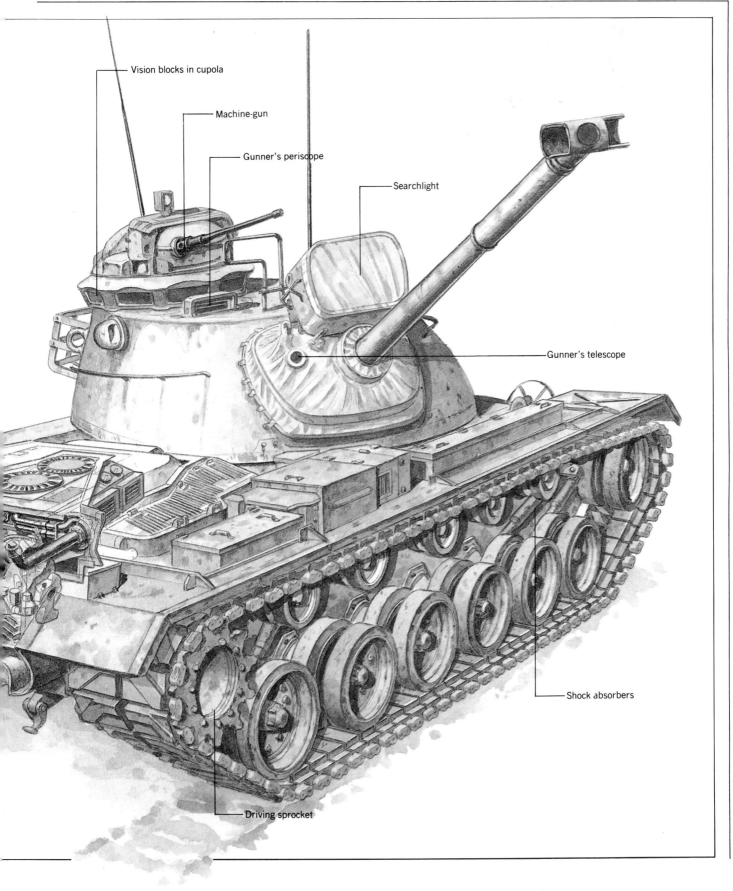

Vision blocks in cupola

Machine-gun

Gunner's periscope

Searchlight

Gunner's telescope

Shock absorbers

Driving sprocket

states in 1948, it depended largely for survival upon infantry backed up by whatever heavy weapons could be begged, stolen or captured. As a result, its tank tactical doctrine was virtually non-existent and its initial escapades under fire were dominated by the wish to support the infantry and dogged by mishandling and breakdowns. There were few encounters with Arab tanks and no recorded tank-versus-tank fights, only encounters between Israeli and Jordanian armored cars and one occasion when a Comet of the withdrawing British mandated power knocked out a threatening Israeli armored truck.

The growth of the Israeli armored forces, as of their armed forces as a whole, was stunted to begin with by the difficulty, due to economic and political restrictions, of purchasing the necessary equipment. Until the supply of imported arms began, from France in 1955, from Britain in 1959 and from the United States in 1965, the Israelis had to make do with whatever they were given – which in terms of tanks meant, for the most part, Shermans of various marks and armament. Israel was guided also by the infantry-biased outlook of most senior officers who resisted the inculcation of tank doctrine even though it was appropriate in large tracts of terrain where the army was likely to be engaged. Two or three realistic exercises and the war of 1956 were needed to swing the pendulum of opinion the way of the tank enthusiasts who were clamoring for priority in the allocation of personnel and material. The decision in their favor eventually came from Prime Minister David Ben-Gurion.

When the Egyptian Army's miscellany of Shermans and various ex-British AFVs were reinforced in 1955 by some 230 T34/85s and 100 SU 100s from Czechoslovakia, the Israelis negotiated the purchase from France of 100 more Shermans and about 100 AMX13 light tanks armed with the German 75 mm L70 gun. Thus when Israel attacked Egypt on 29 October 1956 the tanks ranged against each other were almost entirely of World War II vintage – inferior to the latest Centurion tanks landed by the British from the sea at Port Said on 6 November.

It took the Israelis two days to defeat the Egyptian army at Kusseima on the frontier of Sinai and advance 100 miles to the strategic Mitla Pass, cutting the enemy lines of communication. The fighting at Kusseima was fierce and dictated by the thrusts of Colonel Ben Aris's 7th Infantry Brigade to open up a gap in World War I style. Furious tank-versus-tank fighting broke out, the Israelis minimising their losses by avoiding head-on assaults against a dug-in enemy; preferring instead to reconnoiter ways round to enable their armored task forces to reach the enemy rear, at Abu Ageila, behind the Egyptian frontier positions. It was then only a short time before the Israelis mopped up a defeated enemy and advanced to the relief of the parachutists who had been dropped at the Mitla Pass. It also loosened up the entire Egyptian defense of the Sinai, compelling a wholesale withdrawal to the Suez Canal and by 5 November, the overrunning of the entire Sinai Peninsula before the ponderous Anglo-French landing at Port Said took place.

The Egyptian tank reaction to the Israeli thrusts was tentative. Since the majority of their tanks were allocated to infantry formations and units, and often dug-in themselves, mobility was at a premium. Frequently they were destroyed where they stood. More often than not those which were compelled, by the desperation of the situation, to move into the open were picked off by Israeli tanks, guns and aircraft who maneuvered fluently. Once the general withdrawal began along the coastal road from El Arish to El Qantara, supply trucks and tanks became easy prey. As coordinated measures broke down, rout ensued. Moreover, the Egyptian armored brigade ordered forward to retake the Mitla Pass did not even put in an appearance. Israeli tank losses were few and mostly recoverable; their total number of dead in the entire campaign was only 150. They captured some 55 Egyptian field guns, 110 anti-tank guns, 125 tanks and 60 armored troop carriers – along with 260 hopelessly obsolete ex-British Bren gun carriers.

The after-effects of the 1956 campaign were, for the Israeli armored corps, revolutionary. In 1959 they bought from Britain Centurion tanks with 105 mm guns and in November 1960 used them to engage two old German PzKw IVs which were dug in to support operations by Syrian patrols at Nukheila. Opening fire at about 1500 m, the Israelis shot off 89 rounds in $1\frac{1}{2}$ hours, to raise clouds of dust and smoke but without hitting either PzKw IV, which shot back with equal ineffectiveness. Henceforward, the Israelis under General Israel Tal concentrated upon tightening up discipline, above all gunnery discipline and techniques. With methods similar to those already worked out by the British, the Israeli Centurions began knocking out PzKw IVs and T34/85s at ranges up to 3000 m without themselves suffering much harm. By May 1967 this standard of shooting had been drummed into most Centurion units as well as the units which, in 1965, had begun to equip with American M48s, armed with the 90 mm gun.

THE SIX-DAY WAR
The stage was set for the first major engagement between modern Soviet-built tanks and their British and US rivals when, in May 1967, the Egyptians started pouring troops into Sinai and the Syrians and Jordanians indicated that they too were preparing for hostilities. The Egyptian tank strength had been raised to about 1000, including 60 JS3s, 450 T54s and T55s and 30 Centurions. The Jordanians could field about 50 Centurions and 150 lightly armored Charioteer tanks, both armed with the 83.4 mm gun. Against this combined force, supplemented by some 400 Syrian tanks (including 150 T54s), the Israelis had approximately 1000 tanks, about one-third of them Centurions, one-third M48s, and the remainder an assortment of Shermans and AMX13s. The balance of numbers was not therefore outrageously in the Arab favor, while the quality of the Israeli AFVs went a long way towards correcting any disparity.

The Israelis, taking the Arab build-up as a threat to their very survival, began the war with a surprise pre-emptive strike which virtually eliminated their opponents' air forces on the first day. Their Army struck hard at the Egyptian Army in the defensive positions it had occupied along the frontier from the Gaza strip to Kusseima. The Egyptians deployed to the current Soviet doctrine, as dictated by their advisers. In the forward areas were fortified infantry redoubts with JS3 tanks in place, heavily supported by artillery; in rear the mobile forces, with the T54 and T55 tanks, were held ready either to pounce on an enemy breakthrough or to exploit an invasion of Israel when it was launched.

It was the Israeli intention to stand on the defensive against Jordan and Syria while, on 5 June, delivering a knock-out blow against Egypt with a three-pronged thrust. On the left, Major General Ari Sharon's division aimed at Kusseima and at Abu Ageila; in the center Avraham Yoffe's division made for Bir Kahfan from whence it could cooperate either with Sharon on the left or with Tal's division on the right, as the latter advanced along the coast road to El Arish. Each division made excellent progress and indirectly supported the other. But it is upon Tal's that our attention is concentrated.

BATTLE FOR THE EL JIRADI PASS
The town of Rafah was Tal's first objective, and was captured on the first morning after a ferocious tank battle by a flanking movement involving infantry and armored units. Simultaneously he struck towards El Arish with an advanced guard of 17 Centurions and two M48s belonging to Colonel Shmuel Gonen's 7th Armored Brigade. Keeping to the road (and thus avoiding minefields on either side), it burst through the strongly fortified El Jiradi position by surprise, bypassing a mass of temporarily demoralized Egyptians of their 7th Division. Quickly, however, the Egyptians recovered and reoccupied the concrete emplacements of the Jiradi with infantry, artillery and JS3 tanks which the Israelis had not bothered to destroy. Thus the road to El Arish was blocked and the Israeli tanks, which were already short of fuel and ammunition, were threatened with annihilation if they could not quickly be resupplied and reinforced. Tal concentrated what little armor was immediately available upon the capture of the El Jiradi position. Originally a combined assault by two armored brigades had been intended but now only one, the 7th, already reduced in strength by losses, was to hand. Tal felt he could not wait to execute the more desirable combined night assault. He told Gonen to attack at once. Yet if Sergeant Shuval, the commander of a reconnaissance patrol consisting of a jeep and an armored half-track, had not managed to stop Gonen before the colonel came within full view of the pass in his jeep, somebody else would have had to take charge of the battle.

As it was, Shuval had been lucky to survive when his patrol was knocked out by the defenders of the pass, and luckier still to run back unscathed in time to warn Gonen before he too was ambushed. In the light of Shuval's report and his own rapid examination of the ground, Gonen asked Tal to stick to the original two-brigade plan for overcoming the pass. But with knowledge of the desperate situation of the armored force cut off at El Arish, Tal repeated orders for Gonen to attack at once with a single battalion of M48s, realising that this meant a virtually unsupported effort with sub-units thrown in piecemeal as they arrived post-haste from the fighting at Rafah.

CUT AND THRUST AT THE JIRADI PASS

The Israeli assault on the Jiradi Pass took the strong Egyptian defense by surprise, although after the initial penetration, the Egyptians recovered. Their resistance left the patrol of Sgt Shuval wrecked at the roadside. Nearby are knocked-out M48s of Major Ehud Elad's armored battalion. They had attempted to move off the road, and found the ground free of mines but in deep sand. M48s to the right were crippled by mines, to the left, others were wrecked by gunfire from JS3 tanks and anti-tank guns.

Elad took control in person, and felt compelled to achieve his objective by means of a partially concealed approach farther left among dunes. The panorama shows Elad's M48s fanning out and already under fire. Unwilling to tarry in so exposed a position, and without waiting to organize full supporting fire, Elad choses to lead a suicidal charge. He unhesitatingly crosses the crest onto the forward slope where, a moment later, a shot kills him.

His Operations Officer, Lt Amiran Mizna, at once ordered the tank to reverse and called off the attack. Failing to raise by radio Major Haim, the second-in-command who was fighting a battle of his own down by the road, he had to drive there to report direct to Gonen. He met Gonen at the roadside, as Gonen started to improvize a better coordinated attack.

The state of the battalion was parlous. Several M48s were knocked out, and the rest damaged. Only Lieutenant Ein-Gil's third company was available for a second attack, supported by heavy mortar fire and the guns of every tank from the rest of the battalion which could be brought to bear. He steered clear of the sand and mines by driving flat out at 25 mph along the mine-free road, into the teeth of enemy fire, with his own guns blazing in every direction. He reached the pass almost unharmed, the shaken Egyptian gunners missing such fast-moving targets or deserting their guns which fell silent. Once through, but badly strung out, Haim took charge, ordering Ein-Gil to shoot up the outflanked JS3s on the backward slope. The gunners of the JS3s, with slow-traversing turrets, had been unable to track the speeding M48s; now their vehicles began to erupt under close range fire which ripped through their thinner side armor.   (cont.)

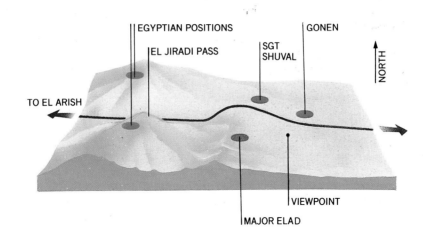

TO EL ARISH

EGYPTIAN POSITIONS

EL JIRADI PASS

SGT SHUVAL

GONEN

NORTH

VIEWPOINT

MAJOR ELAD

CUT AND THRUST AT THE JIRADI PASS (continued)

The defenders of the pass might well have been wiped out at once if Gonen had not intervened to order Haim to press on to the relief of the Centurions in El Arish. Reach El Arish they did, but the pass remained untaken in their rear and this might have spelled their doom had not a fourth assault by infantry that night, followed by a grim four-hour battle, determined the final collapse of the Egyptian garrison.

Dashing though the Israelis were in attack, and staunch as the Egyptians were in defense, it cannot be said that either side could claim much credit for their conduct of this wild episode. It is hard to condone two Israeli omissions to complete the elimination of an enemy daringly taken in flank and rear by penetration of a palpably strong position. Similarly inexcusable were the failures of the Egyptians to block the road with mines after its initial use by the enemy, and to have a counter-attack force clean-up the Centurions at El Arish and reinforce the Pass. But due credit should be given to the Israelis for, despite a certain rashness, always trying hard to benefit in full from their tanks' fire power, protection and mobility – in a way the Egyptians rarely managed in defeat.

THE SIX DAY WAR
JUNE 1967

MEDITERRANEAN SEA

ISRAEL

ONE INF BDE (RESERVE)

GAZA
KHAN YUNIS
RAFAH
TAL
BEERSHEBA
EL JIRADI PASS
BIR LAHFAN
TAL
PORT SAID
SUEZ CANAL
ROMANI
EL QANTARA
ABU AGEILA
YOFFE
ISMAILIYA
AM 8 JUNE TAL AND YOFFE REACH SUEZ CANAL
JEBEL LIBNI
EL QUSEIMA
SHARON
ONE INF BDE (RESERVE)
SOUTHERN COMMAND
GREAT BITTER LAKE
BIR GIFGAFA
BIR HASANA
GIDDI PASS
SUEZ
MITLA PASS
BIR EL THAMADA
NAKHL
EL KUNTILLA
JORDAN
EGYPT
THAMAD
RAS EN NAQB
AQABA
SUDR
EILAT
GULF OF SUEZ

KEY
ISRAELI ATTACKS 5/6 JUNE ➡
ISRAELI ATTACKS 7/8 JUNE ⇨

MILES 0 20 30 40
KM 0 20 40

ISRAEL TAL

ISRAEL TAL WAS BORN in 1924. He joined the British Army in 1941, became a small-arms instructor and fought as a NCO in the Jewish Brigade in Italy. A graduate in philosophy, he joined the Israeli Defense Force and took part in the struggles for his nation's independence and survival. As a permanent member of the Army he earned a reputation for strict discipline, as an expert with machine-guns and explosives, a technologist with the invention of the anti-mole gun to his credit, and for an emphatic enthusiasm for the tank and high-velocity gun as dominant weapons in Israel's defense. His studies of past campaigns convinced him that Guderian's

methods were the models to copy. Experience of the tank battles of 1956 and the subsequent frontier skirmishes showed that the tank was wasted unless gunnery techniques and discipline were tightened up considerably. As commander of the Armored Corps in 1964, he drummed home the vital importance of stricter gunnery procedures with the Centurion tanks and the M48s, with whose procurement he was involved in 1965. In one of the frontier gunnery duels he acted as a gunner, with commendable precision, and had several hits to his credit.

Tal's great moment came on 5 June 1967. As commander of the division which made the series of breakthroughs along the coast road

between Gaza and El Arish, he led to complete victory the force he had trained and equipped, demonstrating the effectiveness of the high standards of vehicle maintenance and gunnery he had instilled into a mainly

part-time force. Subsequently he decried the ATGW as a serious threat and opposed the building of a line of fortifications along the Suez Canal; the gun, he said, would always do better than the missile and static defenses were a prescription for disaster. Though he was proved correct, his arrogant rejection of the missile and absolute faith in the tank did lead to the initial Israeli setbacks along the Canal in the war of 1973.

After the Yom Kippur War, in which Tal was Deputy Chief of Staff, he became adviser to Israel's Minister of Defense on development and organization, and played a leading role in the design and development of Israel's first home-built and original tank, the Merkava.

THE ISRAELIS RUN RIOT

Events had moved so fast and disastrously for the Egyptians that they were unable to intervene with their armored battle groups in time to save the frontier forces. Instead on 6 June, and on the days to come their tanks were either caught on the move trying to mount a counter-attack, or were relentlessly harried as they tried to escape. Across the entire battle front the divisions of Sharon, Yoffe and Tal hunted the vital Egyptian tank force. Brilliant was the action at Bir Lahfan where Tal's tanks, heavily supported by artillery, assaulted a fortified enemy zone and picked off tanks and guns with deadly shooting, driving the survivors onto a line of Yoffe's tanks to the southward. Shabtain Teveth describes how '*T*HE COMPANIES advanced unhurriedly, one section after another, the gunners taking good advantage of the leisure given them and aiming with care and precision'.

This was the pay-off for the hours of training with simplified gunnery drills, allied to the tank crews' confidence in their machines and weapons.

The Israelis were now running riot among the enemy's forward administrative areas and in process of wrecking his logistic system. Yoffe and Sharon headed for the Mitla Pass and found astonishing evidence of a complete collapse of enemy morale. Egyptian supply echelons were being put to the torch by air attacks. The command and control system was breaking down. In the approaches to the pass on the night of 6 June, a company of Israeli tanks became entangled in the dark with a battalion of Egyptian tanks, without the latter realising it. The Israelis did know and kept moving with the convoy until their leader gave orders to swing to a flank, switch on their searchlights, and rake their erstwhile companions with a hail of close-range fire. The entire Egyptian unit was destroyed. Of course, the Israelis too had their logistic probems and their supply echelons rarely were reliable. Several fuelless tanks had to be towed into firing positions at the Mitla Pass, and many a machine kept mobile with fuel tapped from abandoned enemy vehicles. The scale of abandonment was quite astonishing. Near Nakhle, Sharon's division discovered the Egyptian 125th Armored Brigade in perfect order at the road side, their crews escaping on foot without trying to destroy their machines – because they had not received orders to do so, their captured commander explained. A few hours later, Sharon caught up with the remainder of the 6th Division, to which this brigade belonged, and accounted for a further 60 tanks, 100 guns and 300 vehicles.

Here and there Egyptians did fight well but the rot spread too deep to save their army in the Sinai. As the Israelis reached the Canal on the 8th, and fanned out along its banks, the spoils of one of the greatest tank victories of all time were garnered. About 800 Egyptian tanks, hundreds of guns and more than 10 000 vehicles, amounting to 80 per cent of the Egyptian Army, had been captured at a cost of 1300 Israeli casualties (only 300 of them dead). Estimates of Egyptian manpower losses vary between 10 000 and 15 000.

On a slightly smaller, yet no less decisive, scale the Jordanian Army also was ruined. While attention was fixed on the dour infantry-predominant fighting for Jerusalem, the main clash of armor occured in Samaria where two brigades of Israeli Super Shermans fought an almost equal force of Centurions and Charioteers on 5 June. Here the Israelis met their match, the Jordanians at first maneuvering to encircle the invading Shermans and meeting each Israeli charge with unyielding determination in the vicinity of Jenin and Kabatiya. But relentless Israeli tank infiltration and untrammelled use of their air power gradually undermined the Jordanian positions, the Shermans' 105 mm guns proving perfectly adequate to knock out even the Centurion at ranges rarely longer than 1000 m. But it was an Israeli break-through to the route center of Nablus, cutting across the Jordanians' rear and leading to the seizure of all the bridges across the River Jordan, which brought a swift and complete victory on the 6th. Jordanian collapse on the 7th, with the loss of nearly all their tanks, was inevitable.

The fall of Jerusalem on the 7th and the withdrawal of the surviving Jordanian units, gave Israel a free hand on 9 June to assail the Golan Heights, where since the outbreak of hostilities on the 5th the Syrians had been remarkably cautious. Confronted by large numbers of enemy holding fortified high ground, the Israelis depended upon well-balanced infantry and armored units to do the job. In the Cambrai manner, holes were punched in the forward Syrian defended areas and armor pushed through. The sheer pace, across difficult ground, of this exploitation (enhanced by helicopter-carried

CENTURION 3

THE CENTURION MARK 1 APPEARED just too late to take part in WW2, but at last put British tank design back on the map. A distinct breakaway from previous designs, this AFV, with its sloped glacis plate and vastly improved turret shape, had the advantage of being capable of extensive improvement.

Basic principles of gun stabilization

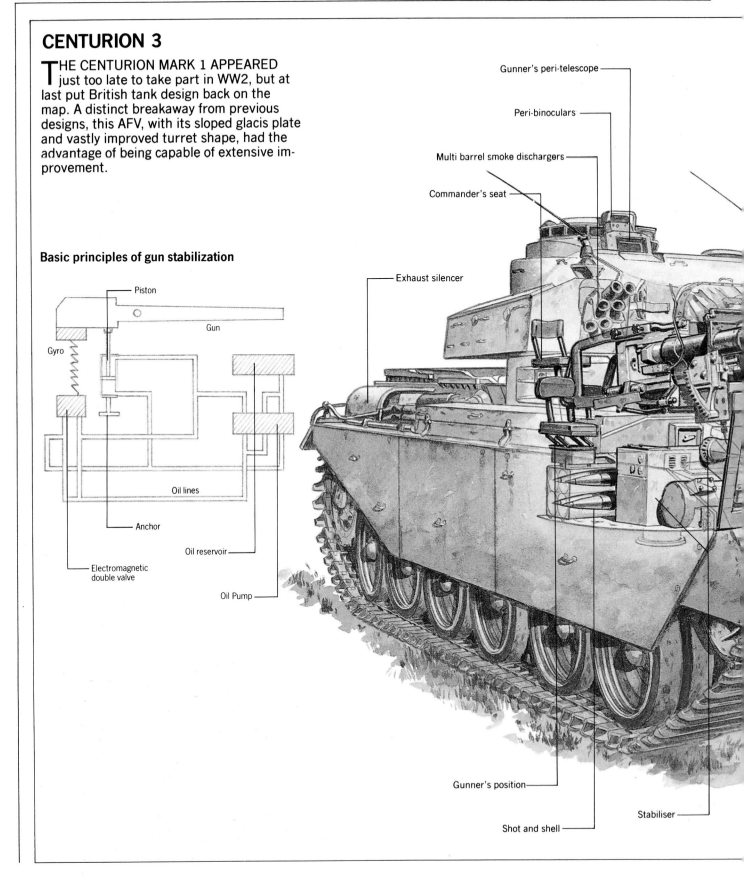

Piston

Gun

Gyro

Oil lines

Anchor

Oil reservoir

Electromagnetic double valve

Oil Pump

Gunner's peri-telescope

Peri-binoculars

Multi barrel smoke dischargers

Commander's seat

Exhaust silencer

Gunner's position

Shot and shell

Stabiliser

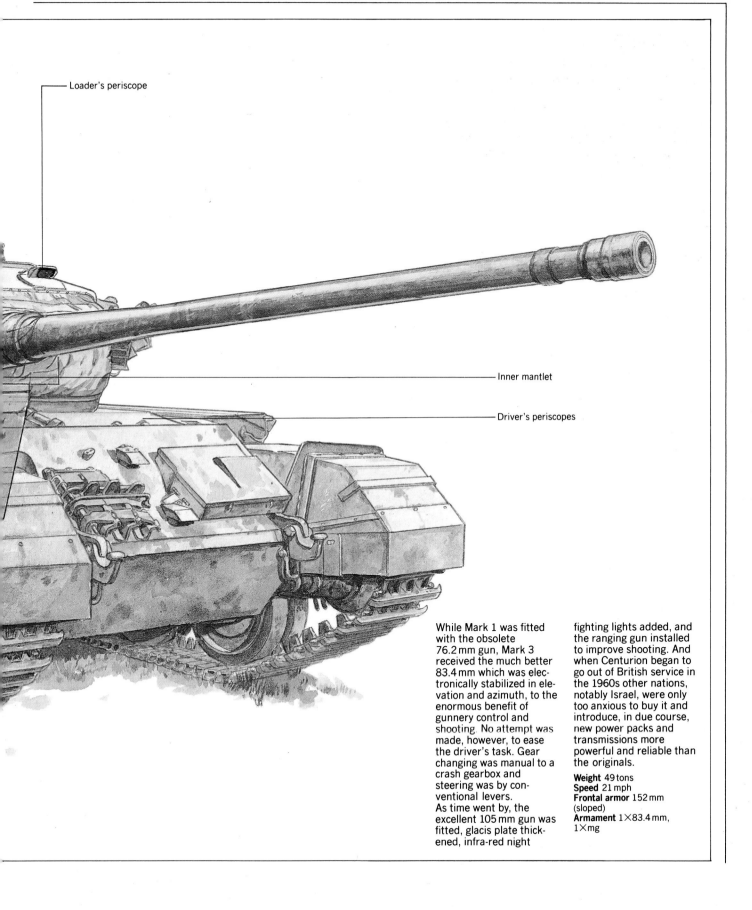

Loader's periscope

Inner mantlet

Driver's periscopes

While Mark 1 was fitted with the obsolete 76.2 mm gun, Mark 3 received the much better 83.4 mm which was electronically stabilized in elevation and azimuth, to the enormous benefit of gunnery control and shooting. No attempt was made, however, to ease the driver's task. Gear changing was manual to a crash gearbox and steering was by conventional levers.
As time went by, the excellent 105 mm gun was fitted, glacis plate thickened, infra-red night fighting lights added, and the ranging gun installed to improve shooting. And when Centurion began to go out of British service in the 1960s other nations, notably Israel, were only too anxious to buy it and introduce, in due course, new power packs and transmissions more powerful and reliable than the originals.

Weight 49 tons
Speed 21 mph
Frontal armor 152 mm (sloped)
Armament 1×83.4 mm, 1×mg

infantry) unbalanced the Syrian will. Their infantry bolted, their tank crews abandoned AFVs in place, and their armored reserve mainly sought safety in withdrawal from the Heights. Such tank-versus-tank fighting as took place was entirely in the more experienced and better trained Israelis' favor.

INDIA VERSUS PAKISTAN
The tank fighting which flared up in the Punjab in 1965 between the M47s of Pakistan and the Centurions and AMX13s of India was of fascinating interest to the West since it pitted US-made tanks against those built in Britain and France. Moreover, it took place on ground over which both sides attempted deep penetrations and maneuver. Yet what transpired was a series of rather costly head-on-encounters in which the Indians, with their simpler gunnery drills and 83.4 mm guns, got the better of the Pakistanis whose hand-cranked ballistic computers were far too slow.

If nothing else, this small but costly frontier war indicated that, contrary to theories held by some in the Indian Army, the well-armored tank retained its importance and

authority as an anti-tank weapon system. For the AMX 13 with its 40 mm armor was hopelessly vulnerable and the M47, with only 110 mm armor, was in trouble against the Centurion with 152 mm armor.

EXOTIC FIRE-CONTROL SYSTEMS
In 1960 the impact of the latest advances in technology, particularly in electronics, began to have a profound effect upon AFV design. The introduction of the transistor in the 1950s and the subsequent development of the microprocessor not only made possible far more reliable and easier-to-operate communications sets, but also made feasible in the 1960s electronic passive night vision image-intensifiers (which enabled crews to see in the dark by use of ambient light without the need for an active light source) and miniature computers all of which fitted fairly easily into the confines of AFVs. Also of considerable importance was the invention in 1958 of the laser which made possible extremely accurate range-finding. By integrating these discoveries it became possible in the late 1970s to create target acquisition and gunnery control equipment which enabled

Russian T 54s and 55s which were captured by the hundred from the Arab nations and, in due course, modified and taken into Israeli service.

commanders and gunners to detect the enemy at night and through smoke and mist, without being detected themselves; to range exactly to the target; and to compute and compensate for meteorological conditions and gun anomalies. The electronic revolution also enabled the gunner, at the press of a button, to be presented with a sight graticule setting which merely required him to aim at the center of target mass and press the trigger to have a good chance of achieving a first-round hit out to 3000 m or more.

At the same time the gunnery control revolution was intensified by more accurate guns and ammunition of increased velocity; to such an extent that people began to question the need for ATGWs even at the longer ranges. This scepticism was stimulated by British research in the 1950s and 1960s which produced Composite Armor. This is a combined or laminated type of plate incorporating steel alloy to resist kinetic energy shot, and a combination of material, such as ceramics, plastics or glass fiber, to disperse the chemical energy jet. To defeat Composite Armor, the caliber of chemical-energy warheads had to be increased considerably – to about 150 mm – and their performance also improved by redesign of the cone shaping the jet. But because the killing power of chemical-energy warheads was suspect, the effectiveness of all ATGWs was also to be thrown into doubt, as will be made plain.

Very few of these latest developments were to be observed, however, in the two major campaigns of the late 1960s and early 1970s, both of which involved very large numbers of AFVs.

WAR IN VIETNAM

AFVs played only a minor role throughout the length of the struggle which began with the French facing Vietnamese nationalists in 1946 and ended with the defeat of US and Australian-supported South Vietnamese forces in 1975. The Vietnam War was a war dominated by infantry and firepower, in which AFVs, initially, were relegated to a limited part because the Vietnamese possessed virtually no tanks of their own and their enemies persisted in thinking of the struggle as a guerrilla war in country unsuitable to tanks. Not until 1967, when the United States carried out a feasibility study, was it discovered that tanks could move in 61 per cent of the country during the dry season and in 46 per cent in the wet; and that APCs could

The French AMX 13 whose 75 mm gun (with automatic loader) was the same as in Panther but whose light armor protection (40 mm) mitigated against close combat.

move in 65 per cent of Vietnam all year round. Thereafter the forces of South Vietnam rapidly raised their armor content to be matched only meagerly, however, by their opponents. As a result, AFVs were almost entirely employed in support of infantry; the principal threat to them was posed by mines and infantry anti-tank weapons, including ATGW. Yet AFVs were rated the most cost-effective weapon system for a country where the helicopter was enjoying a great vogue on the battlefield.

There was only one fight between North Vietnamese and US tanks; a skirmish at Ben Het on the night of 3 March 1969 when two Russian-built light PT76 tanks of 202nd Armored Regiment were seen at about 1000 meters by M48s of 1st Bn, 69th Armor. Infrared searchlights failed to see through thick mist, as Specialist Frank Hembree found: '*I ONLY HAD HIS MUZZLE flashes to sight on, but I couldn't wait for a better target because his shells were landing real close to us.*'

With his second round he set fire to the thinly armored PT76 shortly before his own tank was struck when another PT76 spotted it by the light of flares. A moment later and that PT76 too was in flames after being detected by the light of the burning Vietnamese tank.

It was 1971 before the North Vietnamese tried again with tanks. In the meantime, they had successes with ATGW until the Americans found an antidote by lashing suspected launching-points with fire to disturb the operators' concentration. When

North Vietnamese armor, including Russian-built T54s, did make its debut with 100 AFVs at An Loc in April 1972, the South Vietnamese defense was based entirely on artillery fire, short-range grenade launchers and ATGW and rockets fired from helicopters. In six weeks no fewer than 80 AFVs were accounted for.

But it was another story after the Americans withdrew. The final collapse of South Vietnam in 1975 was accelerated by up to 1000 enemy AFVs which cut loose and overwhelmed demoralized crews about whose last battles very little is known. Suffice to say that over 600 American-built tanks were destroyed or captured and that tank-versus-tank fighting featured only momentarily amidst the general debacle as the North's tank bully dictated.

THE YOM KIPPUR WAR

The essential difference between the Arab attack on Israel on 6 October 1973 and their previous aggressions lay in the combination of surprise with synchronized effort. Not only were the Israelis caught unawares during the holiday of the Day of Atonement, but the Egyptians and Syrians struck heavy blows together, thus preventing the Israelis from concentrating fully against one before the other. Moreover, both on the northern and the southern fronts, Syrians and Egyptians respectively employed tactics well suited to the terrain and the known enemy defenses with their emphasis upon the use of tanks.

In the north, the Syrians, with 1500 tanks and hell-bent upon recapturing the Golan Heights seized their primary objectives with relative ease. But thereafter, despite an initial superiority of 5:1 in tanks (as much as 12:1 in places) they failed to reach the vital bridges across the River Jordan. Upon these bridges subsequent Israeli reinforcement and security depended. The fighting between balanced tank and infantry teams supported by artillery resembled that of many another head-on, set-piece clash in history. Confronted by well-prepared, if relatively thinly held enemy positions, the Syrians had to blast a way through before unleashing their armored brigades in the classic manner. And in the classic manner the 170 Israeli tanks, some emplaced while others provided local mobile counter-attack units, managed to hold on until reserves arrived. The Israeli tactics, made viable only by their well-founded

T 54 (background) and T 55 co-operating with infantry. The man in the foreground is holding the RPG 7 launcher, a short range, rocket-propelled, hollow-charge anti-tank missile of considerable tactical influence since, like all its 'bazooka' predecessors, it placed a useful anti-tank weapon in infantry hands and compels tank commanders to be cautious and work closely with infantry escorts to avoid ambushes. The introduction of modern armor, however, considerably undermines the effect of such weapons with small diameter warheads.

M60

The American M 60, (originally M48 A4) the introduction of which, in 1962, at last rectified the serious gunnery inadequacies of their tank forces by means of the fitting of the British 105 mm gun and further refinements of turret design. It capitalised on the automotively sound M48, with its 865 hp air-cooled diesel engine, and opened the way to a further progression of modifications well into the 1970s. These included fitting M60 A3 with the latest night fighting equipment, laser range finder, improved running gear and electrical system, and schnorkel deep wading equipment.

Weight 48 tons
Speed 30 mph
Armament 1×105 mm, 2×mg

M60 A1 with 105 mm gun

M60 A2 with the 152 mm Shillelagh gun/missile launcher system which had much unfulfilled promise due to the inadequacies of the missile by comparison with the 105 mm gun in M60 A1.

gunnery, depended upon strict economy of
effort, with no rash charges. Their enemy
was well-equipped with, in addition to T54s
and T55s, the latest Russian T62 tanks, armed
with a 115 mm gun and fitted with infrared
night vision searchlights. He was not to be
despised.

Israeli losses at first were high, partly
because they were caught by surprise but also
because the Syrians managed skilfully to
combine their ATGW-equipped infantry tank-
hunting teams with supporting armor; they
virtually eliminated the frontier defenders
within the first 24 hours. Surprised as they
were, the Israelis managed to feed in fresh
units piecemeal and in the nick of time to
block the Syrians a mile from the vital Arik
bridge. Possession of vital ground turned the
scales. The Israelis, with superior knowledge
of the terrain and its best tank-killing sectors,
made no mistakes in this respect. Checked by
the desperate Israeli blocking operation, the
Syrian armored divisions were reduced to
milling about in the midst of the killing areas,
and fell easy victims to Centurion and Super
Sherman gunners who knocked out about 500
AFVs in four days' gruelling combat. Instead
of exploiting the early advances of the
infantry tank-hunting teams, the Syrian tank
columns were squeezed by armored pincers.
Night-fighting with infrared light did not save
them because the Israelis detected the
sources of light through infrared-viewing
devices. But crews who had already fought
hard by day were in poor condition to
continue without rest by night.

By 10 October the Israelis had changed the
balance of strength sufficiently to counter-
attack along the entire front and roll into the
Syrian rear. They drove the Syrians back in
some disorder, picking them off by air and
tank attacks, rebuffing each local attempt at
relief. When a joint Iraqi and Jordanian tank
force, 300 strong, tried on 12 October to come
to the rescue of Syria with a flank attack
against the main Israeli thrust towards
Damascus, a disaster occurred such as the
World War II Allies had frequently suffered at
German hands. In two days of tank-versus-
tank combat, when engagements frequently
took place at the lethal ranges of 200 to 300 m,
the losses on both sides were heavy, but far
heavier among the Arabs. Finally, when a trio
of Israeli tanks suddenly appeared on a flank,
which the Iraqis assumed to be secured, an
abrupt Iraqi retreat left some 60 tanks
burning on the battlefield. At the final count
no less than 1150 tanks were lost to the Arabs

on this front, against 250 knocked-out Israeli
machines, of which 150 were repairable.

In the south, to begin with, the Egyptians
were far more successful, when they
assaulted the Israeli fortifications lining the
Suez Canal. With knowledge of the Israelis'
scheme for securing their strongpoints, the
Egyptians planned their moves with
assurance. By sending across infantry teams
on a wide frontage, to confuse the Israelis, the
Egyptians were able to delay the tank
counterstrokes long enough to establish
strong ATGW and infantry tank-hunting
teams, backed up by tanks, on the east bank.
Clinging to static defenses hampered the
Israelis. Arrogantly counter-attacking with
tanks, unsupported by infantry and artillery,
cost them 100 out of 200 AFVs – a lesson of
improvidence from the past. By rapidly
building bridges across the canal, the
Egyptians, who had some 2200 tanks available, were swift to create a considerable

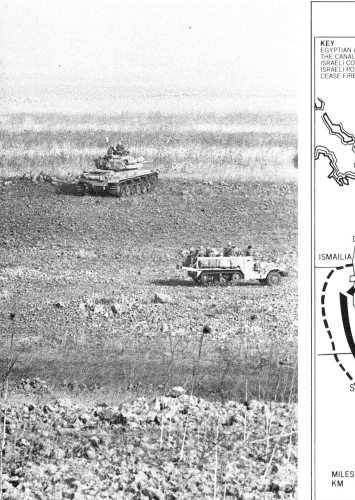

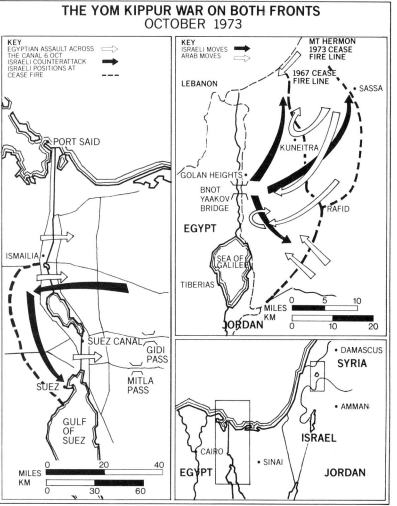

THE YOM KIPPUR WAR ON BOTH FRONTS
OCTOBER 1973

KEY
EGYPTIAN ASSAULT ACROSS
THE CANAL 6 OCT
ISRAELI COUNTERATTACK
ISRAELI POSITIONS AT
CEASE FIRE

PORT SAID

ISMAILIA

SUEZ CANAL

GIDI PASS

MITLA PASS

SUEZ

GULF OF SUEZ

MILES
KM
0   20   40
0   30   60

KEY
ISRAELI MOVES
ARAB MOVES

MT HERMON
1973 CEASE
FIRE LINE

1967 CEASE
FIRE LINE

SASSA

LEBANON

KUNEITRA

GOLAN HEIGHTS

BNOT
YAAKOV
BRIDGE

RAFID

EGYPT

SEA OF
GALILEE

TIBERIAS

JORDAN

MILES
KM
0   5   10
0   10   20

DAMASCUS

SYRIA

AMMAN

ISRAEL

CAIRO

SINAI

EGYPT

JORDAN

Above left: A typical armored combat team of 1973 in which the infantry still travel in American half tracks of 1943 vintage.

Left: Centurions in service with the Jordanian Army.

numerical superiority and forced the Israelis to abandon their defenses on 9 October. Yet they were far too slow to exploit this success, bearing in mind that the Israelis were not only shaken but also had to divert the bulk of their strength to the northern front.

The Egyptians, of course, were facing a problem common in earlier confrontations. Having failed utterly to destroy the opposing armor at the outset, they were faced still by a mobile tank defense which compensated by skill and fire power for any numerical discrepancy. Moreover, the Israelis quickly adopted the use of smoke and harassing tactics to neutralize the ATGWs, thus re-establishing the influence of the tanks with their high-velocity guns. Whenever the Egyptians attacked, they did so piecemeal instead of by coordinated strokes. Inevitably, they were blocked on each predictable line of approach in much the same way as had been the Pakistanis against the Indians in 1965. But in their eagerness to win laurels and to give the maximum support to their hard-pressed allies in the north, they moved the bulk of their entire tank force to the east bank of the canal leaving only 500 on the west side.

EGYPT SUSTAINS BIG LOSSES
The culmination of the Egyptian offensive was reached on the 14th when they made one last effort, spread out in six columns supported by artillery. The Israelis waited in concealed positions, allowing the tanks to come within 100 m in places, before opening rapid fire. Fifty Egyptian tanks were knocked out in the northern sector, another 93 (against three Israelis hit by ATGW) in the center where Sharon's division held the line. Towards the south, where the Egyptians headed for the Gidi and Mitla passes, they lost another 90 tanks, along with many other AFVs. It required only about 500 Israeli M48s, M60s and Centurions to win this victory in a few hours. Afterwards there were those among the Egyptians who said that the attack had been made for political reasons but that, had one concerted blow with all tank formations been made, victory might have been theirs. Maybe! But by then the Egyptian Chief of Staff, General Saad Shazli, had concluded that '

... *I*T WAS IMPOSSIBLE TO ENSURE

the success of any attack – whether by tanks or armored infantry – without destroying or silencing in advance the anti-tank missile defense'.

He overlooked the fact that the Israelis placed little faith in missiles and continued to base their striking power on the tank gun and artillery. And he should not also have overlooked that the Israelis might well deploy prudently to minimize their casualties until tanks returned from the northern battlefield. He must have been aware also that his own latest Russian T62 tanks had a frequent, nasty habit of catching fire whenever penetrated. Be that as it may, he wanted to send back his armored divisions to reserve on the west bank in case the Israelis broke through to the canal and crossed it. But this was refused, for political reasons.

When the Israelis did decide to make that move, it carried with it great risks. On 15 October the approach to the intended crossing place at Matzmed by Sharon's division was intended to open a corridor through the Egyptian lines. In the event it plunged into the midst of two Egyptian divisional administrative areas and set off a fantastic firework display with thousands of weapons opening up against friend and foe alike, setting hundreds of vehicles alight. Potentially more deadly were the tank counter-attacks it invited on the north flank, but which were held at night with the loss of 70 Israeli tanks and twice that number of Egyptian. Yet that was only the prelude to a steady long-range harassment of the Egyptians next day which eventually persuaded them to withdraw. For by then *their* very existence was in peril. The Israelis had crossed the canal shortly after midnight, had brushed off a threat to their southern flank, had constructed heavy-lift rafts and put a few tanks across after first light. But, because the mass of Egyptian armor remained to the east, their counter-stroke could only be launched from there – into the teeth of Israeli tanks which stood ready for them. Crushed by dread, the Egyptian commanders sent their crews on a death ride on 17 October, by which time the Israelis had towed a prefabricated bridge to the canal, reinforced their bridgehead and consolidated the walls of the corridor. Amid sand dunes the Egyptian tanks died to the crack of 105 mm guns. Two attacks from the north were flung back. The assault from the south, consisting of 96 T62s, ran into a minefield trap and lost 86 tanks and all the accompanying APCs.

Meanwhile the first weak Egyptian counter-attacks were enlivening the west bank, though with scant chance of making a serious impression. The bridgehead posed an expanding threat to Cairo when the remorseless erosion of the isolated forces on the east bank continued. With the tank battle won, the surface-to-air missile sites along the canal destroyed or neutralized, and but few tanks available to check the Israelis, Egypt stood ripe for conquest, an event denied by the ceasefire arranged on 24 October.

Paradoxically, a war which had been dominated and won by tanks was portrayed by the so-called experts of the information media as the eclipse of the tank by the ATGW. Yet later analysis showed beyond any doubt that by far the higher proportion of tank losses were credited to guns and that the majority of kills by missiles had taken place during the opening moves – before the Israelis had appreciated the threat and taken tactical remedial action. Those pundits who misguidedly drew the wrong conclusions, and spread them far and wide, failed to take account of over 3000 Arab tanks which had been lost to an enemy who depended almost entirely on the gun. Out of an Israeli force of 2000 tanks more than half were still in action at the end, and many others were recoverable. The 'experts' also overlooked the truth that, once the battle of attrition was settled, the victorious Israeli tanks at once cut loose with sweeping decisive strategic maneuvers.

The British Chieftain. When entering service in the mid 1960s, it set a new standard for main battle tanks with its extremely well-designed armor, powerful 120 mm gun (with two-piece ammunition with bag charges), built-in searchlight, ranging machine-gun, and schnorkel deep-wading equipment. Unfortunately the decision to use a multi-fuel engine backfired because of difficulties over the development of such an advanced aspect of technology. Time, however, has seen Chieftain shake off most of its initial troubles. It has acquired the latest laser-ranging, fire control equipment, and passive night fighting gear, along with even thicker armor. It retains its place as a potent weapon system, and has been used by Iran.
Weight 54 tons
Speed 28 mph
Armament 1×120 mm, 2×mg

CHAPTER NINE

TANK BATTLES OF TOMORROW

BECAUSE IT TAKES FROM 10 TO 15 YEARS FROM THE moment of conception to entry into service of a new tank, the full range of 1960s' inventions did not begin to appear in operational use until the late 1970s and early 1980s. The advent of main battle tanks (MBT) such as the British Shir (later developed into Challenger), the German Leopard, the US Abrams, and the Israeli Merkava revealed radical changes in shape, due to the introduction of Composite Armor, and startling improvements in automotive performance and striking power. In an endeavor to raise performance as well as to deal with weights which had increased to between 55 and 60 tons, engines of some 1500 bhp were installed along with sophisticated hydropneumatic and hydrogas suspension systems. As a result cross-country speeds in excess of 30 mph became feasible without shaking to pieces crews and vehicles. To the ability to detect and recognise targets behind light cover or at night, far infrared thermal-imaging equipment was added to the computerized laser-ranging fire control systems previously described. A commander or gunner, at the touch of a few levers and buttons, could engage targets out to 3000 m, with a high chance of a hit. And a hit from the 120 mm high-velocity guns, superseding the still very powerful 105 mm pieces, could be devastating.

Changes in the demands upon crew members' aptitudes ensued from these shifts in technology. The radio operator/loader no longer needed delicate skills to tune the latest push-button sets, although he certainly needed strong physique to load the heavier shot and charges into very large guns. The gunner, whose ability used to be least-tested, needed now to be far more clever to cope with the complexities of the latest fire-control equipment. The redundancy of the loader came nearer with the introduction of automatic loading devices, particularly by the Russians on their T72 tank. This was a controversial trend, not only because of its added mechanical complexity but also because it increased the danger of breakdowns. For once more the limitations of a three-man crew, with the potential work overload on each crewman, loomed.

The chances of a crew surviving when their tank was hit also improved. Along with wet stowage of ammunition, the suppression of fire by the introduction of fast-acting automatic extinguishers, which dispensed non-toxic halogen gas, was a boon. But the likelihood of penetration in the first place had been so considerably reduced by composite and reactive armor (the latter consisting of appliqué explosive slabs which dispersed the effects of a chemical warhead and just possibly even deflected solid shot) that doubts came to be expressed about even the best high-velocity gun achieving a kill at anything but the shortest of ranges. By the judicious sloping of extremely thick blends of armor, the equivalent of 600 to 700 mm homogenous steel protection was being frontally applied, thicknesses which made it ever less likely that existing ATGW or light infantry anti-tank weapons with their hollow charge warheads would do the job expected of them. Indeed

Left: The American Bradley, with its 25 mm gun and in-built twin TOW anti-tank guided missile system, is an advance on its Russian counterparts. Yet it is rather more conspicuous (though better armored), and tactically inflexible due to the inability to dismount TOW for use in places where the vehicle cannot go.
Below left: Russian Mechanized Infantry Combat Vehicles (MICV) equipped with obsolete Sagger anti-tank missiles and a 73 mm gun. The Russians were front-runners in the trend to place infantry under armor and incorporate heavier weapon systems in MICV, but the trade-off was a cramped and vulnerable AFV.
Below: American M113 APCs showing their inherent swimming capability.

the moment had arrived at which it became essential to place greater emphasis than ever upon attacking tanks through their more thinly armored belly plates and upper decking. Belly attack mines, with special fuses, and target-seeking artillery or air-dispensed munitions assumed a new importance and compelled AFV designers to reconsider the distribution of armor to meet evolving threats.

Another method of attack to which the tank was increasingly exposed came from helicopters armed with so-called 'fire and forget', supersonic ATGW which began to supersede the semi-automatically guided generation of missiles. These weapons had a useful, if complementary, role in the anti-tank battle. But even helicopters fitted with the latest navigation, target-seeking and self-preservation aids were no substitute, (as some claimed,) for the tank. For one thing they themselves were extremely vulnerable to guided weapons, as well as being inhibited by poor weather conditions, darkness and the

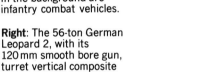

MODERN EUROPEAN AFVs

Above: The Swedish Strv 103 or so-called S tank. It has well-sloped armor and a fixed 105 mm gun which is layed by slewing and raising the whole vehicle. In the background are infantry combat vehicles.

armor, and the latest electronic devices. A 1500 hp engine gives a speed in excess of 30 mph.

Right: The 56-ton German Leopard 2, with its 120 mm smooth bore gun, turret vertical composite

difficulty (sometimes the impossibility) of operating in close country. Therefore, as doubts multiplied about the capability of ATGW, the cost-effectiveness of a machine, which with all the necessary ancillary devices required was projected as costing over $22 million each in the 1990s, began to tell against it.

However, these uncertainties did not make ATGW and their associated carriers obsolete overnight. There remained several very important roles for lighter kinetic energy or chemical energy anti-tank weapons. Not only would these projectiles achieve penetration of the best-protected main battle tanks through their thinner sides, but they also had a vital role against the lightly armored reconnaissance and personnel carriers which might be deployed in mass and be inappropriate 'overkill' targets for the big guns. In fact,

the introduction of light AFVs such as the Russian BMP, the German Marder, the American Bradley and the British Warrior, armed with guns between 73 mm and 25 mm (and in cases with ATGW), ensured that APC-versus-APC combat would be integrated with any MBT-versus-MBT fight.

REVIVAL OF THE SELF-PROPELLED GUN

The desirability of possessing cheaper, effective anti-armor AFVs was also dictated by financial restraints. With an MBT costing anything up to $3 million in 1987, any kind of saving that did not degrade operational performance was welcomed by financially hard-pressed Defense departments. It was essential to examine cheaper means of penetration or failing that, to find a simpler, conventionally armed tank destroyer of

Left: The T72 represents a significant breakaway from previous Russian tank design by its use of a non-Christie type suspension. There have been many misleading announcements about this controversial tank, which has been confused with other Russian AFVs. So far, the most reliable information is about the 125 mm gun with its automatic loader. T72 probably has a speed of 40 mph, although how the new suspension copes across country at that speed is another matter. Far less certain is the nature and quality of its well-sloped armor. No doubt some composite sort is in the offing; perhaps reactive slabs will be attached. Undoubtedly T80 (**above**) will emerge as a derivation of this AFV. But it could be that T90, or its equivalent, will be radically different, to win back for the Russians the lead they have lost in the tank design race.

T72
Weight 41 tons
Speed 40 mph
Frontal armor
Armament 1×125 mm, 2×mg

limited tactical adaptability. And since the 120 mm gun retained its inescapable dominance, the reintroduction of a jagdpanzer type of AFV became very attractive to a number of nations early in the 1980s. It became clear that, by the 1990s, a main battle tank might cost $4.5 million while a tank-destroyer might cost less than half that price.

Several limited traverse self-propelled anti-tank guns had been produced since 1945. Of these the Swedish Strv 103, the so-called S Tank, was the most interesting and publicised because its 105 mm gun, with automatic loader, was fixed along the hull's center line. Elevation was accomplished by raising or lowering the hydraulic suspension; traverse in azimuth by rotating the vehicle on its tracks. However, not only was this AFV relatively expensive, but the gun-laying mechanism did not attain a desirable

standard of accuracy. Besides, there were considerable tactical disadvantages in having to traverse the entire vehicle (not always possible in some locations) to engage a target; in being unable to shoot on the move (and therefore at a disadvantage when caught in open ground); and in being totally disabled if immobilised by automotive breakdown. The original concept of the jagdpanzer, with limited inbuilt elevation and traverse, held good. It lent itself well to very high protective features by incorporating composite armor although, of course, the tactical limitations inherent to all such AFVs remained.

STRANGE NEW SHAPES
While strenuous attempts were being made to improve the effectiveness of conventional AFVs in order to compete strongly in the anti-tank contest, research into unorthodox

THE BRITISH CHALLENGER'S FULL PASSIVE NIGHT FIGHTING AND SIGHTING SYSTEM

Above: The gunner's periscope sight in Challenger which enables him, or the commander, to engage targets simply by sighting on the target, pushing a ranging button to activate the electronic devices, and squeezing the trigger to score a first-round hit with the 120 mm gun out to 3000 m.

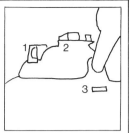

1 The commander's and gunner's sights incorporating laser range-finder.
2 The thermal imaging equipment which displays on a TV screen.
3 The driver's periscope, also with night vision.

machines and components proceeded. The Israeli Merkava, in the design of which Israel Tal played a leading role, assumed an unusual arrangement for an MBT (though not for light AFVs) by locating the engine at the front. This enhanced protection while the ammunition, right at the back, was not only kept in the safest place, but also was quite easily stowed in the vehicle through a rear door, making replenishment in the combat zone much safer. Armed with a 105 mm gun, the Merkava's capability of accepting a 120 mm piece if required is of fundamental importance.

Far more radical than Merkava, however, are the latest attempts to reduce vehicle or turret exposure to the enemy from a firing position, concepts which are embodied in the 'Gun-over-Hull' tank. Project studies have been undertaken, notably in Sweden and the United States (so far as is known) into the practicality of mounting the gun (or a missile) and the sighting equipment in a raisable turret operated by the crew from within the hull below. Loading the gun with such an arrangement creates technical problems, but these can be overcome. The strange-looking new machine which evolves will be well

worth the effort and expense since tactically it benefits from being able, with gun raised, to shoot from a hull-down position with the least exposure of itself to the enemy. Yet it retains the capability of shooting on the move like a conventional tank. Such additional complexity and expense as will accrue must pay off in enormously enhanced confidence and morale among crews who can engage the enemy directly without exposing themselves to direct counter-measures. The misconceived intentions of those who, in 1942, desired to fight tank-versus-tank engagements in the indirect mode, at last will be satisfied without loss of the vital advantages of direct aiming. At a stroke, indeed, tank-versus-tank combat will take a stride forward, placing fresh demands upon revised tactical methods.

Critics sometimes deprecate specifications which appear to place too high a price on crew protection. The expense and trouble, they say, is out of proportion to the advantages gained; war is a risky business and men must take their chance, they argue. Naturally such measures can be excessive, but it cannot be denied that crews who feel their chances of survival are being neglected unreasonably have a legitimate grouse. When crew confidence is lowered, enthusiasm for the fight declines and a damaging reluctance to join in the fight becomes evident. The experiences of French crews in 1940 and of American and British crews in the harrowing out-gunned situations of 1944 are brushed aside and forgotten at any army's peril. One has only to study accounts of the most recent tank fighting in Lebanon between Israelis and Syrian tanks to see that very little has changed in that connection.

Although Israeli and Syrian armor did clash in Lebanon, it was on nothing like the scale and intensity of previous encounters between the two sides. For the most part the Syrians, whose tank strength was of the order of 700, gave way before their enemy's advance and the majority of fighting took place with armor in the supporting role. Very important, however were the debuts of Merkava and the Russian-built T72s. The former did well, earning high praise from its crews for the manner in which it resisted punishment and how well its internal layout and fire suppression equipment kept casualties to the minimum if ever it was penetrated. Similar praise would have been withheld by the T72 crews, for although their 125 mm gun satisfactorily penetrated Centurion and Super Sherman tanks fitted with reactive armor, their own protection fell far short of the designed standard. In one notable action, in which nine T72s were knocked out, there appeared to be no survivors when the tanks exploded. That sort of reputation, once it got around among the crews of the Soviet and other tank forces to which this AFV had been issued, could not fail to be discouraging should a major test come.

FUTURE BATTLES

Indeed, in any prognostication such as follows, due weight should be given to the tank crews' own opinion of their chances of survival in battle, and the tactics they would be called upon to execute. That has been the way of things from the moment crews came to realise that they must take precautions and take evasive action (as did the Whippets at Villers Bretonneux) when confronted by heavy gunfire. Despite the immense difference between the tanks of 1916, (with a speed of 4 mph, armor 8 mm thick and a gun of 57 mm) and the tank of the 1980s (with its speed of 30 mph, armor 600 mm equivalent and a gun of 120 mm) usage has altered little

The unconventional Israeli Merkava with its 105 mm gun, 900 hp frontal engine and fuel tanks, and large rear doors leading into a compartment to carry ammunition or, if required, an infantry squad. This AFV has acquired combat experience in Lebanon and is capable of being up-gunned. It also has a 60 mm mortar and a machine-gun.
Weight 58 tons
Armament 1×105 mm, 2×mg

in principle. Such changes as have occurred are related to scale – to faster movement, and longer ranges of engagement and proportionate variations in resistance to penetration and damage. In battle, armored vehicles continue to perform their best in concert with other arms: they depend upon combining fire with movement, on concealment and the ability to make best use of their armor in defeating the enemy's counter-measures. They remain, in essence, offensive weapons with a role in every phase of military operations – defense, withdrawal and attack.

Over the years, it has become a habit to assume that in any future conflict between the major powers, particularly in a European setting, the land battle will be dictated initially by the onrush of massed Warsaw Pact tank armies driving flat out westward, regardless of the cost. Similarly it has been assumed that NATO armies will seek to check this onrush with a flexible defense based on natural and man-made obstacles, prior to their opponent being worn down and logistically overstretched to the point at which momentum has been stunned. A picture has been painted of battles not so very unlike those during the latter stages of World War II. Then the massive Allied forces, having overcome emplaced German formations, ran amok until they too became weakened at the end of wrecked lines of communication enmeshed in a web of waterways, urban settlements and forest, ripe for a

ABRAMS

THE US ABRAMS, WITH WELL-SLOPED composite armor, was initially armed with the 105 mm gun but is now receiving the German 120 mm gun – to continue the US reliance on foreign tank guns. Easily the best modern tank yet produced by the US, it is powered by a 1500 hp gas turbine engine, is equipped with all the latest electronic vision and sighting devices, and has the gun fully stabilized. At 55 tons it is still, with its sophisticated torsion bar suspension, a very agile AFV but has yet to be tested in action.

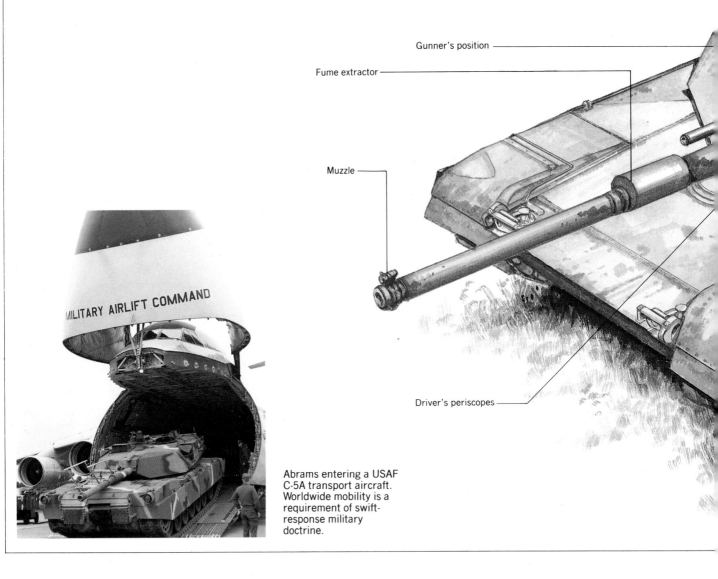

Gunner's position

Fume extractor

Muzzle

Driver's periscopes

Abrams entering a USAF C-5A transport aircraft. Worldwide mobility is a requirement of swift-response military doctrine.

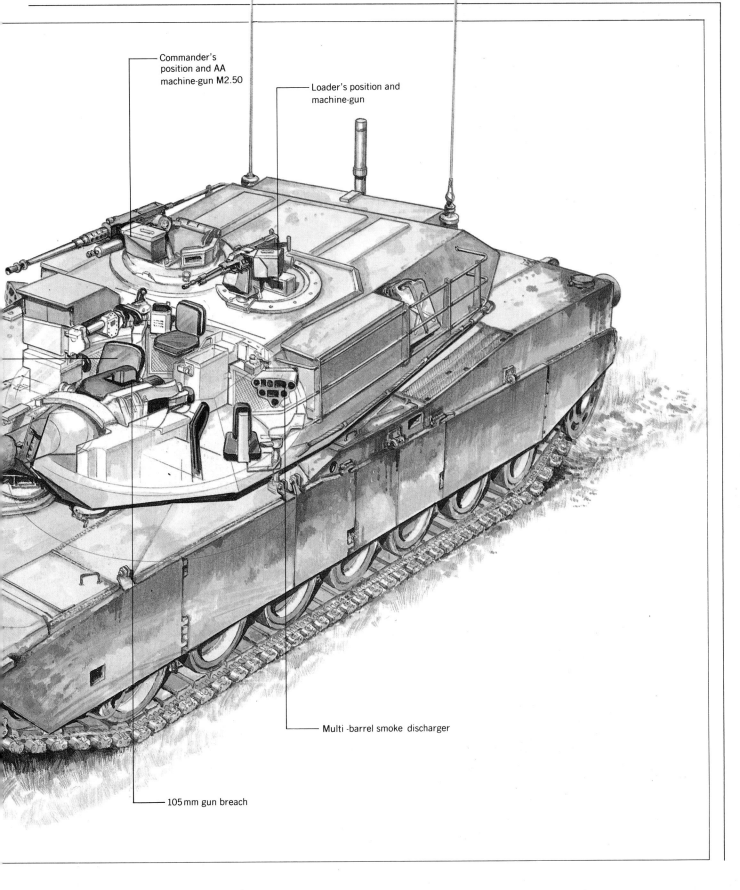

Commander's position and AA machine-gun M2.50

Loader's position and machine-gun

Multi-barrel smoke discharger

105 mm gun breach

Manstein-like counter-attack which would stop and then roll them back with disastrous losses. It is an image founded upon traditional methods, on a belief that the central theme in combat will be the prosecution of the armored struggle in which tank-versus-tank encounters will predominate. Yet that image could be false even though its tank-versus-tank element persists, as persist it must. Let us first, therefore, examine the shape of tank-versus-tank fighting which might evolve when the latest AFVs collide.

ATTACK UPON A BLOCKING POSITION

In our future war scenario, Warsaw Pact Tank and Motor Rifle Divisions advancing against determined NATO opposition in prepared positions are expected to be supported by overwhelming artillery fire intended to prepare the way for their armored battle groups by destroying or neutralizing the large number of ATGW they expect to encounter. They hope that their smoke screens and the clouds of dust churned up will create confusion and, · above all, obscure their advancing vehicles to enable them to close the range before being shot at. Once infiltrated among the fixed NATO positions, at relatively low cost, they hope to dominate the vital ground and catch their opponent's armor at a disadvantage, destroying it in position during a series of tank duels, primarily because of their numerical superiority.

In response, the NATO forces will do all in their power to counter the enemy artillery and, at the same time, channel the advancing armored columns into killing zones, where terminally guided munitions, ATGW and tank-destroyers take their toll. By mining gaps through the natural obstacles which bar the way to the enemy, by demolishing bridges and basing defense upon towns, villages and tank-proof copses (just as had their forebears from the 1930s and 1940s) any advantage in numbers possessed by the Warsaw Pact assailants could be nullified without the involvement of NATO tanks – a policy made all the easier to implement in a part of the world where urbanization has flourished since 1945. It would be the earnest desire of

The British Challenger, with its superbly sloped composite armor shape, and rifled 120 mm gun. Challenger's 1200 hp diesel engine gives a smooth ride, with hydro-gas suspension, across country at over 30 mph.

the defenders to conserve their main battle tanks in readiness to take concentrated offensive action against a weakened, unbalanced opponent.

Ideally the defenders hope to benefit from early warning of every Warsaw Pact thrust so as to minimize the element of surprise and conduct action from vital ground at maximum range. Reports from air reconnaissance, including Remotely Piloted Vehicles (RPV), from artillery observers, and from light tanks and armored cars of the reconnaissance forces screening the front and exposed flanks of defended localities, would contribute to intelligence needs until the first direct contact between the principal forces. Skirmishes at ranges of about 1500 m between light AFVs would eventually give way to the longer-range clash of heavier units. In open country, Heavy ATGW (HAW) teams might be lucky enough to spot targets at their maximum ranges of 3500 to 4000 m, and score a few kills to start the attritional process. Perhaps a few lurking ATGW helicopters would contribute. But ATGW, regardless of their launch platform, would be exposed in their unreliability when smoke and dust prevented their engaging or when counter-fire disturbed their operators' concentration. Alternatively and more ominously, hits might fail to penetrate because the warhead was inadequate for the job.

Not until the range closes to 3000 m would tank-destroyers, or tanks dedicated to the main anti-tank defense, move into their previously reconnoitered positions to open the gun duel with their 120 mm guns. Regardless of their prior knowledge of the ground and the range to critical points, they would depend upon their computerized laser sights to pour a deadly but economical fire upon an enemy whose reply might not be so well-founded. As so often in the past, tanks in ambush opening fire by surprise hold the key to local victory. The attackers' main chance of success lies in taking evasive action, in locating the sources of resistance quickly, and in maneuvering for positions from which to fire with equally deadly effect from flank and rear upon their adversaries. As routinely in the past, the struggle would hinge on maneuver with the decision more likely to go in favor of the most mobile, best informed and controlled side.

However, as was rare in the most recent Arab-Israeli wars, the impact of electronics would be crucial. For while profuse use of radio communications and radar improves

Russian-built armor (T55s and T62s) in action in the Iran/Iraq war of the 1980s.

command and control and creates better operational flexibility than in the past, it also considerably multiplies the perils inherent in electronic counter-measures. Frequency-hopping and secure sets certainly reduce the risks of radio intercept, but it is still possible for an enemy to acquire sufficient information from the radiation of 'signal signatures' to draw adequate conclusions about what is in train. It is also possible to adopt positive counter-measures by homing in on targets, particularly against centers of command and control. Similarly there is the double-edged backlash of imaging devices which see in the night and through battlefield obscuration during daytime. For operational purposes, night must be treated like day. Total concealment can never be guaranteed. As a result there is superimposed upon the age-old complexities of night fighting, the compulsory obligation to move and take the same concealment precautions as in daylight. No longer can darkness or smoke be assumed to cloak movement: movement requires fire support, even at night. No longer can a tank be assured of occupying a fire position at night without being observed. Thermal detection and hits at long range by a sniping enemy tank or ATGW launcher are possible. And since the protection of darkness is now largely illusory, the stress and strain of the *intensified* 24-hour battlefield day places unheard-of stress upon fighting men to the extent that without relief and rest, they rapidly become exhausted. Exhausted crews must either be relieved by reserves or be reduced to combat impotence.

EUROPE: THE NEAR FUTURE?

TANK–V–TANK IN THE 1990s

Picking his moment, on radio orders from the American tank platoon commander (whose three Abrams hide in ambush in front of the village) the commander of the Goliath tank destroyer tucked in between buildings in the village, orders his vehicle to crawl forward into a previously selected turret-down position. Unseen by the Russians, he confirms the location of the targets described by his American ally. He lines up his vehicle, lasers for range onto the center of the leading T90, instructs his gunner to tell the driver when the tank has moved forward far enough to make the gun crest-clear, and orders the driver to advance into a fire position. At the gunner's word, the driver halts and the commander presses the trigger [the computerized fire control system having already made full adjustments to gun-lay by compensating for range, barrel bend, temperature, wind drift and so on]. The ambush is complete when a first-round hit is obtained with APFSD. Penetration seals the destruction of the T90.

AN INCIDENT OF THE 1990s

Tank-versus-tank engagements adhere to past principles and retain a recognizable historic shape. The majority of engagement ranges are conditioned by terrain – meaning that few take place much in excess of 2000 m with the majority below 1000 m. Nor is the rate or scale of destruction so very different to the past. Take, for example, the thought processes of an Abrams tank commander faced at 3000 m by a hull-down Russian T90 (an assumed vehicle) which, he has been led to believe, is protected by composite armor and armed with a high-velocity gun as good as his own 120 mm piece. His suspicions about the high quality of the enemy armor have been confirmed by witnessing the failure of the TOW ATGW, fired by a nearby Bradley Infantry Fighting Vehicle (IFV), to knock out the T90 with a hit square on the glacis plate – and that Bradley has now been reduced to a flaming wreck by the undamaged (or slightly shaken) Russian tank. The Abrams commander has now to decide if he can hit such a small target and penetrate the T90's thickest armor at extreme range. For the sake of prudence he decides to hold his fire until either the T90 advances to present an easier mark at closer range, or until something more vulnerable turns up. Meanwhile he keeps under cover, turret-down, and resists the temptation to engage a couple of Russian IFVs, flaunting their presence at a distance of 1500 meters. It is not worth letting rip at such an obvious lure to disclose his position to the

lurking T90 or to any of its companions which are probably lying in wait. Likewise the T90 commander holds his hand when another Bradley shoots at the Russian IFVs with its 25 mm gun: he too is hunting bigger game. The American contents himself with reporting events and rests more content when he hears his platoon commander re-deploying a sub-unit to deal with the next enemy move. He is interested and pleased also to hear that one of the Canadian Goliath tank-destroyers (an assumed vehicle) is coming forward, tasked specifically to snipe at those T90s which stand off at long range.

The appearance of the Goliath puts the commander of the T90 in a quandary. The Russian does not recognise the squat AFV or realise that its extremely thick frontal armor might defeat his own 125 mm gun. In all innocence he inches forward, ordering his gunner to engage. He notes the results of laser range-finding on his own sighting instrument. There is not a moment to lose because experience of the enemy's Visual and Infra Red Screening System (VIRSS), which automatically deploys a grenade-launched local smoke screen when it detects a laser probe, has taught him that targets thus protected are fleeting in the extreme.

But the Goliath's commander has deliberately switched off VIRSS because he is spoiling for a duel and does not want his intended victim obscured in any way. Fully briefed by the Abrams commander of the T90's position, the Goliath commander has told his gunner where to look and had him line up his sights before ordering the driver to advance to the crest line. Feeling fairly confident that his sloped composite armor would deflect or defeat the Russian APFSDS at that range, he is prepared to slug it out, but nevertheless prefers to make best use of surprise by laser ranging, laying and shooting before his opponent. As it happens he has the edge by a few seconds – the difference between his gunner actually acquiring the target and the Russian commander moving forward into a fire position. With its first shot the Goliath strikes home, penetrating the T90's good armor and wreaking havoc within.

As a prelude to the next main Russian surge in this sector, this incident is characteristic of the crucial command, control and training advantage enjoyed by NATO's professional troops over their shorter-service conscripted opponents. Good though the Soviet equipment is, it is not always employed to its best

The Russian Hind helicopter, armed with guided missiles, is shown here merely as an example of the latest threat to AFVs. Dangerous though armed helicopters are, they too are extremely vulnerable to missiles, while their strike capability has been downgraded by the protection given against HEAT projectiles by composite armor. In tactical terms, the armed helicopter is just another weapons system to be incorporated in all-arms combat teams. It is no substitute for the tank and is very expensive.

AFVs OF THE FUTURE

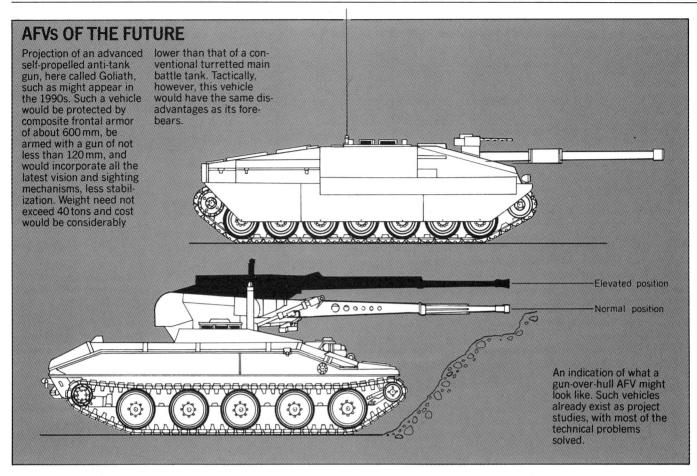

Projection of an advanced self-propelled anti-tank gun, here called Goliath, such as might appear in the 1990s. Such a vehicle would be protected by composite frontal armor of about 600 mm, be armed with a gun of not less than 120 mm, and would incorporate all the latest vision and sighting mechanisms, less stabilization. Weight need not exceed 40 tons and cost would be considerably lower than that of a conventional turretted main battle tank. Tactically, however, this vehicle would have the same disadvantages as its forebears.

Elevated position

Normal position

An indication of what a gun-over-hull AFV might look like. Such vehicles already exist as project studies, with most of the technical problems solved.

technical advantage. But the Soviet attack which now develops is formidable nevertheless. The clouds of dust kicked up by an intense artillery bombardment, which engulfs the assault objectives, are condensed by smoke fired to disturb ATGW operators and those among the defenders who remain determined to fight back. The defenders' reactions are pragmatically multifarious. Some, chiefly those caught in the open without the protection of armor, are cowed and supinely await their fate. Those in trenches lie low and hope for the best. Occupants of light AFVs take advantage of their mobility to withdraw under orders from the maelstrom, seeking alternative positions of greater safety from which to strike back at the enemy when he enters the designated killing zone. Some among the best-armored tanks stay where they are, dedicated to make the enemy pay dearly for every yard even though, at the shorter ranges against fast-moving targets, they might be overwhelmed by pace and sheer numbers. Nothing has changed so very much since 1944 in the approaches to the German frontiers.

As the advancing Soviet tank phalanx begins to appear (despite the dust and smoke) on the thermal-imaging screens, the Abrams and Goliath commanders who stand fast to fight take account of the fact that feed-back from the dust might upset their laser range-finders. They mostly choose, therefore, to let the T90s draw closer to ranges of about 1500 meters, where the chance of a kill is almost guaranteed. Only when an enemy target reaches or stops near a topographical feature, whose range has been precisely established and recorded prior to action, are gunners permitted to expend ammunition. Two T90s and an APC are disabled by this method without loss to the NATO AFVs. For the Russian gunners are inhibited in firing back by the obscuration of their own making. Indeed, by placing so much emphasis upon the area coverage of massive indirect artillery fire (which is by no means guaranteed to score a high rate of kills against AFVs) the Russians tend to deny themselves the extremely accurate and deadly direct pin-point shooting from which they might otherwise benefit in support of their advancing assault waves.

EUROPE THE NEAR FUTURE?

THE BATTLE UNFOLDS

Depicted here, as one facet of the scenario of an imagined Soviet offensive against NATO ground forces in Europe, is the moment of first contact between the Advanced Guard of a Red Army mechanized Division and the forward edge of an American/Canadian blocking position.

Advancing as fast as they dare – perhaps a little too fast for safety – the leading T90 tanks of the Advanced Guard have bypassed a village and, in medium terrain, are within sight and range of what they have had reason to believe is a defended enemy position. Already, scouting armored car patrols have come under fire from the high ground ahead. Some have taken cover in hedgerows, copses and folds in the ground; others, cautiously, are seeking unguarded ways via the flanks round the village ahead. Meanwhile the Advanced Guard commander, ordered to make the utmost haste, has had no choice other than to chance his arm and drive head-on at the village in the hope that it is not strongly held or that the enemy will carelessly expose himself to fire from tanks, missile launchers and artillery lying back in support.

The ploy has worked. From the northern end of the crest some sort of American missile launcher, which he guesses might be a Bradley IFV, has let fly with what was probably a TOW. It has hit one of the leading platoon's T90s but, to the immense relief of the shaken crew, has not penetrated. The T90 has used maximum acceleration to get under cover while one of its comrades, whose commander had been lucky enough to catch sight of the Bradley, has got in a first-round hit. Smoke now marks the funeral pyre of that Bradley, which was unwise enough to expose more

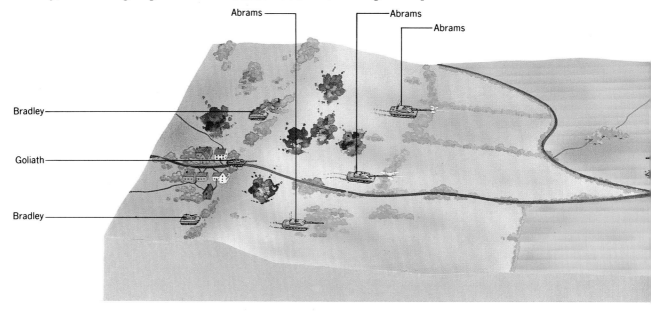

Not until the range closes to about 800 m do the three Abrams and the Goliath open rapid fire to exterminate a foe they can hardly miss or fail to penetrate; a foe who is unable, moreover, to reply at once because he cannot easily pick out hull-down enemies in previously undisclosed positions. T90s on the move are devastated, the survivors compelled to concentrate upon running for cover without shooting back; those in support at long range are hard-pressed to penetrate their opponents' Composite Armor. Only when a T90, which has found cover at 400 m, manages at last to get in an aimed shot is an Abrams hit and penetrated by a 125 mm round, a strike which inflicts serious damage and casualties but fails to set the Abrams alight because the fire is instantly snuffed out by its automatic chemical extinguishers. On this sector the Soviet attack wilts, a fate so frequently recorded in the history of unsupported tank charges. Only to a flank, of its thinly armored hull than was prudent. Meanwhile the Advanced Guard's reconnaissance helicopter is busily popping up and down, to spy out the opposition, itself trying to keep out of trouble from the Surface-to-Air missiles its pilot realises will be heading his way if he hovers too long. As a result, he fails to make any substantial contribution except to report his suspicions that one or more enemy tanks are lurking in cover near the village.

The Advanced Guard commander tries to tempt the enemy into exposing those tanks. He orders forward two BMP 2s as bait. But this does not work out quite as hoped. For it is another much more skilfully deployed Bradley which ineffectually engages one BMP 2 with its 25 mm gun; and something else which tackles his own T90s. At this moment, the Goliath comes into action as described on page 184.

Thereafter, as the encounter follows its predicted course, the American combat team maintains its position by skilful local maneuver while making best use of its composite armor against Russian ATGW and terminally guided munitions fired by artillery. Smoke and dust accumulate as both sides try to get a clear sight upon the other without exposing too much of themselves to view. The T90s, with their 125 mm guns, are always at a significant disadvantage compared to the Abrams and the Goliath. They are caught in the open where such speed as they can generate is not enough to throw off NATO gunners who hardly need to aim off – so high is the velocity of the shot from their 120 mm guns. Only at a high price in casualties do the T90s move to positions where they can both see and penetrate their foes. And by then the Advanced Guard has had its sting drawn. The battle now becomes the responsibility of the oncoming Main Guard and flanking units.

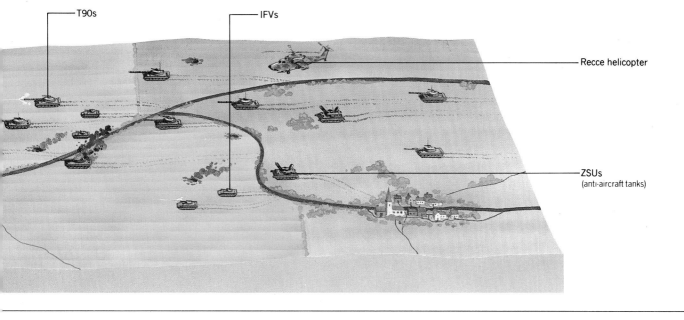

where a company of Soviet tanks and APCs find a gap and pour through, does the battle swing their way, forcing the NATO units to maneuver in an attempt to both block and hit this penetration in flank.

In these more mobile conditions, the Russians also make better use of their anti-tank weapons to score hits and put their enemy under pressure. NATO infantry anti-tank weapons are frequently in danger of being overrun or destroyed when they disclose their positions without instantly wiping out their antagonists. Similarly the Goliath tank-destroyers have to take care for fear of being caught in flank and thus unable to swing the entire vehicle to bring its gun to bear. It is at this stage that the main battle tanks impose their authority, both as an offensive and defensive weapon system, when their commanders operate totally unsupported by other arms, especially when the moment arrives for a counter-stroke.

THE COUNTER-STROKE

Riposte in the Manstein manner is as demanding of perfect timing in the 1990s as it was in the 1940s. The enemy must have reached that point of overstretch which makes him ripe for collapse as a prime dividend of applied shock. But shock is applied by the tank only at the core of offensive action; it is the archetypal instrument of shock, yet the moment for application is acquired through the combined use of all weapons available in wearing down both the main battle tanks and the anti-AFV weapons of the enemy. Most likely, therefore, NATO forces are committed to the counter-stroke when the interdiction of the Soviet lines of communication by air attack, demolition and harassment have weakened their logistic arrangements; when indirect artillery fire of all natures (including scatterable mines and terminally guided projectiles) have destroyed or disabled significant quantities of equipment; and when the NATO soldiers have weathered the storm of the original enemy assault without forfeiting their belief in victory to the extent that they have retained a sense of superiority over a shaken opponent. A successful counter-stroke can do more than check the much vaunted Soviet onrush, as the Arras counter-stroke in 1940 momentarily checked the German drive to Dunkirk. It can hurl back the enemy in such confusion that his basic spirit is subverted in much the same way as German morale was shaken by the Russian counterstroke before Moscow in the winter of 1940–41.

In the classic manner the counter-stroke may well be directed against an extended enemy flank, to drive a wedge into the enemy wedge (as did Manstein before Kharkov in February 1943). In the overtures to this performance the attacking Russians will have been distracted by a series of anti-tank ambushes in which tank-destroyers would have been in their element – punching the enemy AFVs by surprise at ranges up to 3000 m before backing off to repeat the battering elsewhere. In this phase, too, ATGW helicopters will play their part, while mines of all kinds and bomblets take their toll. It would be counter-productive, however, for the counter-stroke to repeat the Soviet errors of ramming a tank charge into a coherent defense of the threatened NATO flank. By excellent reconnaissance and intelligence work, the Soviet weak spots have to be pinpointed. By deception and concealment, the Soviet intelligence system must be denied warning of the impending blow. By rapid concentration and swift advance, the blow must be launched but not as a blind charge.

The principle of seizing vital ground as a base for destruction of the enemy remains as valid today as it did in the 1930s when Guderian propounded it. Armor in the counter-stroke should be infiltrated among the enemy, seeking to avoid centers of strong resistance in order to minimize losses prior to reaching positions from which devastating fire can be launched against a confused enemy whose troops are thereby compelled by sheer necessity to launch desperate hasty local counter-attacks to recover the lost vital ground. Always the commander of the counter-stroke force should be trying to free his main battle tanks for further offensive moves against enemy weak spots. As of doctrine, he should replace them at the point of enemy counter-attack by tank-destroyers and ATGW which will inflict still greater punishment through ambush. Above all, that commander will be trying to throw the enemy into confusion at the same time cutting off his supplies, wrecking his logistic system, demoralizing him, and smashing his will to stand – let alone his capability to advance any farther.

At the heart of each encounter of mounting scale, executed by individual weapon systems, complete all-arms units, and groups or formations, the main battle tank will stand supreme as the dominant factor, in much the same way as it has since its inception. And because modern armor provides such a high level of protection it has been granted a lease of additional life, which few at one time could have foretold. For that very reason the tank has less to fear from its detractors and battlefield enemies than in the past, yet most to fear of all from its own kind armed with the high-velocity gun.

The tank, therefore, fares well with an assured future. Even if it were far more vulnerable than it is, it would continue to stalk the battlefield simply because it has been built and paid for in very large numbers. Also, as yet, no equally satisfactory means has been found to dominate combat by terror and by immense striking power, high mobility and a reasonable level of protection in one, albeit very expensive, vehicle. Therefore, tank-versus-tank combat will be with us for a long time to come, tactically varied, slightly yet not fundamentally, by each shift in the balance of invention by the technologists.

INDEX